ALSO BY JULIA MARKUS

NOVELS

Uncle
American Rose
Friends Along the Way
A Change of Luck
Patron of the Arts: A Novella

BIOGRAPHY

Dared and Done:
The Marriage of Elizabeth Barrett and Robert Browning

EDITIONS

Casa Guidi Windows by Elizabeth Barrett Browning
Sonnets from the Portuguese:
Illuminated by the Brownings' Love Letters (coeditor)

ACROSS AN
UNTRIED SEA

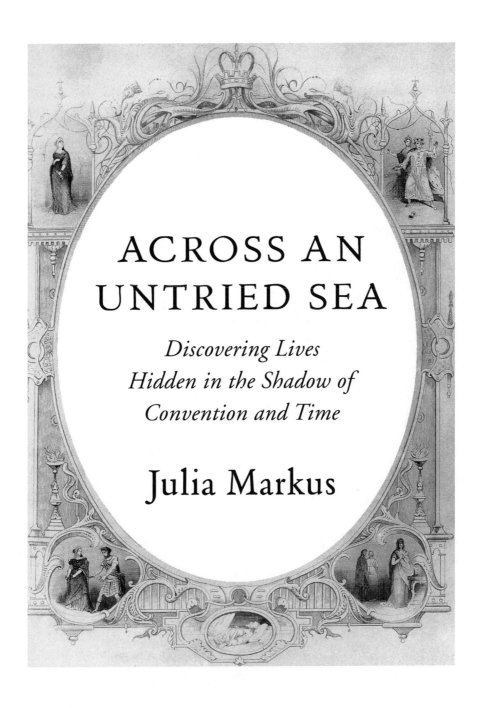

ACROSS AN UNTRIED SEA

*Discovering Lives
Hidden in the Shadow of
Convention and Time*

Julia Markus

ALFRED A. KNOPF  NEW YORK 2000

THIS IS A BORZOI BOOK
PUBLISHED BY ALFRED A. KNOPF

www.aaknopf.com

Knopf, Borzoi Books, and the colophon are
registered trademarks of Random House, Inc.

ISBN 0-679-44599-4
Library of Congress Card Number: 00-108133

Manufactured in the United States of America
First Edition

Dedicated to the memory of Diane Cleaver

Get leave to work
In this world—'tis the best you get at all.

Elizabeth Barrett Browning
Aurora Leigh

Contents

Acknowledgments

THE AUTHOR is grateful to so many libraries in the United States and Great Britain that she consulted and read at as she worked on this biography, most particularly: the Manuscript Division of the Library of Congress, the National Library of Scotland, the Schlesinger Library at Radcliffe College, the Pierpont Morgan Library in New York, the Library Company of Philadelphia, the Victoria and Albert Museum, the Carlyle House in London, the Manuscripts and Archives Division and the Berg Collection at the New York Public Library, the Theatre Collection of Harvard University, the Brander Matthews Dramatic Museum Collection at the Rare Book and Manuscript Library at Columbia University, the Alexander Turnbull Library of New Zealand, and the Folger Shakespeare Library.

The staffs of these libraries have been so kind and helpful. It is a pleasure to thank Fred Bauman at the Library of Congress and Carol Johnson, curator of photography there, Iain Maciver and the Trustees of the National Library of Scotland, Helene Gold and Jacalyn Blume at the Schlesinger Library, Georgina Ziegler at the Folger Shakespeare Library, and Jean Ashton, director of the Rare Book and Manuscript Library at Columbia University. I would like to thank, as well, the Marquess of Northampton, who graciously gave me access to Harriet Hosmer's letters to Louisa Lady Ashburton, the editors of the invaluable and ongoing Duke/Edinburgh edition of the letters of Thomas Carlyle and Jane Welsh Carlyle, and the very helpful Timothy Lovett-Smith of the Alexander Turnbull Library of New Zealand, who enthusiastically e-mailed me with so much information concerning the Jewsbury–Mantell correspondence.

A month's grant at the International Writers' retreat at Hawthornden Castle outside of Edinburgh gave me the time to consult the National Library of Scotland daily and to come to some knowledge of the Carlyles' Scotland as well. I cannot thank the staff and the beneficent Drue Heinz adequately for true hospitality and kindness which added so much to this biography. The Scottish experience was further enriched by a week in Dumfries, where I consulted the city records and library, as well as visiting more of 'Carlyle

Country'—Templand, Craigenputtock, and Ecclefechan—from my perch on the River Nith.

Many thanks to Virginia Surtees, Louisa Lady Ashburton's biographer, and to Dolly Sherwood, Harriet Hosmer's biographer, for conversations and support, as well as to both Fred Kaplan and Ian Campbell for conversations on matters pertaining to Thomas Carlyle, to Elizabeth Milroy for the photograph of her great-aunt Emma Stebbins with Charlotte Cushman, and to Gilles Rousseau for his generous help with the photographs. To Hofstra University for research and materials grants, as well as for a special leave to initiate this book, I am, as always, quite grateful.

To all my enthusiastic friends who encouraged this project, warm thanks. To my literary representative Harriet Wasserman and to my editor Victoria Wilson, for support, wisdom, and constant inspiration—more than words can say.

ACROSS AN
UNTRIED SEA

A Home in Rome

ROME, LONDON

1852–1857

S OMETHING NEW under the Roman sun: a household of unmarried women. Independent women they were called in 1852. The
famous American actress Charlotte Cushman, always paterfamilias,
leased the house on the Corso and filled it with her friends. The actress was
thirty-six years old at the time. Having raised herself and her family from
poverty to riches, Charlotte was retiring from the stage. She came to the
Eternal City with her companion, Matilda M. Hays, British translator of
George Sand. Matilda was a few years younger and more feminine in
appearance than Charlotte, though they both dressed like men from the
waist up, wearing tight, lapeled bodices, handsome waistcoats, and elegant
bow ties.

A third person in this party of 'jolly bachelors,' as they called themselves, was a young woman of twenty-two, short, chubby, and daring, who
soon dressed like a man from the waist *down* as well as up. She rode her
horse, 'scrambling about,' going anywhere in Rome and its countryside that
she desired—alone.

Harriet Hosmer was her name; 'Hattie' she was called. Hattie's hair was
cropped, and when she joked around or talked seriously about the art of
sculpture, she pushed her fingers through it like a boy. The popular British
actress Fanny Kemble, who knew Hattie since she was a child, worried that
Hattie's 'peculiarities,' as she phrased it, might be held against her genius.
But not in Rome. Or in Florence, where residents such as the Brownings

fell in love with that fun-loving, free-spirited American. Elizabeth Barrett Browning, who found Hattie strange at first, soon found her pure, pure, pure.

Three other independent women joined them on the Corso, justifying Charlotte's friends' joking remark that the actress was never seen with fewer than six people in tow.

Charlotte took care of the household expenses, her fortune recently increased by a long and profitable 'farewell tour' in America. She had been absent from her homeland for five years, during which time her spectacular success on the British stage turned her into a legend. *Cushmania* marked her return. In New York and Philadelphia the actress had trouble wending her way into her dressing room through the crowds that lined the streets to greet her, to touch her. She was escorted through the throng by Sallie Mercer. Sallie, part of the Cushman mystique, was with her in Rome. She was Charlotte's prompter, her skilled dresser, her housekeeper—her 'right hand,' Charlotte called her.

Charlotte had hired the bright, outspoken, literate Sallie in Philadelphia when Sallie was only fourteen and Charlotte at twenty-eight was about to try her luck abroad for the first time. Charlotte always had an instinct for the right people. She saw Sallie's intelligence and determination in the high cast of her forehead, in the brown sheen of her skin.

'Sallie,' she'd write, and then list a complicated set of instructions for the girl—people's houses to go to, what to say, messages to deliver and return—signed 'Charlotte.' Though Sallie's mother objected, Sallie was eager to accompany Charlotte to London—and since then hardly ever left her side.

In Rome, the slim, strong-minded Sallie Mercer did not dress like a man from the waist up. But being a Negress, not a slave in bondage, but a *free American* Negress, had its own exotic appeal among the expatriates, and among the Romans, who were known even then for their live-and-let-live enjoyment of novelty, their finely honed sense of irony, and their ability unabashedly to stare.

William Wetmore Story, the aspiring sculptor who was at the head of the English and American expatriate community in Rome, entered the household of e*man*cipated women, as they were slyly called. He arrived to pay his respects to the only male among them, Hattie Hosmer's father, whom he knew from Boston days.

William Wetmore, a lawyer who wrote a definitive work on contracts, was supposed to return to New England after sculpting a memorial statue of his father, the deceased Supreme Court judge Justice Joseph Story. But he was actually in the process of giving up law—and Boston—and devoting his life—and his inheritance—to sculpture and poetry—from the vantage point of the *piano nobile* of the Palazzo Barberini. Already he was the poet Robert Browning's best friend.

Hattie called her father into the room.

Dr. Hosmer entered rather meekly. Being there in Rome among these jolly bachelors was not his idea.

A year and a half before, Hattie insisted on going from Watertown, Massachusetts, into Boston to see Charlotte Cushman play Hamlet and it changed her life.

Hattie was overwhelmed by Cushman's portrayal of the Danish prince, and with her usual aplomb, went backstage—where Charlotte immediately took to her. Hattie told her straight out that she planned to be a sculptor. No matter that there were no professional women sculptors at the time. It was even a peculiar choice for an American man. Most Americans believed all those naked statues were better left to the ancients and the Europeans.

Harvard did not admit women and Dr. Hosmer could not persuade the medical school to allow his daughter to study anatomy there. So Hattie traveled to St. Louis, Missouri, where she was able to study anatomy and to live with the family of her best friend Cornelia Crow—Cornie. Even the way she traveled was brimming with fun. Leaving St. Louis with her certificate of proficiency in anatomy in hand, she smoked a peace pipe with a Dakota chief in Lansing. She beat the boys in a race up an unnamed bluff four hundred feet above the Mississippi. It became—and remains—Mount Hosmer.

Hattie's youthful determination reminded Charlotte of her own.

If Hattie wanted to be a sculptor, she had to go to Rome. It was the center of the art world, according to the best tables in Boston. Charlotte had never been there, but she and Matilda Hays might be going next autumn. Would Hattie join them?

She might be going to Rome! Hattie wrote to her friend Cornie in St. Louis, 'Isn't it strange how we meet people in this world and become attached to them in so short a time?'

Months later, Charlotte went to Watertown to persuade Dr. Hosmer to allow his daughter to travel, but she did not win him over. Only when word came from St. Louis that the wealthy businessman Wayman Crow, Cornie's father, would sponsor Hattie did the doctor agree—reluctantly.

Charlotte thought Dr. Hosmer cheap, could not imagine a father not giving his daughter what she wanted when he had the wherewithal. Look at all she did for *her* family, her *belongings,* she called them. Born and bred in Boston, she left school at the age of thirteen to help her mother run a boardinghouse in nearby Charlestown, after her elderly father went bankrupt in West Indian trade. Elkanah Cushman, who began his working life as a hairdresser, hadn't even the business sense to put paper between him and his partner. Young Charlotte, the oldest child, dreamed of saving her family. There were the music lessons she paid for by becoming an indentured servant. She whose family boasted Mayflower roots. Then the successful debut in Boston on the opera stage, followed by the disaster in New Orleans where her voice deserted her and the critics on the *Bee* and the *Picayune* panned her. She did not give in, she turned to acting, tutored by one in the company.

By the age of nineteen, with only a few months of professional training which aimed at getting below the surface of her Unitarian-girl reserve, Charlotte found her calling and made her acclaimed debut as Lady Macbeth. Her Lady Macbeth was a young, ambitious, energetic, unsexed force, possessed with one mad desire, ready to peril all that was high and holy to attain her end. The same newspapers that had humiliated her now extolled her. And every adversity since then, every attempt of her enemies to thwart her, she turned from defeat to advantage through talent and brute determination. Never for herself, she made sure everyone knew. All she did, all she had ever done, was done to support her *belongings,* her mother and her younger siblings. For *them* she had become an actress. It made her almost respectable.

Dr. Hosmer, with only one belonging spared him by God—his wife and other children all died of tuberculosis—held his purse shut until wealthy Wayman Crow opened his. That was how Charlotte saw it, but the doctor was fearful as well as parsimonious. He had raised his daughter to a rigorous outdoor life to save her from the dreaded illness. He gave her a spirited horse, a dog, a *gun.* A boathouse. Their Watertown home had gardens that reached down to the Charles River. Young Hattie rowed and swam in the summer, ice-skated in the winter. Unheard-of activities for girls. Of course she adapted to the boy's regime of exercise and hard play like a duck to water. Hattie was a handful with her wild pranks and her wit and her 'peculiarities.'

As a child she was unruly at school, coming home with notes of reprimand pinned to her back. She ran off to Boston at night; once she uncoupled a railroad car, hoping the engine would go on its merry way, leaving all the passengers behind. Her father had to pay for that one.

The frugal doctor warned beneficent Wayman Crow that reckless spending was Hattie's incurable disease. Open a purse and she emptied it.

Because of her wild streak, Dr. Hosmer was almost forced to send his daughter to Mrs. Charles Sedgwick's home school for girls in Lenox, Massachusetts. Mrs. Sedgwick was known for her way with difficult cases. Hattie soon became the wittiest girl, the life of the party. Away from her father, she had the most wonderful time. And she met Cornie Crow, who became her roommate there.

'Come, Hattie, do give us some fun tonight!' Cornie remembered the actress Fanny Kemble saying.

Mrs. Kemble kept a cottage in Lenox and would read Shakespeare to the girls when she was in town. On Saturdays the girls were invited to her 'Perch,' where they would play charades or put on amateur theatricals or sing and dance, Kemble accompanying them on piano.

Always a punster, Hattie composed doggerel. One was a mixture of English and French. It convulsed them at the Perch when Hattie became an Anglo-Frenchman, energetically reciting to his lady love:

> *Regardez-tu, Regardez-tu*
> *L'amour sublime que j'ai pour vous.*
> *Oh Arabelle! je ne puis pas dire*
> *L'amour pour vous, si fort, si fier.*

For all the trouble Hattie caused him, his daughter was all the doctor had and he feared lest anything befall her. He brought her to Rome personally, and she repaid him in her usual irrepressible manner, this time by insisting the household of women call him 'Elizabeth.' You have to be one of us, she told him, to live with us.

William Wetmore Story, his artist's beret in his hand, his other hand quizzically stroking his well-kept yet luxuriant beard, was visibly surprised at Dr. Hosmer's compliance with the house rule. It was 'Elizabeth' this, 'Elizabeth' that, all through the whole visit. Were the women playing with Story as well? Story thought Dr. Hosmer almost *fou* in his concern for his daughter, while he wasn't quite sure Hattie cared for the good doctor at all. And that 'Elizabeth' nonsense!

William Wetmore Story, sculptor and poet. Henry James' two-volume biography *William Wetmore Story and His Friends* established Story's posthumous reputation as the central figure in the Anglo-American community of artists living in Italy during the Victorian period—a community equally influenced by Charlotte Cushman and her friends.

Story might have provoked Charlotte Cushman on that visit. For *she* was giving Hattie this opportunity in Rome, not he. Charlotte was already entertaining the delightful British and American expatriate community and expected to use her connections to find Hattie a teacher. But W. W. Story looked at the girl's two daguerreotypes of her one sculpture bust, and he introduced Hattie to the renowned British neoclassical sculptor, John Gibson. Hattie charmed her fellow bachelor on the spot. Though Gibson rarely took any students, Hattie became his first and only female student—and dear friend. Gibson even gave her a hallowed studio to work out of—it once belonged to the great master of their Sublime art, Antonio Canova.

After that, 'Elizabeth' fled from Rome as fast as he could, leaving Hattie to her friends and to what turned out to be her destiny.

Charlotte took to the city immediately, just as Hattie had. Italy was not yet a nation, but it was a state of mind. One could be oneself there under the bluest of skies, buoyed by the best of exchange rates. Charlotte entertained. The winter society in Rome was of the finest, such a grand combination of dedicated artists and wealthy travelers. She had her portrait painted by William Page, called 'the American Titian,' and he succeeded in rendering her flat, blunt, no-nonsense face with its broad forehead, dent of a nose, and wide jaw with some adherence to truth—Charlotte was Yankee plain. Page caught the glint of sadness in her gray-blue eyes.

Nobody knew what she suffered. Her first year of retirement from the stage should have been heaven. But not unusual in her history, the reward of her labors was a living hell. Charlotte's companion Matilda and young Hattie were making love, flirting outrageously, as was Hattie's wont, right in front of Charlotte's eyes. And then an old flame of Matilda's, one Miss B., who thought Charlotte had stolen Matilda from her some years back, arrived in Rome.

Charlotte Cushman and Matilda Hays had what was termed a 'female marriage.' In the privacy of their love and under the eyes of God they pledged their troth. When Elizabeth Barrett Browning met the women on their way to Rome, she was confused by the arrangement and wrote back home to her sister that Charlotte and Matilda 'made vows of celibacy and of eternal attachment to each other—they live together, dress alike. It is a female marriage.' She had never heard of such a thing, she told a friend, who answered, 'Oh, it is by no means uncommon.'

In Charlotte and Matilda's case, it had never been a stable marriage, and now it was coming apart, no matter Charlotte's constant efforts to keep it intact. The whole two-and-a-half-year 'farewell tour' of America was a way of having some privacy, an ocean separating the women from Charlotte's disapproving mother. Charlotte resettled her socially conscious mother in London, close to brother Charlie and within traveling distance of Liverpool, where Charlotte's beautiful sister Susan—her mother's favorite—lived. The divorced Susan left the stage, where she was in Charlotte's shadow, and remarried into British society, just as their mother wished.

Charlotte Cushman, seated, and Matilda Hays, by Albert Southworth and Josiah Hawes, taken during Charlotte's successful American tour, 1849–51, when Matilda Hays translated George Sand's *Fadette: A Domestic Story from the French*. Hays dedicated the translation to 'Charlotte Cushman, True Artist and Yet Truer Woman . . . In Affectionate Remembrance Of Our Travels In The Country Honored By Her Birth.' Charlotte and Matilda's own domestic story did not run as smoothly as the dedication suggests.

Matilda replaced Susan on the stage, and played opposite Charlotte in the British provinces. But that new career was short-lived and Matilda resumed her literary life and her translations of George Sand—work she could do while keeping house for Charlotte.

During Charlotte's American tour, the poet Henry Wadsworth Longfellow noticed the vague sense of sadness that enveloped Matilda, as well as her bitterness, one that he intuited came from disappointment. Charlotte's companion had not quite found her niche and had the earmarks of a dissatisfied wife.

Returning to England, what was to keep the couple there during the winter—the disapproving look in Charlotte's mother's eyes?

It was always the same. No matter how hard Charlotte worked, no matter how high she raised her family, no matter how much money she invested wisely—she, unlike her now deceased father, had excellent business sense—she could not please her mother. Mary Eliza always considered her overinfluenced by strangers and particularly by her girlfriends. Her mother felt she spent too much on them, money that should be spent on her *belongings.*

Concerning Matilda, Charlotte's mother might have been closer to the mark than she usually was. Matilda seemed to have Charlotte on a string.

Mary Elizabeth Babbitt Cushman, mother of Charlotte. From an undated photograph in Charlotte's album. The actress lifted her mother from genteel poverty to wealth and took care of all her physical needs. Still, Mary Eliza favored her other three children, particularly her beautiful daughter Susan, and disapproved both of Charlotte's acting and of what she considered her elder daughter's foolish and excessive female friendships.

Charlotte knew it herself. She had never asked for the relationship, yet once it happened, she grew morbidly dependent on her spouse.

Before Matilda entered her life, Charlotte had been with another Englishwoman, Eliza Cook. That was eight years before, when Charlotte traveled abroad for the first time, to improve her fortunes by a six-month exposure to the British stage. However, for the first five months in London, 'we lived on a mutton-chop a day,' Charlotte's right hand, the young Sallie Mercer, remembered. 'And I always bought the baker's dozen of muffins for the sake of the extra one and we ate them all, no matter how stale they were. We never suffered from want of appetite in those days.'

It was only by clever horse-trading that Charlotte seized her opportunity. The devious Philadelphian actor Edwin Forrest arrived in London and wanted her to play opposite him in *Othello*. 'I cannot begin with Emilia,' she told the small, shifty stage manager J. M. Maddox, who had earlier rejected her from his Princess Theatre. Suddenly Maddox wanted her to debut in a role that would in no way demonstrate her range. It showed much about her business sense that although she had given herself six months in England and time was running out, the twenty-eight-year-old realized that the wrong start in London would be worse than no start at all. The only way she would play Emilia, she told Maddox, was if he gave her her own London debut the night before, in a play of her own choosing.

That was ludicrous, Maddox replied.

Why?

'She's not good-looking.'

He didn't say that to Charlotte, but to a British critic, who responded, 'You're a fool, Maddox.'

Charlotte responded by showing Maddox she could act. Before leaving his office the second time, she stopped at the door, turned to him, and said, 'I know I have enemies in this country!' Then she threw herself down on her knees, clenched her fist, and cried, 'So help me! I'll defeat them!'

Had she made a fool of herself? she wondered early the next morning in the London flat she shared with Sallie. Why had she done it? she asked the girl. Her big scene was not going to budge Maddox.

Sallie was looking out the window. She turned to Charlotte with a big reassuring smile on her face and motioned her over. Below them, chilled, was Maddox, pacing the street, his collar turned up, knowing it was still too early to call.

'He is anxious,' Charlotte said. And then, without the slightest hesitation, she told Sallie, 'I can make my own terms.'

For her British debut at the Princess Theatre, she chose the role of the betrayed wife Bianca in Henry Hart Milman's melodrama *Fazio,* just as British Fanny Kemble chose Bianca for her American debut.

The passion Charlotte Cushman brought to the role of the betrayed wife made the American a sensational discovery in a city ever ready to glamorize the new. After the act in which she threw herself down into a broken heap in front of her husband's beautiful mistress, the small audience got up on the benches and waved handkerchiefs, while the previously dismissive cast applauded her as she went through the greenroom to her dressing room.

'You've got 'em,' Sallie cried as she dressed her for the next act. 'You've got 'em.'

The reviews in the London papers were ecstatic. Maddox sent them to her. 'I was never more delighted,' he wrote. Before her performance, when she complained about the flimsy sets and cheap costumes, he asked her what had she expected, to set the town on fire?

Charlotte was never one to brag—or even talk about her acting. She was stating the unadorned truth when she wrote home to her mother, '*All of my successes put together since I have been upon the stage would not come up to my success in London.*' Everyone who was anyone wanted to meet her. She was invited to every important breakfast and dinner in town. Within a year, there would be only one attraction that outdrew her at the box office—P. T. Barnum's presentation of another American, Tom Thumb.

Eliza Cook, herself a fine, independent, self-educated woman, a poet, illustrator, journalist, saw Charlotte in her London debut as Bianca. She was so swept away that she sent the actress a poem:

> *I did not deem thou could'st awake the sob*
> *Of choking fulness and convulsive start*
> *But thy pale madness, and thy gasping woe*
> *That breathed the torture of Bianca's pain*
> *Oh never would my bosom ask to know*
> *Such sad and bitter sympathy again!*

When the two women met, they recognized each other immediately. Eliza described that knowledge in a poem subtle enough for careful Charlotte to keep with her memorabilia:

> *There are sealed pages in my heart*
> *traced with illumined hand,*

That none can see, and if they did
oh who would understand?
But thou, by some strange sympathy
hast thrown a searching look:
And read at sight the hardest scroll
embossed within the book.

Though they read each other's 'hardest scroll' with that first searching look, mannish Eliza was not really Charlotte's type. Charlotte, sailing to England for the first time, had given her desserts, which she was too upset to eat anyway, to a tall lady in a cabin near her, one with a beautiful face who reminded her of Rosalie Sully, the lovely daughter of the Philadelphian portrait painter Thomas Sully.

Charlotte had moved her acting headquarters from New York to Philadelphia at the age of twenty-four, to manage the Walnut Theatre and to act in it and the Chestnut Theatre. It was hoped that under her management, theatre in Philadelphia would become a respectable cultural activity, a place fit for the family.

The Cushmans were Unitarians, and one Sunday at church in the city of brotherly love, the pew owner next to them abruptly gathered up his wife and children and conspicuously left the service because he wouldn't have his family sit near an actress. Charlotte had her work cut out for her.

The portrait painter Thomas Sully, on the other hand, welcomed Charlotte and her family into his spacious four-story brick house on Chestnut Street and introduced them to his wife and daughters, Blanche and Rosalie. Rosalie was two years younger than Charlotte, and the actress was struck by her beauty, her grace, her gentle, shy nature. Rosalie was a painter in her own right—a painter of miniatures, as her uncle had been before her. The two began to see each other every day.

Thomas Sully painted Charlotte's portrait. You made my unfortunate mug beautiful, she told him. He had in fact taken liberties with her blunt, no-nonsense face, turning her as softly pretty as one of his daughters. For shy Rosalie she was indeed the siren's call.

Before she left the States, on a hot July evening outside of Philadelphia, Charlotte put a ring on gentle Rosalie's finger and they swore eternal love. They considered themselves married—just like Romeo and Juliet, only without the benefit of a sympathetic friar. Charlotte's daybook for July 1844 was filled with her love of Rosalie, squeezed in among her business accounts.

Charlotte Cushman by Thomas Sully, 1843. 'I have established in my mind that I am beautiful,' Charlotte wrote to Sully after viewing the girlish, idealized image, one of two portraits he painted of her.

On various days: Clover Hill with Rose—Saw Rose in morning—Slept with Rose—Burned letters.

Rumor was driving Charlotte from Philadelphia. Before she fell in love with Rosalie, she was with another Philadelphian, Anne Hampton Brewster, a brilliant and cultured young woman with exquisite literary and musical tastes. Anne was educated by her mother. Her father had abandoned the family to live with his mistress and their children. Anne continued her studies at home, while her older brother was sent to Princeton, the first time the siblings were separated. Burnt-faced Ben, Anne's brother was called, terribly disfigured as he was since the age of five when his clothes caught on fire. As a man he compensated for his deformity with clothing out of a storybook. Tall sheer white beaver hats, velvet vests, light-colored pants, white alligator spats, patent leather British shoes. He was quite a dandy and—once he charmed a woman past his face—quite a lover. Burnt-faced Ben, profligate in his ways, became a powerful Philadelphia lawyer and later President Chester Arthur's attorney general. For many years he lived with his sister, keeping tight hold on the purse strings and keeping Anne, who adored him, dependent on his largesse.

He had no use for Charlotte Cushman. Tyrannical by nature and jealous to maintain his sister's undivided attention, he openly deplored Charlotte and Anne's love. He told everyone who would listen that Charlotte's friendship for his sister was unnatural; he no longer allowed Charlotte's daily visits to their house. It did not help that Charlotte's Romeo, a breeches part she played with great success in New York, puzzled Philadelphia, to say the least.

Charlotte was made much more welcome in the Sully household. How many hours had she and Rosalie spent upstairs on the sofa in the back room. *Our* sofa, Rosalie called it. And then they had Charlotte's spot at Clover Hill for privacy.

Eventually, like Romeo fleeing Verona, after secretly marrying Rosalie, Charlotte fled Philadelphia. The things people said about her there were untrue, she wrote to her mother. She knew her safety was in flight. She would return vindicated with money enough to support not only her family but an independent life with Rosalie.

Her success in London was so unprecedented that she called for her family to join *her*. 'I am doing well, and I hope my star may continue in the ascendant,' she wrote home to her mother. 'I have given myself *five years more,* and I think at the end of that time I will have $50,000 to retire upon; that will, if well invested, give us a comfortable home for the rest of our lives, and a quiet corner in some respectable graveyard.'

Perhaps if Rosalie had more courage—she was always so self-effacing, so shy—she would have come too. Rosalie wrote to Charlotte that she was not even brave enough to ask for her father's portrait of Charlotte to be put on her bedroom wall, now that it was returned to them for safekeeping. She hadn't dared call out for them not to place it in the picture gallery. 'No no, I want it in my room.' She labeled herself a fool. Not only that, she was forbidden to write to Charlotte anymore.

Rosalie never lied by word or action, she told Charlotte. All the actress would have to do to ascertain that 'I am as fondly yours as I was the 6th of July last' was to find out through others that Rosalie still wore Charlotte's ring. She would never take it off.

'Dear Dear Charlotte my grief is too deep for expression . . . never never question my love for you. I am unalterably yours for ever.' She often threw herself on *their* sofa 'alone and heartbroken, praying for death to end my misery.'

That couldn't have made Charlotte feel too easy about herself. She had already broken her vows with Rosalie and taken up with a lovely woman in

London, Louisa Oakley. Squeezed into her daybook for 1845: wrote to L.O—note from L.O—went with Miss Oakley to hear Easter Service—L.O. slept with me.

But L.O. left her for a man, brother Charlie remembered. Charlotte's blond brother, less than two years younger than she, had already arrived in London, as tall and handsome as any British aristocrat. (All of Charlotte's siblings were swans, she the only duckling.) Charlotte used a form of black-mail to have her mother send him first, telling her mother she could make a fortune in England but was perhaps too homesick to remain. Couldn't Charlie come out by the packet from Philadelphia on the twenty-fifth of March or the eighth of April? (She kept a sharp eye on the shipping news.) 'He will have no need of getting anything, for I can furnish him when he comes. So send him as he is—as fast as he will come.'

Charlie arrived in April in time to witness Eliza Cook, who really over-whelmed Charlotte with poems and letters, take L.O.'s place. Charlie thought Eliza the superior woman, if not such an attractive one. And he knew of course his sister was not one to be alone.

As Charlotte planned to tour the provinces with Eliza Cook, she tapped into her own experience of longing, exile, and frustration. She passed through the pain of her own frailties and Rosalie's innocent faith, to the vir-ile, boyish, impulsive lover.

Charlotte wanted to play Romeo again—but not that season.

She would wait for her beautiful younger sister Susan to arrive to play Juliet before she dared it in England.

She asked Charlie to speak to her manager Maddox to tell him she would not play Romeo as he requested. Her run at the Princess had been extended through June, but after her tour of the provinces that summer she secretly planned to seek another theatre. In the meantime, she'd do any of her other roles for Maddox—except Meg Merrilies. It was a character role. Charlotte portrayed Meg as a brutally withered, almost demonic old Gypsy queen who had once been the loving baby nurse of a highborn Scottish child. Through Charlotte's interpretation, Meg became the best moment in the melodramatic stage version of Sir Walter Scott's *Guy Man-nering*. The long stick the witch-like hag leaned on became a valued tro-phy; one exists in the room Edwin Booth died in—the New York Players Club today.

But Edwin Booth's father warned Charlotte about character roles. In America, she played Nancy Sikes in *Oliver Twist*. Actors supplied their own costumes in those days, and for Nancy Sikes Charlotte had gone to the slums of lower Manhattan, the notorious Five Points, to pick her rags, rusty old key, and attitude out of the garbage there. In so doing she turned a minor role—meant to insult her—into a sensation. 'No! No! It is a great part, Charlotte—one of your best; and you made it; but never act it in London,' the elder Booth advised. 'It will give you a vulgar dash you will never get over.'

Well, Meg Merrilies could be considered a Gypsy Nancy Sikes. Charlotte always caused a gasp in the audience when she swooped onstage as the frightening hag of a Gypsy, and ovations when the curtain fell and Charlotte dramatically took her bows, shedding her disguise, revealing herself as a young woman. Definitely 'a vulgar dash.'

Charlie muddled her instructions (as her male relatives would all through her life) and came back having given Maddox his sister's word that she'd play Meg in London and on tour that summer in the provinces.

What could she do, but the same as when that malicious New York manager had first assigned her the role of Nancy Sikes. 'It was midwinter,' she recalled for Eliza Cook. 'My bread had to be earned. I dared not refuse.' So, she held back her anger. 'I meant to get the better of my enemy. What he designed for my mortification should be my triumph.'

She would do what she always did when her hands were tied. Do the best that she could. Turn around defeat. She riveted London with her Meg Merrilies. Eliza Cook was thrilled and drew a lively caricature to immortalize the moment. Charlotte as Meg, in her hermit-like rags, on the Scottish plain. A long branch in her withered left hand, bracing her. But Meg's face is young, pencil lines of radiance spark round her head and her cheeks puff up as she blows her own trumpet. The scroll descending from her horn lists the journals that have lauded her and the writers as well. Eliza Cook's name heads the list. The caption reads: 'Yankee Hanging out her Banner.'

When Susan Cushman arrived, the sisters brushed up on their unbowdlerized Shakespeare. 'American Indians' they were called by jealous London players—not without wit. Fourteen American Indians from the Northwest Territory had recently landed in England to be stared at for profit. Why not two more?

The sisters ignored the antagonism of their fellow players and took their unique *Romeo and Juliet* to the provinces to try it out. Sallie Mercer assisted as Charlotte's dresser, and Eliza Cook, of course, came along. In Manchester the play went well, but in Scotland, in Edinburgh, people were shocked

Left: Eliza Cook; right: 'Yankee Hanging out her Banner' by Eliza Cook. One of eleven children, the popular poet was forced by circumstances to work outside the home as a governess. While in the employ of a widower, she was accused of some shadowy impropriety relating to the daughters under her care and was dismissed. She created *Eliza Cook's Journal,* dedicated to issues relating to a wide audience of middle-class women striving to find their place in an industrialized society.

to watch two sisters making love. That famous phrenologist George Combe (Fanny Kemble's nephew) wrote to Charlotte expressing his—and his neighbors'—concern.

Two sisters? Charlotte questioned in reply, with maidenly confusion and hurt. How could that be improper in any way? Did not such casting banish the very idea of impropriety? It would be different if Susan were making love to a man. What a strange idea—'entirely *new to me*'—Mr. Combe was forcing her to entertain. Why, she was only doing her duty, playing Romeo in order to give her sister the appropriate showcase for a respectable British debut as Juliet.

When Combe kept peppering his letters to Mrs. Kemble with questions about Charlotte Cushman's virtue, Kemble told him she knew no more about Miss Cushman's private character than she did of the man in the moon. Why didn't the phrenologist read Miss Cushman's *skull* if he was so interested, she finally complained to a friend.

In London, despite her fears of a breeches part tarnishing her British triumph, Charlotte took the plunge. After all, as she told them in Edinburgh, she wasn't the first woman to play Romeo.

But no woman played it like her. For when Cushman put on her leggings and buckled her sword, she *became* the virile youth.

Romeo's sword fights rang with danger. His passionate love rushed toward physical consummation. All the erotic undertones of Shakespeare's play were fulfilled. The London critics gasped in appreciation. Hers was a Romeo for new times. And so her extraordinary star rose even higher and she managed to slice her sister a piece of the sky, as everybody ran to the Haymarket:

> 'But what's the attraction? Why thus do they rush, man?'
> 'Don't you know? Tis Romeo, played by Miss Cushman.'

In the midst of popularity and success so great it invited parody, life retaliated with tragedy. Almost three years to the day that Charlotte put a ring on Rosalie's finger, Rosalie Sully, who had prayed for death to end her misery, caught the fever that had just claimed her brother, and she too suddenly died. After her tour of the provinces, Charlotte herself collapsed at the baths of Malvern. The American papers reported the great Charlotte Cushman was barely rescued from 'the tomb.'

Back in Philadelphia, Anne Brewster, reading that Charlotte was terribly ill, confided in her diary: 'I love my mother & my Brother dearly and my friends, but my love for C was a love that is felt but once in one's lifetime. . . . And we were separated—never to meet again . . . the only being I ever truly loved or shall ever love. . . . Oh Father above is such love wrong? Can a feeling which seemed to elevate & refine my nature as did that love for her be wicked? Oh! no it cannot be my inner self whispers, and I feel assured though separated in this life, in another world we shall meet & never know the wretchedness of separation!'

At the baths of Malvern, Eliza Cook tended Charlotte with the utmost devotion as the actress regained her strength.

It was through Eliza's influence, particularly after the success with Romeo, that Charlotte dressed in a way she wouldn't have dared in America. She often wore a man's collar and cravat and Wellington boots. 'Charlie de Boots' she was nicknamed in Edinburgh. In Yorkshire, when Eliza Cook and Charlotte's host William Forster gave Charlotte a bolt of steel-blue

'The Rose and the Lily,' Thomas Sully's double portrait of his daughters, 1842. From left to right, Blanche Sully (the Lily) and her younger sister Rosalie (the Rose). When parted from Charlotte, Rosalie wrote, 'Fate has done her worst for us,' but still, 'I am unalterably yours for ever.'

alpaca from his textile mills (Charlotte would always be interested in textile dyes as an investment), she had it made into identical dresses for Eliza and herself, with tight-fitting lapelled and ruffled shirtfronts. They dressed as twins, these two masculine-looking young women.

When the two women parted company, Eliza was so desolate that she developed a chronic malady. She also began *Eliza Cook's Journal,* a weekly she edited, wrote, and illustrated for five years. It dealt with the concerns of middle-class women, affected by what she called the 'Canker of Gentility.' Imagine any woman in her right mind wishing to be a governess! Yet literate women who considered the occupation *genteel* were flooding the papers with ads. Well, being a governess was an ill-paid job, in which a woman stood utterly isolated and alone and was treated as a kind of upper servant, a better-bred sort of menial. One who got paid less than a cook or butler. Eliza had been one, and knew.

The snobbish set vilified and abused Eliza Cook, though she was a very popular writer among others. The *New York Times* ridiculed Eliza for wearing red plaid and sable cuffs in July and for her masculine gestures when she plunked herself down in a tavern and ordered beer. 'The finger of calumny pointed at Eliza Cook,' brother Charlie remembered. 'She was a woman who treated the world, the flesh & the devil with the utmost & the most deserved contempt—in my own estimation not a more deserving, upright & honorable woman ever walked the earth.'

Now in Rome, Charlotte had even greater reason for empathizing with Eliza's pain. She had never asked for her relationship with Matilda Hays. In Manchester, a mutual friend, the novelist Geraldine Jewsbury, introduced her. Then Matilda simply knocked on Charlotte's door, asking was there anything, anything at all, she could do for her? Why, *why*, had she become so bound to her? Matilda and Hattie, acting so coy. Matilda seen all through Rome with her ex-lover, Miss B. That woman thought Charlotte once stole Matilda away from her and hated Charlotte accordingly. For the first time Charlotte felt like Rosalie Sully, but she didn't pray to die, she thought of killing herself.

This was insanity. She knew it, but she was lost. She thought it would be better if she and Matilda returned to London. But in London Matilda soon walked out on her and went back to the household of women in Rome and it was much worse.

No one knew her sufferings in those days, Charlotte wrote to the red-headed American journalist Grace Greenwood, one of the household of women on the Corso who witnessed it all. Finally, she grasped onto something beyond herself to save her. 'My old religion of labour fell upon me like a soft & fleecy shawl & "work!" "work!" "work!" was the mystic word which was to open this rock which was meant to crush me.'

Only two years after proclaiming her retirement in a 'farewell tour' through America, Charlotte returned to the London stage. She was no longer received with the unanimous acclaim she had garnered when she made her debut, but she won the audience over. By the New Year, Matilda came back, begging forgiveness. She had almost been forced away by Miss B.; she knew she had been terribly wrong. After an excursion with a delightful little new friend of her own, Charlotte took Matilda back. 'Never again perhaps to be what she once was to me, but still, perhaps, better for us both that I am not so dependent upon her.'

Charlotte bought a four-story Georgian house for them in Mayfair close to the theatres at 1 Bolton Row. She hired a staff for Sallie and a very British butler, Wilmot, and the women settled down into their domestic routine:

Charlotte working, Matilda translating, there when Charlotte got home. Then, after a few years of this life, she and Matilda tempted fate. Why not try Rome once more, during the winter season?

Rome meant Hattie, who was having quite a success. Charlotte hadn't seen Hattie in three years, and if she still smarted from Hattie's earlier fling with Matilda it certainly didn't show. Matilda was absolutely delighted to see Hattie and raved about her development in a letter to Hattie's best friend, the now married Cornie. 'To begin, she has added an inch or so to her height, of which, between ourselves, she is very proud; and more than an inch considerably in her circumference.' Hattie might be rounder, but Matilda reported her at the same time having a charming little waist and figure, not to mention having darkened hair which suited her admirably.

'So much for externals. Better than all, she is the same frank, unaffected darling as in old times. Her spirits more boisterous and sustained than ever; in fact, she is the happiest human being that I know and thinks herself so. Her progress in art is wonderful.'

Harriet Hosmer in Rome in the 1860s. 'Now that I am supporting myself I feel so frightfully womanly that I cannot describe my venerable sensations.' . . . 'It never entered my head that anybody could be so content on this earth, as I am here. I wouldn't live anywhere else but in Rome, if you would give me the Gates of Paradise and all the Apostles thrown in.'

The neoclassical sculptors lived for beauty, for the Sublime. For them
the Greeks and Romans had set a universal aesthetic standard for all time.
In the decades before Rodin, in his Parisian studio, pressed his fingerprints
into his clay and changed sculpture forever, all that mattered was the Ideal,
the uncluttered, proportioned, and generative Idea, floating in a space high
above changing fashions and smiling down on golden-hued Rome. For
Hattie to be able to go to the Capitoline Museum and experience those
timeless monuments, to be exposed daily to the great standing ruins of an
ancient world glinting under the lively sun, to be trained in the studio
of the man who had studied under Canova, to be free of prudish Miss
Grundyism and the restraints of genteel womanhood—all that mattered
was the Ideal—well, everything came together for Hattie.

She couldn't wait to bring the women to her studio. She had completed
a series of bare-breasted sculpture busts of such mythological women as
Daphne and Medea. Pure white Carrara marble—not a vein in sight. The
laurels under Daphne's nubile breasts lifted them; the serpent wound under
Medea's only emphasized their roundness. Circles in themselves, they
needed no support.

For Cornie's father, her patron Wayman Crow, she had completed a full-
length statue. 'I don't know how I shall ever express to you what I feel for all
your fatherly care of me,' she wrote to the man who within a year of her
arrival in Rome was supporting her. Dr. Hosmer had bowed out—at least
temporarily—pleading 'ill fortune,' and Hattie even sold her horse to
remain in Rome—till Mr. Crow took over and gave her what New Englan-
ders phrased 'a good start.'

'When I look around and see other artists who have been here for years
and still are waiting for a "start" and then think what a friend I have in you,
senza complimenti, I wonder why I have been so much more blessed than my
neighbors. Every successful artist in Rome, who is living, or who has ever
lived, owes his success to *his* Mr Crow.'

She chose to render a half-naked and grieving Oenone for Mr. Crow.
History has all but forgotten Oenone, and though Cornie begged to know
the literary reference—statues told stories in those days—Hattie teased her
and would not tell her for the longest time. Oenone was the woman Paris
rejected when he chose Helen. Hattie assumed herself rejected. She had
been very upset and shaken when Cornie married Lucien Carr. With a
sense of Puck-like mischief, mixed with regret, Hattie fashioned her first
large-scale commission for Cornie's father, adding in a secret kick.

Cornelia Crow Carr and *Oenone* by Harriet
Hosmer. The eldest child of a wealthy St.
Louis merchant, 'Cornie' was Hattie Hos-
mer's best friend and future biographer.
When Cornie told Hattie she was engaged,
Hattie responded: 'I am beaten—don't say
a word. Don't mention it—don't in any
way, even the most distant, allude to it.'
Oenone (1855) was commissioned by
Cornie's father and reflected Hattie's mixed
feelings about losing her friend to matri-
mony.

Puck himself was sitting there in Hattie's studio, looking as though he
were alive. Charlotte was taken at once, as was her generation. The mischievous sprite of Shakespeare's was a thirty-inch winged baby, sitting on a
toadstool, hard white marble translated into softest baby skin. Beyond his
chubby cheeks there was the baby pout, and in his pudgy hand he held a

scorpion he aimed to throw. Part angel, part scamp, part and parcel Hattie. She had sold more than one copy to the British aristocrats—the Prince of Wales was not yet old enough to buy one for his college room, but he would soon come to Rome and do just that. Mr. Crow had already suggested she raise her price from five hundred dollars, since they were going so well. (And she was spending so much of his money.)

Perhaps Puck holds the secret to Hattie. Everyone who knew her, from the Brownings to Grace Greenwood to Cornie (who became her biographer), speaks of her sense of fun. Half child, half woman, Grace called her. Pure sprite was Elizabeth Barrett Browning's designation. Madcap Hattie was Charlotte's frequent call. If the Greeks had a goddess of fun, she would have come down from Olympus to play a trick on Hattie. But fun has never been deified the way it was in that young artist.

Take the reclining full-length Beatrice Cenci she was working on. What could be more serious than the subject of that woman, involved in the killing of her incestuous father, then condemned to death by beheading. Hattie could not wait to show her to Charlotte and Matilda. The half-draped tragic beauty is in her cell, stretched out on a prison block. She seems asleep or in a languid swoon, her left arm dangling off the side of her harsh bed, a rosary in her hand. That arm is also pressed against her firm breasts, slightly squeezing them and pointing them toward the viewer. Hattie used female nudes in her studio, at a time when nude male models were used in Rome as the basis for both sexes. In the Beatrice Cenci she went one step further. She convinced her good friend and patron Lady Adelaide Talbur to pose for her. Had anything so daring been done in Rome since Princess Borghese took off her clothes for Antonio Canova?

Visiting Americans might say they found such nudity shocking, but that did nothing to make Hosmer's open-studio hours less popular, nor did it stop wealthy gentlemen—and their wives—from returning.

British aristocrats, male and female, took to Hattie immediately.

And Charlotte? Why, Hattie's growing fame had much to do with her. She was the woman who brought Harriet Hosmer to Rome. Whatever pain Hattie had caused Charlotte, Charlotte did what she always did, turned it around and cut her losses. Like an overly proud parent of a precocious child, Charlotte took her credit by doting.

'Ma,' Hattie called her.

Living with Hattie at the time was a woman Charlotte's age, Miss Emma Stebbins, an accomplished amateur artist from New York. On tour

Puck by Harriet Hosmer, 1855. Based on Shakespeare's Puck, who spreads confusion and pain by causing people to fall in love, Hosmer's mischievous imp was created at the time of Cornie Crow's marriage and was immediately understood as a 'laugh in marble,' appealing to its audience's sense of fun. When the Crown Princess of Germany viewed it in Hosmer's studio, she exclaimed, 'Oh, Miss Hosmer, you have such a talent for toes.'

with her mother and sisters in Rome, Miss Stebbins was encouraged by Hattie's success to entertain the thought of staying longer and pursuing her own art. Hattie might be the first, but, Charlotte quickly realized, she need not be the only professional woman sculptor in Rome.

Charlotte in fact was an integral part of a new development of the times: opening up professions other than teaching for women. Professions other than the 'genteel' slavery of governess-ship as well. 'Respectable' women had no other options. Just as Charlotte had discussed the plight of working women with Eliza Cook, she discussed the issue with her novelist friend from Manchester, Geraldine Jewsbury. It was in Manchester at the Queen's Theatre eleven years before that Charlotte Cushman tried out her Romeo for the first time in England, with her newly arrived sister Susan as her Juliet. Geraldine, like many with poor eyesight, took an extra relish, and extra delight, in what she saw.

Geraldine Jewsbury had just made a name for herself, having published her first novel, *Zoe: The History of Two Lives*. It dealt with the love between her heroine, the married Zoe, and a disillusioned Roman Catholic priest. Zoe and Father Everhard (yes, Ever hard) have a steamy love scene in the chapel of a burning castle. The novel caused a sensation.

Geraldine's publishers, Chapman and Hall, insisted she modify many of her sections before printing. Her unpublished letters to them during the editing process began compliantly and in good humor, new novelist that she was, but by the end of the process she was totally perplexed and put out. What they really wanted was a different book, a *domestic* book. At first she joked that if they were so very desperate about having heroes and heroines marrying and living happily ever after, she had another novel, partly written, that would end in a marriage in the parish church. But when the publishers actually suggested that they wait to publish the second novel rather than *Zoe,* she became quite serious and snapped that the reception of the book was her concern, not theirs. They knew as well as she that women did not begin to write novels without first counting the cost of the unjust and sneering speeches that might be made about them.

She didn't care a penny's worth what people might say, except as far as their criticism suggested practical hints for doing better next time. And when they asked the slightly built but fiery redhead how she wanted her name to read on the title page of her first novel—Miss Jewsbury or Geraldine Jewsbury—she told them, 'My own impression is that the name of *Miss* anybody, gives no weight to a book.'

Perhaps she should use a masculine nom de plume. She would ask her friend Jane Welsh Carlyle, the great philosopher's wife, for her advice and would abide by Mrs. Carlyle's decision. After the battles with Chapman and Hall, if not before, Geraldine must have realized the gentlemen might not have taken the book if it hadn't been urged on them, personally brought in and handed to them, by the brilliant and somehow always irresistible Jane Welsh Carlyle.

In the long run Geraldine entered the literary scene with her own name intact. The *Manchester Examiner* described Geraldine Jewsbury's *Zoe* as the vehement protest of a young, clever, susceptible Englishwoman against the thousandfold dullness of narrow provincial life.

Geraldine, with her red hair, whisper of a frame, and startlingly flamboyant manner, was anything but dull. At thirty-three years of age, she scorned the word 'propriety,' smoked cigars when she wished, used profanity, at times wore plunging necklines, at times men's clothing. She could become overinvolved in relationships with unavailable partners: priests, revolutionaries, younger men, and complexly committed married women. She was extremely conscious of the social restrictions that kept women from preparing for or performing 'meaningful work' and was interested in what Eliza Cook had to say on the subject, though the two women did not get along. 'Miss Cook,' Geraldine wrote to Charlotte, 'wd think me very good if she cd *believe* that another person might love you as well as she does.'

Geraldine and Charlotte had sworn eternal friendship almost as soon as they met. Didn't that give Geraldine the same rights? 'Do my darling love me as long as you can & as much as you can for I am superstitious about my friends & if I lose *one* it would be a breaking of the magic ring,' Geraldine wrote. 'Love me & believe that I love you a great deal more than I ever told you in words.'

There would always be an 'unweaned' quality to Geraldine's emotional life—she realized it herself. Perhaps it had to do with her mother dying when she was so young. Geraldine, born in that auspicious year 1812, the fourth of six children, believed she had hardly known mother love. She lost her mother when she was seven. Her sister, the poet and essayist Maria Jane Jewsbury, twelve years older than she, took on maternal duties and was a powerful influence on her, though Geraldine was eventually sent to boarding school for her education. Maria Jane married an Anglican minister when Geraldine was twenty and died in India the next year—leaving Geraldine in Manchester taking care of her father, a retired cotton manufacturer and insurance agent, and her dear youngest brother Frank.

Geraldine believed the age of the New Woman was about to dawn. She wrote of it to Mrs. Carlyle. She spoke of it with Miss Cushman. The time would come when women would be able to fulfill themselves with meaningful work. A time would come when marriage would not be the be-all and end-all of a woman's life. 'Women will be taught not to feel their destiny manqué if they remain single. They will be able to be friends and companions in a way they cannot be now.' Geraldine and Jane and Charlotte too were all in the forefront, imperfect examples of an evolving species. Love preoccupied women because they were expected to stay at home and think of nothing else. Charlotte must meet Mrs. Carlyle in London; no words could capture that extraordinary married woman. They would have so many things to talk about.

There was nothing Charlotte would rather do than meet Jane Welsh Carlyle. She had heard of Thomas Carlyle's wife through so many, including Ralph Waldo Emerson, an early influence on Charlotte's own life. For Charlotte had been in the choir of the Unitarian church in Boston when she was thirteen to sixteen, before the young Emerson, as if to answer Carlyle's call, left the ministry. A trust in yourself was not false pride but true piety, Emerson preached in his unorthodox sermons. The only true morality was being true to yourself. Follow the God within. Work hard. *Yourself* is what you earn by the sweat of your brow. *Herself.* Her individual self. Emerson's doctrine of self-reliance strengthened young Charlotte Cushman's resolve.

When as an adult she met up with Emerson again, in Manchester, England, in Boston, Massachusetts, he was full of enthusiasm concerning Carlyle. Everyone who was anyone came to 5 Cheyne Row in Chelsea to hear Thomas Carlyle talk, and most left captivated by Mrs. Carlyle as well. Geraldine raved about Mrs. Carlyle to Miss Cushman—and she raved about Miss Cushman to Mrs. Carlyle. 'Geraldine . . . is all in a blaze of enthusiasm about Miss Cushman the Actress—with whom she swore everlasting friendship in Manchester,' Jane growled.

At a moment when all London wanted to meet Charlotte Cushman, Jane Welsh Carlyle refused to know her.

Was it because she was an actress?

Geraldine swore on their friendship it had nothing to do with that. Charlotte wasn't 'too greenroom' for Mrs. Carlyle. Geraldine's own great enthusiasm for Miss Cushman turned Mrs. Carlyle sour. She was jealous. That was all.

An old slight, which still stung. For Charlotte still yearned to meet the Sage of Chelsea's wife. But she was in Rome now, where she entertained as always, bringing everyone to her. Hattie's success invigorated her. She had reached forty, but in Rome, this second season, she felt young.

When Matilda (a woman Geraldine Jewsbury *had* been able to introduce her to in those heydays) packed her bags and walked out yet again, Charlotte did not want to stop her. Let her go back to London as a writer on the newly formed *English Woman's Journal.* No matter that its publisher, soon to be recognized as George Eliot, thought she was given a job on the basis of her having nothing else she could do. Let her go back to the new friend who helped get her that job, the poet Adelaide Anne Procter. Adelaide Anne Procter, a pivotal champion of work for women, was also helping in the development of an all-women's printing press: Emily Faithfull and Company, Victoria Press (for the Employment of Women). Matilda seemed to gravitate toward women more famous then herself. And Charlotte had already found a new duty. Something of a higher nature that would demand Work.

Miss Emma Stebbins, staying with Hattie, remembered the first time she saw Charlotte. It was at a typical expatriate occasion. A man who thought he resembled Shakespeare, dressed like him, and invited everyone to his reading from the Bard. Shakspere Wood, an English sculptor and journalist who lived in Rome for over thirty years, was a fast friend and early supporter of Charlotte and her housemates on the Corso. From the beginning Shakspere called the women by their first names and escorted them to balls and dances, mincing and stuttering as he moved along, according to William Wetmore Story, who once referred to Charlotte and her friends as Shakspere Wood's 'harem (scarem).'

Charlotte came in late, as usual, to Shakspere's reading—punctuality was one of the few Yankee virtues she never mastered. She arrived in a flock of friends—including Matilda.

Miss Stebbins watched her sweep into the room. Such a stately bearing. Right from the first moment she saw the beauty within, which came to the surface only in the rich understanding of her deep-set gray-blue eyes. Stebbins, middle-aged herself—she was approaching forty—could appreciate the fine consideration Charlotte showed for her friends, doing small things that put their comfort ahead of her own.

Then Shakspere manqué began his reading of Shakespeare. The actress known for her Lady Macbeth, her Queen Katherine, her Romeo, her Hamlet, paid quiet attention. All aspiration to art, whether successful or not, Cushman respected. And that had to appeal to Miss Stebbins. For as fine an artist as Stebbins could be, there was not one piece she ever completed that she felt should not have been made better.

Hattie, who had the daredevil's ability to flaunt who she was at the same time that she disguised it, wrote to Mr. Crow: 'I have taken onto myself a wife in the form of Miss Stebbins, another sculptrice, and we are very happy together.' Were the sensitive, refined Miss Stebbins and the boisterous Hattie lovers? If they were, given Hattie's nature, they wouldn't be for long.

Miss Stebbins had been an artist since she could hold a crayon. There were no art schools in New York that accepted women, but she worked in oil painting, watercolors, pastels, crayons. In the 1840s, while Hattie was still detaching engines from trains, skipping school, and driving 'Elizabeth' crazy, Miss Stebbins developed a love for clay modeling.

That happened when the young sculptor Edward Bracket came from Vermont to New York to exhibit a group of his own clay models. Stebbins was fascinated by Bracket's tabletop pieces and became acquainted with him. She took the hints on sculpture he gave her and found out she had the sculptor's thumb.

Working in earnest, Stebbins did a bas-relief of one sister, a bust of another, and a bust as well of her brother Henry. Then she did a model of a boy catching a ball, which was looked on as very promising in its clay state. However, the figure was injured in casting, and true to her self-doubting and depreciating nature, such a mishap discouraged her. 'But the passion only slumbered,' her sister Mary Garland noted. When she came to Rome it awoke. For there she found a woman sculptor working. A younger woman, so different in temperament than she.

Miss Stebbins had the soul of an artist—always striving to bring out the voice she knew was within, yet never feeling confident that she had translated its call into her work.

When she met Charlotte, she spoke with that self-effacing quality, genius cloaked by timidity, that poor Rosalie Sully had. Rosalie never appreciated her own talent as an accomplished painter of miniatures. Here was Miss Stebbins, modestly asking Charlotte, Dare she imagine becoming a sculptor like Hattie?

She was *not* like Hattie; that Charlotte saw immediately. She was a woman of the most refined intellect and delicate sensibilities—a genius— who had so very little faith in her own ability that she needed Charlotte Cushman more than Hattie ever had.

Charlotte looked at this sweet-faced woman with her gentle eyes, as Jane Carlyle would one day describe them, who did not know her own worth. Why was she living with Hattie? Hattie was too busy with her own career to pay proper attention to another. True, Hattie had introduced her to John Gibson, who even commissioned a work, but Hattie would remain Gibson's only student. Hattie couldn't give this woman the support and encouragement she needed. Hattie only thought of herself.

Charlotte took Miss Stebbins up, in the fantastically generous and expansive way only Charlotte could. Her years of uncontrollable dependence (and youth) were over; she found what she called her 'own work' plainly marked out for her in her new friend. It was as if Miss Stebbins had immediately become a belonging, a loved one Charlotte could work for, a loved one that Charlotte could save.

The very dominance of Charlotte's nature turned Miss Stebbins' dreams into resolve. Never in good health, and with a chronic lung condition, Stebbins found the strength to throw aside her New York life along with her oils and pastels and devote herself to the rigors of the sculpture she loved. Many years later she would wonder to another scuptor, Anne Whitney, whether an artist didn't owe it to herself to pick the easiest mode of expression she could find. She certainly hadn't.

Miss Stebbins soon moved in with Charlotte and continued lessons in Paul Akers' studio, with an old Italian artist. Her sister Caroline stayed too. She married the painter John Rollin Tilton. No doubt about it, in those days Rome was magic. Or as sister Mary Garland discreetly wrote, everything in Rome was 'Creative.' And 'large-hearted Miss Cushman' had found the way to cater to Miss Stebbins' '*inner* needs.'

When Charlotte and Miss Stebbins exchanged rings and wed, Charlotte vowed eternal fidelity once more. And Charlotte seemed to predicate her attachment on a singular idea: Miss Stebbins could not live without her. Charlotte would lease out her London house on Bolton Row with all of its expense and obsolete associations with Matilda Hays and move to Rome. She had the most rewarding reason now for retiring from the stage and making the Eternal City her winter residence—to advance Miss Stebbins' career.

The relationship between Charlotte and Miss Stebbins has always been described as a mature love between equals: two middle-aged women who, through a mutually satisfying female friendship with somewhat hazy 'romantic' overtones, were able to dedicate themselves to each other and because of this more fully to their own work.

Charlotte's biographer Joseph Leach avoided the sexual issue. He pictured the compatible women in their black bowler hats on their daily rides to the Borghese Gardens, where they picnicked on wine and cheese under the pines. Lillian Faderman in *Surpassing the Love of Men* placed Miss Stebbins and Charlotte in her chapter about love and women who live by their brains. She concluded that their love was an equal balance, all of its harmonious energies enhancing both their careers. 'Their relationship worked on every level,' without any kind of male-female competition, and, in her opinion, without any 'genital' sex. To most twentieth-century critics it seemed as if human nature itself skipped a generation when it came to Victorian women.

Charlotte Cushman, seated, and Emma Stebbins, taken around 1859, after the couple exchanged rings and vowed eternal fidelity and love to one another.

Certainly the quick marriage between the 'sculptrice' who had been so fleetingly Hattie's wife was not as sexually charged a relationship as it was an emotionally charged one for Miss Stebbins and a psychologically charged one for Charlotte—if one could, momentarily, put a finger on such shifting things. But the couple were, after all, doing more than swearing eternal friendship with one another; they *were* married—with as much or as little sex as that institution implies.

And there appeared to be no special ingredient in female marriages that made them run more smoothly than male-female marriages. In matters of love, women of genius who worked with their brains seemed to have no less difficulty than their male counterparts in living by them.

'The winter of 1856–57 passed swiftly, and only closed too soon,' Stebbins remembered.

It was brought to its end by financial chaos. Right after their union, Charlotte found that her business manager in Philadelphia had not credited the interest due on seventy thousand dollars; worse yet, he had falsified the records of what was owed her.

Charlotte had done a lot of investing during her profitable 'farewell' to the American stage. She scouted prime real estate in Delaware and New Jersey, bought a house for Sallie's mother in Philadelphia. But now there was an economic downturn sweeping the States, and in that crunch she found she had an untrustworthy manager. Once more it was necessary to come out of retirement and return to America, in order to straighten out her finances and earn some more money for her new life in Rome.

Miss Stebbins put her career on hold. She left the copies and the casts she was working on in order to accompany her spouse. A separation from Charlotte was unthinkable. The need Stebbins had developed for Charlotte was for Charlotte a satisfaction.

Before they sailed, they found the perfect setting for their future life together. A fine tall house at 38 Via Gregoriana at the top and to the left of the Spanish Steps—a wonderful location at the very height of things. They were less than a block from where Percy Bysshe Shelley once lived and John Keats died; they were at the hub of expatriate life. Charlotte leased the property. Extensive renovations would be made while they were away. Dear Hattie would look after things—when she had the time.

Hattie, cheerful as ever, seemed not to flinch when Charlotte took over Stebbins' life. She even suggested, since Charlotte would be acting in St. Louis, why didn't she consult Wayman Crow about her bungled business affairs? Here was a man of impeccable honesty and tremendous business ability who appreciated women artists. Mr. Crow handled all of Hattie's finances, and all of Fanny Kemble's. She gave Charlotte a note of introduction and she wrote to Wayman Crow that Charlotte Cushman was coming.

Lady Love

NEW YORK, ST. LOUIS

1857–1858

ROME, PARIS

1859–1860

C HARLOTTE ALWAYS characterized her returns to the American stage in the same way—she had to make more money. This time it was true. Not only had her Philadelphia manager failed her, but America itself was in a deep financial slump.

The theatre too was suffering. Yet during the worst November for the box office that New York had ever seen, Charlotte Cushman's name sold tickets. It seemed to have a mysterious, exotic, international appeal. Theatre people jealously rumored that Miss Cushman shrewdly planned this dramatic return to the stage. But of course, Matilda Hays left her, Miss Stebbins arrived, her Philadelphia manager cheated her. Sheer coincidence brought her back to a financially troubled New York thirsty for her 'foreign' glamour.

Charlotte was pleased the Stebbins family could see her success, but would have been more gratified if they were less supportive of Miss Stebbins' career, would have left it financially as well as emotionally up to her. But Miss Stebbins' brother Henry had his home walled with his sister's earlier oils, crayons, and pastels. Henry, a banker and member of the New York Stock Exchange, insisted on footing his sister's Roman bills. The only member of the Stebbins family who seemed to view Charlotte without some amount of genteel unease was Miss Stebbins' old mother, who loved her right away. Like many a good local wine, Miss Stebbins did not travel well. So Charlotte left her spouse with her family on Gramercy Park and went on tour with Sallie by her side. Less than a year after she and Miss Stebbins exchanged rings and married, in January 1858, Charlotte arrived for a two-week run in St. Louis.

She opened at Wood's Theatre and the very next day met with Wayman Crow in his office. Mr. Crow's bearing was strong, his high-foreheaded oval face both serious and sensitive, his blue eyes intelligent and quite lively. It was not surprising that his business office was lined with books. He, like Charlotte, was self-educated and had a deep respect for the books he found for himself.

Wayman Crow was as much a self-made man as Charlotte Cushman was a self-made woman. There was not that much difference in age. He was approaching fifty, Charlotte was half a year away from forty-two. They were both Unitarians. Like Charlotte, Mr. Crow had a quintessential American success story. He had gone to school in a log cabin in Kentucky, was apprenticed to a country store keeper at the age of twelve. Before he was twenty-one (legal age), he was so respected that not only was he appointed postmaster of his town of Cadiz, he bought out control of an entire dry goods business on credit—and paid back all his notes before they were due.

Charlotte went to England for six months and ended up living abroad. Wayman Crow went to St. Louis on a business trip and became ill. This lucky misfortune gave him time to realize the young city's potential as a commercial center to an America expanding west. Beginning with a Philadelphia partner, he established in St. Louis what would through the years evolve into Crow, Hargadine & Company, the largest and best-known wholesale dry goods business in the West. He would see his firm successfully through every financial crisis the country went through from 1835 to his death in 1884. Every business endeavor he connected himself to, including rails, was a success. He became a Missouri state senator (on the Whig ticket) and was as charitable as he was wealthy. He gave freely and intelligently to educational causes, and to the arts—particularly to women artists. Married young to Isabella B. Conn, he had four strong daughters and one rather challenged son.

Both Charlotte and Wayman had unending faith in their young country and the resolute tenacity it takes to rise from nothing and stake a claim.

They were willing to work flesh from bone if needed in order to succeed. Wayman Crow had as well an absolutely unblemished integrity. But then again, he was a man in a man's world; he spoke the right language.

Charlotte realized at once the benefit Mr. Crow could be to her. How lucky of Hattie to have met him through Cornie. But now there *she* was, facing him across his sturdy desk.

She listened attentively, the way she always did with important men, careful to make them feel important. (Nothing coy or greenroom in her attitude, just a sensible, intelligent spinster lady seeking advice.) She listened to astute Wayman Crow tell her that her money should be kept where it was, at work in railroads, mines, and city real estate. Conditions were poor at the time, but things ran in cycles, investments would appreciate. Charlotte was on the right track and would need patience to ride out these bad times. Mr. Crow offered to be of service to her in any way he could. After her disastrous experience with her Philadelphia manager, Charlotte did not feel herself free to sign away control. No need to. Wayman Crow was willing to advise Miss Cushman as she wished.

She stood up to leave, telling him how grateful she was for his time and his help. What endless trouble we are with our money matters, we spinster ladies.

He stood up. Could she stay a minute? He knew there would be someone waiting outside his office more than eager to meet her.

Of course.

He ushered in his daughter Emma, one of Cornie's younger sisters.

Emma Crow was nineteen years old. There was something of Hattie in her, Charlotte thought immediately, except that Emma was a beauty, and she dressed, not like a boy, but like a lady.

Emma had been in the audience the night before, when Charlotte opened her St. Louis run with *Romeo and Juliet*.

The girl had never seen the play acted before. And when Miss Cushman appeared onstage as Romeo, a thrill ran through her. It was as if the actress read her mind. Charlotte's Romeo was the literal incarnation of the ideal lover that Emma fancied, the perfect, virile lover Emma dreamed of at night: 'It was an epoch in my young life.'

The part of Juliet was played by a protégée of Miss Cushman's, the ever so small and pretty Mary Devlin, who subsequently became Edwin Booth's first wife. The young actress had the luxuriant head of thick dark hair Emma wished she had:

Charlotte Cushman as Romeo with her Juliet (here her sister Susan), in a lithograph by Margaret Gillies, 1846.

'She wore her own beautiful hair in ringlets down her back and everyone must have felt a thrill when in the balcony scene at the moment of impassioned parting, Romeo returned again and again for a last embrace and finally pressed one of those ringlets to his lips.'

It was one of Charlotte's inspired bits of business, running back for the last time, twirling Juliet's lock of hair between her fingers, then kissing it passionately before parting. With that gesture, as Emma phrased it, Romeo won more hearts than Juliet's.

In her father's office, her hands trembling, her cheeks reddened, Emma Crow, as usual, spoke her mind. Perhaps it was because Miss Cushman was a woman that she understood what girls dream?

Mr. Crow attempted to cut through his daughter's enthusiasm. Her naïveté? As he spoke, Charlotte studied the privileged young girl. She was not unlike Anne Brewster. Fair Anne reading out Shakespeare for Charlotte in those early Philadelphia days. Charlotte hearing from her fine, cultured lips the very *poetry* of the dramatist. It had been a revelation, a 'new world.'

Finances were no longer on Miss Cushman's mind. Her middle-aged Romeo, it would appear, could still make a maiden swoon with desire—right in front of her father's eyes.

When the unexpected happens, it follows no common route. It was the nineteen-year-old Emma Crow who actively pursued the forty-one-year-old woman.

For the two weeks of Charlotte's stay, every day, Wayman would send a carriage and Charlotte would visit at the Crows' grand house overlooking the Mississippi. Wayman Crow had freed his household slaves only four years before. One wonders if this intimacy would have developed as smoothly if he hadn't. For Charlotte always assured Sallie's safety and comfort before she left the Eastern states. As it was, Charlotte mingled with the family at home and took rides along the Mississippi with Emma. (One wonders what the Crows made of Sallie.)

And just as Hattie had in her Watertown days, Emma Crow came to all of Charlotte's performances. Charlotte showed the girl the scene room, the greenroom, her dressing room.

Emma wanted to return to New York with her. Well, Miss Stebbins was waiting there.

'But you will come to Rome.'

Charlotte left St. Louis on a steamer to Memphis. Caught in a snowstorm, she wrote to Emma, 'The Enthusiasm of Youth is too precious not to be gathered up, so I gather you dear. We shall meet again——.' She hoped to return to St. Louis in early April, but if not, she'd find some way to see Emma again before she left the country in June.

Emma coyly revised history, remembering that it had been Charlotte who initiated their relationship that day she came to Charlotte's hotel room.

'I don't *believe a word of it*!' Charlotte replied. 'You were "got up"—as the slang expression is—in a very womanly and *dignified* way.' Yet Emma's pretty, childlike nervousness, her hesitation and blushes, betrayed her. They had not a bit of the 'dignified lady' in them. So don't accuse Charlotte of breaking down the walls of decorum! When she asked Emma, 'Do you love me a little,' she already knew the answer. She just wished to hear it from Emma's lips.

Which she certainly did.

They embraced after the acknowledgment, kissed, petted in the hotel room. But they went no further. They were still technically in the realm of female friendship, which could be very effusive and intoxicating—and diffused. Women swore eternal friendship all the time; had romantic friendships not predicated on sexual consummation. Charlotte thought it best, as much as she was still thinking, to keep their love on this emotionally ambiguous level. She was a newly married woman with a dear new little friend. Hattie had Cornie Crow. Charlotte had Emma Crow. In short Charlotte kidded herself.

Emma signed herself 'little lover.' Charlotte signed herself 'your not ungentle mistress,' and at times 'your ungentle mistress.' Often she called herself Emma's 'ladie love.' This role reversal, with the beautiful young girl pursuing the strapping mannish actor, Charlotte found amusing, certainly part of the irrepressible Emma's charm. 'All that is young and fresh & enthusiastic has especial charm for me. I see my own young aspirations & feelings reflected— . . . wondering how I ever should excite such feelings which others have excited in me.' She told the girl she released a mixture of sensations in her at an age when such pleasure was rare. Like Cupid's arrow released on so many a Roman wall and frescoed ceiling, this hit was entirely unexpected.

'Do you really love me? How funny!' Emma wrote. Charlotte would have none of that.

'Is it funny dear or only strange or does your "*funny*" mean "strange," you dear little patronizing monkey. Explain your meaning. "Funny" to me implies something *ludicrous!* and that is an element I don't like in love!'

Right from the beginning of their relationship, there had to be careful scripting. Emma must remember that when Charlotte came back to St. Louis to visit her, even if the actress was talking to Papa or sister, she was there only for Emma. And Emma must burn her letters.

As for Emma's dream of coming to Charlotte's hotel room to *sleep* with her: 'I think if I were your Papa or Mamma . . . I should be sorry to have you do such a thing. I need not assure you of the true pleasure it would be to me—your own heart which tells you that you are dear to me will speak for me—if you doubt that *I want you.* . . . If I were on a visit to your house I would open my own gladly to such a visit. You should talk to me & keep me awake all night if you would—but I don't like my "pretty white bird" coming to the Hotel to sleep.'

The erotic undertones of the letters were driving Emma to distraction. Emma was far from fond of her own fine-textured, medium brown hair. Charlotte was very fond of it: 'If I do sleep with you—I will cut off one of your curls as you lay sleeping by my side.' And as far as Emma calling herself a *goose* rather than a swan: 'I will *punish* you for all these things when I see you.'

Emma, strong-willed when she was not flushing under Charlotte, made sure the actress was invited to sleep at the Crows' home when she returned to St. Louis. And Charlotte did return, later than she wished, in time to become very troubled by Emma's condition. 'You seemed so very poorly & I did not like your symptoms at all. Pray Heaven you are not ill.'

They had no privacy. Charlotte went to church with the Crow family. She involved herself with Emma's older sister Mary and the much younger children—six-year-old Wayman Junior and two-year-old Isabel. But for all of that careful scripting, Wayman Crow declared he would not bring his daughter to Rome with him that winter.

Emma wanted to go with Charlotte anyway. She wanted to live with her—forever. And Emma was used to getting her own way.

All this forced Emma's 'ladie love' to be a very ungentle mistress indeed: 'Do you not know that I am already married, I wear this upon the 3rd finger of my left hand?'

Emma would have to content herself with knowing that the married Charlotte loved her.

They must be thankful for the time they had together and trust that in the future they would find ways to meet and be together again. At nineteen Emma hadn't the older woman's patience—or her other ties. She did have a

Emma Crow, the third daughter and middle child of Wayman Crow and younger sister of Cornie, soon after Charlotte met her. Charlotte advised from Rome: 'My darling must try to *make a purpose* for herself & this *may* perhaps bring her more surely to me next year!'

mama and papa who were not at all pleased by this excitement aroused by Miss Cushman.

Charlotte succeeded in having Miss Stebbins sail back to Europe ahead of her. She extended her own engagements in New York, ostensibly while her mother Mary Eliza and sister Susan came on a visit.

The Crows summered in the East, as usual, in fashionable Newport, Rhode Island, and Charlotte got to see Emma again—in Pittsfield, Massachusetts. Emma and her family were on their way to Lenox to visit the Sedgwicks and the actress Fanny Kemble, whose money Mr. Crow managed. Emma wanted Charlotte to continue on with them. Impossible.

'And how is it with you, dear little lover mine?' Charlotte wrote from the

Metropolitan Hotel in New York. 'Are you glad to get rid of your "ungentle mistress"? Or are you thinking more tenderly of her as your "ladie love?" I am very much afraid I was a burden to you during my last few hours. You seemed pre-occupied & troubled. I hope my objections to going to Lenox will be productive of no disagreeable result. . . . Had Mrs Kemble not been in Lenox I would have.'

When Charlotte began her career onstage, Fanny Kemble was her idol and inspiration: 'I had a real hero-worship for her.' But it was actually another British actor, William Macready, who led her to her craft.

Charlotte was only ten years old when her seafaring uncle, Captain Augustus Babbitt, her mother's brother, took her to the theatre. The captain was a bachelor and Charlotte was his favorite niece. 'He took great interest in me,' she remembered, and 'offered me prizes for proficiency in my studies, especially music and writing.'

To others, she could be a handful: 'I am afraid I was what the French call "un enfant terrible"—full of irresistible life and impulsive will—living fully in the present looking neither before nor after, as ready to execute as to conceive—full of imagination.' This imaginative faculty was often thwarted by her parents, who feared she was lying, neither she nor they realizing she was really, quite spontaneously, quite intuitively, acting.

Uncle Augustus was the only one who understood her. 'My uncle had great taste and love for the Dramatic profession,' and took it upon himself to introduce her to the stage 'in one of his return voyages, which was always a holiday time for me.' At ten years old, she watched the famous British actor William Macready perform Shakespeare's *Coriolanus*, with great passion and grand gesture, yet in a human, natural voice. The first of many plays Uncle Augustus took her to.

Charlotte was always a great mimic—'*Imitation* a prevailing trait'—and the little girl added Macready's deep, resonant voice to her repertoire of farm animals and odd clerics. By deepening her own voice she could speak like the man. She insisted on male parts from then on at the theatricals she held in her big old Boston attic with her friends, and for the first time, in school, she lost her shyness and spoke up, giving a startlingly apt recitation as Brutus. 'No wonder she can recite,' jealous classmates opined. 'She goes to the Theatre!'

Eighteen years later, the same grand William Macready requested that Charlotte be his Lady Macbeth when he toured the States and played in New York and Philadelphia. Unusual for Charlotte, she became frightened.

She restudied her Lady Macbeth till she almost drove herself to distraction. Then she had to put it aside: 'I must do something to get back my unconsciousness' till opening night. She found working with Macready like walking on eggshells, never knowing when the arrogant, explosive ego of the actor might erupt at her expense. He walked on eggshells as well. As much as she praised him, he had a paranoid's sixth sense and did not trust her.

They looked very much alike, the same height, stance, jutting chin. Even her mother Mary Eliza found it eerie. When Charlotte played Lady Macbeth to his Macbeth in Philadelphia, a child in the audience piped up, asking which was Macready and which was Miss Cushman, to which the father replied, 'Whichever you please, dear.'

When she played with Macready in New York, he reiterated what she already knew, but from a more utterly British point of view. The *only* audience that counts, the *only* acting that counts, is in England. She simply must go there if she wanted to arrive. So she set sail on the *Garrick,* against her mother's inclinations, particularly since Uncle Augustus had recently been lost at sea. Charlotte arrived safely in Liverpool to find no letters from her mother, though many from Macready. He wanted her to play against him in Paris. But as hungry as she was in those early days, she was too shrewd to begin with him—or to replace and thereby insult Helen Faucit, a well-respected British actress. As angry as he was, as much as he fumed, after she was established, he later played against her in London. There was even a rather unremarkable if chaotic royal performance. And there was as always the inevitable comparison:

> *What figure is this which appears on the scene?*
> *'Tis Madame Macready—Miss Cushman, I mean,*
> *What a wondrous resemblance! the walk on the toes,*
> *The eloquent, short, intellectual nose—*
> *The bend of the knee, the slight sneer of the lip,*
> *The frown on the forehead, the hand on the hip;*
> *In the chin, in the voice, 'tis the same to a tittle,*
> *Miss Cushman is Mister Macready in little. . . .*

There were deeper similarities as well. Both were of a literary intelligence, both abhorred the tinsel and trappings of their trade, both were uneasy about their social position as actors, both, Charlotte less obviously, were snobs.

No fault with the striking resemblance we find,
'Tis not in the person alone, but the mind.

Their similarities added to their distrust of each other.

Macready was her first taste of the stage; but British Fanny Kemble, whom Charlotte saw on her first American tour, was her intoxication. She sent the actress who played Juliet flowers, messages, gifts.

'It is too early in the year to be beginning your flower bounties to me,' Mrs. Kemble pleaded in one note to her, '& I *beg* you not to waste your money so terribly for . . . it gives me annoyance rather than pleasure.' Charlotte wrote poetry and some of it was published. But her poems to Mrs. Kemble were of a personal nature: 'Thank you for the verses & the book but I have a whole library of yours already' was the response.

And then when Charlotte arrived in Philadelphia at the age of twenty-four, as luck would have it, Fanny Kemble was living there, and of course a constant visitor to her relatives the Sullys. Thomas Sully was British by birth, from a theatrical family, and Rosalie's full name was Rosalie Kemble Sully. Charlotte commissioned a miniature from Rosalie and greatly admired the result. She sent it in a locket to Mrs. Kemble, who admired it as well but would not accept Charlotte's miniature any more than she would accept a box for the opera. She previously heard the same music performed perfectly well outside of Philadelphia, thank you.

Fanny Kemble had married a socially prominent Philadelphian, Pierce Butler, who at the beginning was madly in love with her. She did not realize the extent of his slaveholdings until they moved to Butler Island, Georgia, when it became her husband's turn to manage the family's plantations. Slavery appalled Fanny. That slave families were separated, mothers or fathers sold off without a second thought, particularly horrified her. She did not keep her views to herself, and when she could fought against the system. Nor did it escape her attention that some of the house slaves resembled her husband, who had not given up claiming his master's right. It was a very contentious, ill-fated marriage on many levels.

By the time Charlotte arrived in Philadelphia, Fanny was separated from her husband, who maintained jurisdiction over their two daughters. He had carried out his threat: if Fanny left him, she would lose her children. This terrible injustice infuriated Charlotte, who let Fanny know she had a plan by which the actress could claim her children, even as she divorced her husband. 'My dear Miss Cushman . . . There is one thing in your note &

Fanny Kemble by Thomas Sully, ca. 1844. The British actress and writer told Wayman Crow that she feared their adored Hattie Hosmer's 'peculiarities' would stand in the way of her artistic success with people of society.

one alone having reference to my affairs which I will answer. You say that I have become convinced that you cannot serve me—it is perfectly true. I am so convinced I am certain that *nobody* can as my lawyers & friends one & all have been obliged to admit.'

Charlotte seemed to have suggested a way of entrapping Butler sexually. Fanny found the suggestion quite unseemly—if not downright tawdry. And it gave her a rare, unfiltered glimpse into Charlotte's soul and the lengths she was willing to go to for those she loved.

Though she would socialize with Charlotte after church on occasion, Mrs. Kemble avoided all other social contact.

Emma, in Lenox with her family, was surprised to find that Fanny Kemble, who had so many glowing things to say of Hattie Hosmer, said nothing—not a word—about Charlotte. 'We have had some passages in our lives full of trouble & vexation & mortification to me. And Mrs. Kemble does not love me more from misunderstanding than any wrong in me. So you must not be surprised if you find her silent in regard to me.'

Fanny Kemble was a woman of the world. Imagine Charlotte arriving at Fanny's 'Perch' in Lenox with their financial advisor's young daughter trembling by her side.

Emma would have to wait till their week together in New York. Even though Wayman was against it, Charlotte was so sure of Emma's powers of persuasion and her father's love of indulging her that when a knock came on her door one Tuesday morning at seven o'clock, she called out, 'Open the door for Miss Crow!'

In walked Charlotte's mother, returned from a trip to Niagara.

'I was just heartsick.'

When the Crows visited Charlotte in New York, they did *not* bring Emma with them. Mrs. Crow explained that their daughter would have had to spend too much time alone in Charlotte's hotel while Charlotte worked.

'Emma knew that my mother & sister were here, who would have taken care of her!'

'I did not know *that,* or she should have come,' Mr. Crow replied.

'So darling,' Charlotte instructed, 'if you had asked a reason for their decision you would most likely have been able to get away to your loving friend, who *bitterly regrets* missing you!'

But Emma did know her parents' reason for not bringing her, no matter how politely they covered it up.

Hattie had not helped matters by writing jovially to the Crows from Rome that she had heard Charlotte and Emma 'are what we this side of the ocean call "lovers"—but I am not jealous and only admire Emma for her taste.' Hattie thought she was playing. 'Lovers' in her day could mean nothing more than romantic friends. When the term signified sexual passion as well, Victorian women became quite discreet.

Charlotte was very careful in addressing her letters to Emma. Every one began with terms of endearment, yet not one salutation would ever bear Emma's name. That safeguard was hardly enough. She instructed her lady love to destroy her letters.

'Darling mine. I wish you would *burn* my letters. I have asked you to also—you do not know into whose hands an accident might make them fall—suppose anything should chance to you—suddenly—& your papers were—*looked* through. If you do not promise to burn them I shall have to be careful how I write & you will not *like that.* You can always keep *one* and when another comes then destroy the old one.'

That had always been Charlotte's method. She would keep the last letter her lover wrote until the next one arrived. That old letter from Rosalie Sully, for example, that one in which she told Charlotte she prayed to die, was probably the last letter Rosalie was allowed to write, for it is the only one that remains.

Charlotte was destroying Emma's letters right from the beginning, and was concerned, as well as touched, by the girl's reluctance to do the same. Well, she would have to now that her lady love was returning to Europe. Emma was forced to promise, and without the two having opportunity to meet again, Charlotte went on her way.

AN OCEAN between a forty-two-year-old woman and a nineteen-year-old girl, even an extraordinary girl with a mind of her own, should have created a large enough 'field of force' to put things in perspective for Charlotte. (Michael Faraday's recently published work on the field theory of electromagnetism was already being incorporated into the language of love.) But by the end of the year Charlotte was compelled to write to Emma, 'Love is so eminently *subtle* that it cannot be controlled.'

She had hardly written to the girl over the summer. When she did, she spelled out her commitment to Miss Stebbins, how anxiously the sculptress awaited her in London, how the two went to Great Malvern for the water cures and afterwards to Tintern Abbey, where she showed Miss Stebbins that lovely ruin.

Emma's long letters followed her from place to place. Charlotte excused her own lapses. If she lived for herself alone, she would have more leisure time. But she sometimes allowed herself to be molded according to the will of the one she was with. 'Forgive the writer for making a lady wait. But then you are not a lady if you are my lover &—I am by all woman laws—justified by precedent in making you wait!'

Charlotte returned to London to make arrangements for the leasing of her big, costly house at 1 Bolton Row. Her mother was brimming with disapproval of Charlotte's new life in Rome, with yet another woman to drain her. It would be useless to explain to her mother that Miss Stebbins, of the New York banking family, paid her own way.

It was a shame that she could not stay in England long enough to see her nephew Ned—sister Susan's son by her first marriage. Charlotte had lived with Ned for most of his first twelve years—until Susan remarried and moved to Liverpool. Soon after that second marriage Charlotte adopted her young nephew in order to make him her legal heir. She did not see her 'handsome boy' often, but she paid his bills. Now Edwin Charles Merriman Cushman—Ned—was twenty years old and in the merchant marine. She had just received a letter from Calcutta telling Auntie he'd be in Liverpool in early October. She wrote to Emma, 'I long to see the dear "fellow" who is believed to be his auntie's darling—but his auntie has another darling. Do you know who she is & where she is?'

In Rome, Miss Stebbins, pale and ill from the journey, found the house not ready; the workmen were still busy at 38 Via Gregoriana. Since neither she nor Charlotte could speak Italian, the alterations were taking even longer, and Hattie was too busy at her studio to help. If only Hattie's luck would rub off on Miss Stebbins. The younger sculptor was 'fat and jolly,' leaping with her horse, as reckless in her pursuits as she was free. Miss Stebbins was setting up her studio too. She was working on a commission that Charlotte had secured for her in St. Louis—by pressuring Mr. Crow: two crayon drawings of Hattie.

Hattie had so many commissions. She was working on a full-scale *Zenobia*. That ancient Queen of Palmyra, a famed warrior, intellectual, and patron of the arts, was brought to Rome in chains. And it looked as if with Mr. Crow's help she would be awarded the monumental Senator Thomas Benton to be erected in St. Louis. Her mischievous *Puck* was still a favorite among the British aristocrats. While Charlotte was in America, Hattie had sold copies to the Duke of Hamilton and Earl Fitzwilliam.

With a rather full plate of complementary motives, Charlotte offered Hattie free quarters in her house on Via Gregoriana, to do up as she pleased. And Hattie promised 'Ma' her own copy of *Puck*—for which Charlotte was wise not to hold her breath.

Meanwhile, Hattie terrorized Pa with the bills for the renovations she was making on her free flat at 38 Via Gregoriana. Charlotte had a theory about Dr. Hosmer that she confided in Emma. He was faking his terror. For if Wayman Crow believed the doctor meant to restrict his daughter's expenditures, he would come to the rescue, once more sparing the doctor's paternal purse. 'Of course this is *entre nous* & a private opinion,' one which Emma was still not burning.

While Charlotte whispered such things to Wayman Crow's daughter, Hattie, responsible for Charlotte's entering her patron's life, shrewdly explained her living arrangements to Mr. Crow. By moving in at 38 Via Gregoriana, 'I shall keep a sharper lookout on Miss Cushman and not allow her to go on in this serious manner with Emma—it is really dreadful and I am really jealous—furthermore, it is a bad lookout for Emma, for, and you may tell her if you like, that unless she restrains her emotions, she will never get a husband. Tell her I speak from experience.'

Mr. Crow told her. But Emma had no intention of restraining her emotions.

Hattie was just jealous of any other person knowing a bit more about the Crow family than she did, Charlotte explained. Recently she said to Charlotte, 'I hear Mr Crow has made an investment for you in Liberty Bonds.'

'Indeed,' Charlotte answered, '& this is all I know.'

She allowed Hattie to believe she was still the queen of the Crows. 'Never mind if she approves or not dear. I love you very much & shall continue to do so.'

Living at the hotel while the workmen finished, Charlotte gained firsthand knowledge that English was widely spoken, making it easy for American and English travelers. Emma's father should be informed of this.

'I wish I could hold you to my heart for ten minutes just to show you how hard I love you & how much I want to see you. You *shall* come to me when you will & you *shall* stay with me as long as you like. Can I say more?'

But Emma would not come that season. Her father was finally persuaded to bring her with him to Europe, but at the last minute changed his mind about going himself and would not allow his daughter to travel alone. Had Fanny Kemble said something? 'She does not love me & does not speak of me well or kindly.' Or was it possible that Papa was jealous of Charlotte's influence on Emma?

'I hope not! He is too good & noble for that. Yet if it has been suggested to him that your association with me was not well for you, he would be justified in not wishing to bring you within my world.'

Charlotte would look on the bright side and not doubt. 'All will be well!'

All was well at 38 Via Gregoriana. Finally Charlotte and Miss Stebbins and Hattie moved in. A new household of women, with Sallie, as usual, the right hand.

Miss Stebbins remembered those days in terms of staffing and the Italian penchant for exhibiting a *bella figura*. There was the cook Augusto, with the most orderly kitchen, he himself a picture of cleanliness in his white uniform. But as soon as dinner was served, 'he became quite an elegant gentleman and went forth, probably, to *flâner* with the best on the Pincian, leaving the cleanup to his staff.'

There was the handsome waiter or majordomo, who, though he could neither read nor write, was so impressive to look at that more than one young lady visitor declared he was closer to their ideal of what a Roman prince was like than any of the genuine article.

Rome itself could be epitomized by their own back gardens, with their luxuriant growth and artfully placed shards of antiquity. One looked out over to Via Sistina with its artist studios and its apartments from which Italians conducted the drama of family life window to window in very high-pitched voices. Not at all *musical,* according to Miss Stebbins.

But for Charlotte, all this local color underscored desire. She looked out over the back gardens thinking of how to get Emma to Rome. She could see St. Peter's dome in the distance, and past it uninterrupted countryside and wide sky. In that soft, evocative clime, in that unhurried village atmosphere of *Roma, com' era,* she could walk up the street to the top of the Spanish Steps, where the Church of Santa Trinità dei Monti stood; she could hear the French nuns' voices at twilight while Bernini's fountain splashed silently far below. All sites sang: Love is too subtle to be controlled.

Yet plans could be made. As Charlotte would one day write to Emma: 'My professional position has brought me before the public so that my life & character is known, more than that of women generally. This influences your idea of my ability & worth.' Added to Charlotte's celebrity, Emma looked at her through the eyes of her love and found in her a superiority that Charlotte failed to see.

'I do not for a moment propose that I am not as women go a tolerably clever woman. I understand my fellow beings better than most women have an opportunity of doing—because women primarily living an indoor life get their ideas of men and things through their family or books.'

She would use her worldly wisdom to bring her love to Rome. Emma must involve her older sister Mary in her European plans. Cornie was already married and mother of a daughter named Hatty. And of course Isabel was still a child. But if two of his daughters were planning a European excursion, Papa could no longer have the excuse of not wanting Emma to go *alone,* whether or not he came along.

She kept an empty apartment just waiting for the girls—and for a chaperone if Mr. Crow insisted. The rooms connected with Charlotte and Miss Stebbins' apartment so that Emma could be with them as much as she liked. Hattie's rooms adjoined, she could tell her father. She would have the benefit of Hattie's protection as well, if Mr. Crow doubted Charlotte's alone.

Then, out of the blue, Emma wrote to Charlotte that she had a marriage proposal and was deciding what to do.

'Your letter gave me unnecessary pain,' Charlotte answered, but not very quickly. Had she expected Charlotte to jump, begging her not to accept her gentleman? 'If so, darling, you have mistaken me.'

Marriage was a 'very, very' serious subject, one about which Charlotte never joked in her life. She could not believe Emma was simply *flirting* with her, that would be too unworthy of her little lover. So she would take this marriage proposal in dead earnest. Marriage without love was too miserable a contract for any woman who had either intelligence or heart. In fact, it was a sin which brings its own punishment.

Emma should see more of the world, and then if she told Charlotte she had found a companion upon whom she could rely in every way, Charlotte would be among those blessing the union.

Although Charlotte signed this letter 'Your faithful "Ladie," ' she'd given Emma a well-deserved dressing-down. Only an unfortunate accident—a bad fall before she posted the letter—jolted her, and brought her to add a warmer postscript.

For an uncanny thing happened. Her handsome young nephew Ned, after visiting his mother and half sisters in Liverpool, had come on to Rome to stay with his adopted mother for a while. Just back from India—and getting over fever—Ned was being encouraged by Auntie Charlotte to end his seafaring days. That life was destroying his health as well as abetting his dissolute tendencies.

Everything had been handed to Ned all his life—and not by his no-good father. In Rome, barely twenty-one, he was dancing to his heart's content, as was his wont, and out riding with Auntie on her splendid horses as much as he could. Well, Ned knew absolutely nothing about Emma, but he had seen her picture on Charlotte's piano and found her quite striking. He was very much moved.

'Ned has run away with your picture. It seems a strange coincidence.'

Either Ned wrote to Emma or convinced Auntie to send her his picture. Charlotte hoped Mr. Crow would not see it, not that he need be alarmed. 'Ned is such an absolute sailor *boy*, that my "little lover" will never take a fancy to him, she will find that he has not sufficient weight of character or rather force of character to be a life companion.'

Miss Stebbins captured Ned's rather dissolute charm and his considerable virility in a tabletop marble. He stands open-shirted, slim-waisted, hands on hip. Broad-foreheaded, wide-eyed, full-lipped. The sensuality of the piece is notable, right down to the bulge of his tight trousers. Its blatant masculine virility went beyond anything Hattie would even think of rendering. Her male nudes were passively erotic, fey, sleeping fawns, not muscular American men. 'The Sailor Boy,' Charlotte called the work while Stebbins modeled it. It was exhibited as *Commerce: The Sailor* to favorable reviews.

While visiting in Rome, life handed the immature Ned a blow. A telegram came from Liverpool. His mother, Charlotte's sister Susan, was ill with pneumonia. Ned rushed off immediately. Charlotte followed more slowly, as she was weakened from fever herself.

So many thoughts of her sister Susan must have occupied Charlotte on that voyage. How her baby sister was literally tricked into her first marriage. Susan was left in Boston with their feeble father when Charlotte was first acting in New York, living with and supporting her mother and brother Charlie.

A friend of their father's, a Mr. Nelson Merriman, wanted to adopt the pretty child and see to her education. Mary Eliza wouldn't allow that. She immediately said no, though years before when her New York relatives

Edwin Charles Merriman Cushman, the adopted son of his aunt Charlotte Cushman, seen here as the model for Miss Stebbins' tabletop marble *Commerce: The Sailor*, in 1859, when he was twenty-one. His sailor life and habits taught him 'to throw off responsibilities,' Charlotte complained.

offered to adopt Charlotte, Mary Eliza thought it over carefully before she decided no matter what the financial consequences, a child was a child. With her usual ambiguity in such matters, Mary Eliza continued to accept Merriman's financial aid for the girl. Then Merriman became deathly ill. He sent Mary Eliza word that he wanted to marry Susan on paper so that she could be his heir.

Susan didn't want to marry an old man, the way her mother had, but Mary Eliza went to Boston and convinced her. It was only a marriage on paper. So Susan, at fourteen, became a different kind of Juliet, one who obeyed her mother and married Paris. Immediately marriage without love brought its own punishment. The bridegroom leaped from his deathbed to his marriage bed and claimed his child bride.

At fifteen a very pregnant Susan arrived at Charlotte's door in New York. Her husband had fled, leaving Susan to the creditors knocking on her door.

Charlotte would have two more mouths to feed. Not that she minded. She had recently lost her youngest brother Augustus, whom she considered her son. She had raised him and paid for his boarding school. The youngest of four siblings, Augustus had been born into more poverty than Charlotte, Charlie, and Susan. And he was the brightest and best of them all; of that Charlotte was sure. He wrote her the most lovely notes from school, in a childish yet decorative hand—they remain preserved among her papers. On vacation in Vermont with his schoolmaster, he had a terrible accident. A runaway horse, a terrified child, a rutted, muddy road, an awful fall. The farmer who witnessed Augustus break his neck picked him up, brought him into his house, and bathed him with camphor till the boy seemed to fall into a deep sleep and quietly died. 'I do not know as there can be any blame attached to any one,' the farmer ended his report. Mary Eliza's eyes said something different. The boarding school, the horse, both profits from Charlotte's ungodly profession. God had sent retribution.

It was a loss Charlotte only survived through work. She carried the jacket Augustus died in with her for the rest of her life.

In New York, the pregnant younger sister Charlotte barely knew read Charlotte her lines, giving Charlotte time to study the girl. Such patrician good looks. Dark brown hair, slightly confused blue eyes, even more deeply set than Charlotte's, a good chin, hardly Charlotte's jaw, and that fine nose. Susan felt the lines she read; she had a flair for tragedy.

Soon after Ned was born, while filing for divorce, 'S. Cushman' made her debut as the ingenue in *The Genoese* at the Park Theatre. Charlotte played her lover.

Now Susan was in her middle thirties, with a new family. And another marriage their mother Mary Eliza helped to arrange with Dr. Sheridan Muspratt of the socially prominent Liverpool family. *His* masked balls her mother approved of. Better yet, Dr. Muspratt had taken Susan off the stage—and away from the callow, mustached actor she appeared to be in love with. But had she been any luckier in husbands? Ned, used to being the apple of three women's eyes—his mother's, grandmother's, Auntie's— was treated shabbily by Muspratt, who beat the spoiled boy. When Charlotte saw her young nephew after the marriage, he was disoriented, uncommunicative, distant—that was why Susan, fearful of his fate, willingly allowed Charlotte to adopt him. As years passed, Charlotte was afraid that her sister might suffer as well from Muspratt's hard hand. He was unbending with his two little daughters. Susan named the elder Rosalie, bless her. Eventually he was mean to Mary Eliza and openly contemptuous of Charlotte. A day would come when Charlotte fantasized Ned horse-whipping Muspratt in the town square, giving the brute the public beating he deserved.

Arriving at the Muspratt estate, Charlotte felt only relief to find Susan looking much less ill than she had expected. Naturally, Susan was very much reduced in strength, but the mirror her big sister held up to her convinced Susan of her recovery. Though Charlotte's possessiveness and prominence had at times oppressed her, Susan now radiated her sister's strength. Charlotte sat with her, talked with her, planned. It was a good visit.

On the ninth of May 1859, the doctors ordered that Susan's room be changed, and she was calm and happy and cheerful. But that afternoon as she and Charlotte chatted, Susan was taken by one of her dreadful fits of coughing. Nothing relieved it. It went on for an hour. It weakened her so. Charlotte was thankful when she fell off to sleep.

'She's sinking rapidly,' the doctor whispered.

'What do you mean?'

'She is going very fast.'

'You don't mean to say she is dying?'

In utter disbelief Charlotte sat there and watched her sister's life ebb from her like the going out of the tide. 'The bitter hand of death was laid upon her.'

That summer in England, Charlotte wrote to Mr. Crow on the black-bordered stationery of mourning. Her sister's death made Charlotte more indifferent to life, she told her financial advisor. Still there were money matters to discuss.

She had been disappointed not to see Emma over the summer, she added, but was quite pleased to hear that Mr. Crow might be sending *both* Mary and Emma on a European tour in the autumn. What a good idea.

'If you could find protection for them over here—& would like to entrust them to Miss Stebbins & myself—two careful spinsters of an age to be trusted, we would take very good care of them.'

Wayman Crow hired a careful spinster of his own before reluctantly sending his daughters abroad.

By the time the Crow sisters arrived in Paris, Charlotte was mourning in Rome. 'Not that I am sad, darling, when with happy people around me like my mad-cap Hattie—, but personally I find myself less capable struggling with circumstances.'

Having Emma and Miss Stebbins under the same roof would be such a circumstance. Miss Stebbins was not at all pleased about Charlotte's affection for her dear little lover. And Miss Stebbins meant 'lover' in the platonic sense. What was she to do? Charlotte uncharacteristically asked the younger woman.

What was madcap Hattie to do? Mr. Crow was her patron, not to mention the father she wished she had. Charlotte had come along, blithely insinuated herself into the family, and stolen his daughter's heart. And it was on Hattie's advice that Charlotte looked Mr. Crow up in the first place. What if he implicated *Hattie* in these Roman arrangements?

Hattie wrote to her patron most bouncily, 'We have all decided, that is, "the three old maids" of the Gregoriana, that when everything else fails, we'll go in for lecturing. Miss Cushman will hold forth upon Dramatic Art, Miss Stebbins upon Pictorial Art and I upon the Art of Sculpture.'

What could be more harmless than allowing his daughters to visit the house of three old maids?

And when Emma and Mary arrived in Rome, Hattie presented Mr. Crow with a pretty picture of innocence abroad. The girls had just come to Rome for a few days, but soon they would return for three long delicious months. 'They are such darlings in every way, that I stand straighter in my shoes when I call them sisters mine.'

Why, Miss Cushman told her, 'they are just the nicest American girls I know.'

Hattie replied, 'Myself excepted.'

To which Miss Cushman looked at her pityingly. 'You fiend!'

What fun.

When the American girls and their chaperone Miss Whitwell—or the Ass, as Charlotte came to refer to her—arrived for their long winter visit, staying from the end of November to the beginning of March 1860, the visit caused a dangerous, sexually charged atmosphere at Via Gregoriana. The Ass saw what was going on. She made snide remarks to Emma, always prefaced by 'Your dear friend Miss Cushman.'

That was simply womanish spite, and Emma shouldn't let it affect her, Charlotte advised.

'I was born under Mars, a fireish planet,' she told Emma. But she admitted that as delicious as this love of Emma's was, it made her fearful for herself and for *all* of her darlings. She was afraid of fire.

She was terribly torn by what she had wrought. Prudence and constraint were called for, particularly under the jealous eyes of Miss Stebbins and the concerned eyes of Hattie. But Emma was burning with desire. How do you convince a twenty-one-year-old that passion must not be allowed to destroy the balance of a household? That she must have patience. Emma was so charged with emotion that her temper often erupted and those hands of hers visibly shook. She couldn't sit still.

Miss Stebbins spent the season making much of Charlotte's fine horses, Ivan and Othello, and their dogs. 'Nothing so absolutely loving, faithful, disinterested and sympathetic as the dog nature,' Stebbins remembered.

A friend brought them 'Bushie,' a Skye terrier from Edinburgh, remarkably behaved on a long train ride to Rome. Bushie had been neglected by her previous owners and she arrived her coat all in tangles. Sallie rolled her eyes at the mess of a dog.

'Sallie, you will do your duty by the little dog,' Charlotte told her.

To use Sallie's own words: 'I carried her in my arms down stairs, and the little thing licked me all the way down, and by the time I got to the kitchen I was completely won over.'

So was Miss Stebbins, who loved Bushie mightily. 'Endless was the pleasure and comfort the dog afforded to all genuine dog-lovers.'

With her eye pointed resolutely toward posterity, Stebbins described the joys of the expatriate life. 'Riding in the Campagna is one of the most esteemed pleasures of the season, and an excellent and very needful stimulant against the enervating Italian climate.'

Charlotte and Emma and Ned and Mary and Hattie and Miss Stebbins rode.

Ned followed Auntie's advice after his mother's death and gave up the merchant marine. He addicted himself to pleasure, which was his wont, and spent as much time as he could with the sisters. Mary, who picked up Italian quickly—on Hattie's insistence—was as beautiful and as fashionably dressed and as indulged as Emma, and she liked boys—a lot. She was attracted to handsome, carefree Ned, but could see he was hopelessly drawn to Emma. So Mary became Ned's 'friend,' which gave her the right to give him confidante-like advice. Charlotte didn't trust her; was sure she was two-faced and jealous and warned Emma to watch her step.

'O, those unsurpassed days,' Miss Stebbins wrote. 'Days of glory and beauty, in which the very air seemed like golden wine burning and tingling in the veins! An atmosphere so pure and translucent it seemed to bring down heaven to earth or lift earth to heaven.'

Life was almost like that in 1860 among these Americans abroad. It could have been just like that if in life, as in Miss Stebbins' *Charlotte Cushman: Her Letters and Memories of Her Life*, Emma Crow needed only one mention.

It had to be a painful, if confusing, time for Miss Stebbins. It was during this winter season that Charlotte sat for her portrait bust, another commission Charlotte procured for her spouse while she was west on her American tour. As the tension on Via Gregoriana mounted, Miss Stebbins chiseled. The stark whiteness of Carrara marble did nothing to soften Charlotte's broad forehead or her jutting jaw. Nor was it the best aesthetic solution to close off her eyes with blank marble.

Many of Stebbins' contemporaries considered the frozen likeness wonderful, including Anne Brewster, Charlotte's early Philadelphia love, who was traveling in Italy that season. It would be another eight years before her brother Burnt Ben manipulated her inheritance and she lost everything. Then she moved to Rome permanently, supporting herself as a correspondent for the American papers. Whatever her bitterness over Ben, her new-found freedom, she confided in her diary, meant more to her than the injustices involved.

Her whole writing career began because of her grief over Charlotte. When her brother separated them, Anne had to do something new, something that she and Charlotte hadn't done together, in order to find some meaning in her life. It couldn't be drama or her beloved music. So, she began to write.

'My old magnetic power is coming back to me in full force,' she confided in her diary right before making this first trip to Italy. 'And why do I care to possess this mysterious magnetic power? Because it gives me happiness. It gives life, spirit and vigor to my imagination. . . . Charlotte Cushman had it and she gave me intense deep rest.'

Remeeting Charlotte in Italy, Anne was disappointed to find Charlotte had grown hard, as hard as Miss Stebbins' portrait bust: 'She looked as if made out of white iron—if one could imagine such a substance—not painted iron, but some substance harder and sharper than marble in its points.' Brewster wrote this not in her diary, but in her novel, *Compensation; or, Always a Future,* to describe Tante Octavie, cast not as an American actress, but as a German school director.

Duty is the German aunt's great word—as it was Charlotte's. Yet she has one weakness, for her good-for-nothing, overindulged, spendthrift sensualist of a nephew.

Isn't it odd, the young woman narrator opines, that when such people as Tante Octavie do have a weakness, it is apt to be a worse one than the frailties of others combined and that they will sacrifice blindly so much because of it?

At the end of the novel, the young woman, once engaged to the nephew, becomes a substitute for him in Tante Octavie's life. Tante Octavie tells the girl she loves her so much she wants to monopolize her, keep her all for herself.

'Never fear, Tante Octavie,' the girl, kneeling at her feet, reassures her, 'I shall never marry.'

'And you will be my child.'

'I will so help me God.'

With that, she lies in Tante Octavie's arms, clasped tight to the older woman's breast, feeling, at last, at home, and no longer alone in life. This is their 'sweet troth-plight,' when the girl chooses to serve and live evermore with her 'mistress-mother.'

'She kissed me fervently again and again, and a large, round tear, a second tear, rolled down her cheek, hallowing the contract; and this is how I came to be Tante Octavie's daughter.'

With something less than delight, Anne Brewster watched Tante Charlotte claim her own mistress-daughter.

After the winter season, when Emma and Mary and 'the Ass' left to continue their European adventure, Charlotte believed the separation would be for the best, allowing things to go back to normal in Rome.

Ned and Hattie accompanied the girls as far as the Swiss border. They stopped in Florence on the way, where Emma visited a girlfriend she had

Bust of Charlotte Cushman by Emma Stebbins, 1861. 'To me it seems when God conceived the world, that was poetry. He formed it, and that was sculpture. He varied and colored it, and that was painting. And then, crowning it all, He peopled it with living beings, and that was the grand, divine, eternal drama.'
—CHARLOTTE CUSHMAN.

grown up with in St. Louis, the young and beautiful journalist Kate Field. Suddenly, the octogenarian poet Walter Savage Landor realized advanced age offered him a saving grace. It allowed him to kiss Kate Field, to whom he wrote the most beautiful poem, and it allowed Kate Field not to demur.

Fresh from Rome, where the Brownings were wintering, Emma told Kate that Robert Browning had just paid her a tremendous compliment. Kate wrote to her Aunt Corda, 'I was dying to know what, but modesty forbade.'

Kate was in a position to understand Emma's feelings for Charlotte. Kate's feelings for her Aunt Corda, only fourteen years older than she, were as intense. (Fourteen years was not considered a big age difference between women in those days.) Kate's friend and biographer Lilian Whiting would write that Aunt Corda and Kate's 'absorbing affection' had elements of tragedy in it—because they were relatives who shared a romantic love, not because they were of the same sex. 'The young aunt satisfied the more impassioned side of the girl's nature.'

It was Aunt Corda—Cornelia Riddle Sanford—married to wealth, who brought Kate to Italy for the first time. They stayed in Rome at Charlotte

Cushman's, where Kate mingled with the likes of the wintering Brownings and recent visitors such as Nathaniel Hawthorne and President Franklin Pierce.

'You are very ambitious,' Robert Browning later told her in Florence.

She laughed and asked him how he arrived at that conclusion.

'Oh, I can tell by your eyes.'

'How so?'

'I can detect it in their glisten.'

'Well,' she said, 'it is no great crime to be ambitious, is it?'

'No indeed. I admire it,' Browning replied. 'I would not give a straw for a person who was not.'

Kate's mother, Aunt Corda's sister, was visiting Kate, and Kate wrote to Charlotte from Florence, heading her letter, as usual, 'Dear Romeo': 'I am tranquilly happy to have my loving loved Mother caring for me, trying to make me a moral woman and forgiving me though I don't much profit by her efforts.'

That day her mother said, 'Well Kate, I suppose it is useless to attempt alterations or repairs in you; people will have to take you as you are, and if you are "misunderstood," you must make the best of the misunderstanding.'

So you see, she told Charlotte, 'Mother is forgetting her propriety most rapidly and very shortly will be qualified for our set.'

'Our set,' Florence branch, had at its center Isa Blagden. Once, after Charlotte left Rome that first season, Isa Blagden joined the independent women on the Corso. Afterwards she settled in a beautiful villa in the hills ringing Florence, becoming, as Kate Field called her, 'Our Lady of Bellosguardo.' Isa was a novelist known for her hospitality and her kind heart. She was a great friend of the Brownings, and had the same nurturing, nursing spirit that Robert Browning had. Fifteen months after Emma met her, Isa would accompany the distraught Robert and his son Pen back to England after the death of Elizabeth Barrett Browning. She was a great comfort to them during those dark days. And though Robert never again returned to Florence, he and Isa wrote to each other on prescribed days each month until she died.

Henry James, in his biography *William Wetmore Story and His Friends*, remembered her gentle, gay black eyes, and the visible hint of her East Indian blood. James alluded to the sexuality of 'our set' in Florence in tones so hushed in shadowy illusion that he could as well be referring to lichen on a villa wall.

Isa Blagden, British novelist and poet who was at the center of the Victorian Anglo-Florentine community, and a close friend of Elizabeth Barrett and Robert Browning, Charlotte Cushman and Miss Stebbins, in a photograph from the 1860s in Charlotte Cushman's album.

Isa was not rich and derived most of her income from her writings. She was living at the time at her villa with the Irish feminist and writer Frances Power Cobbe. She generally shared her home with a woman. In her novel *Agnes Tremorne* she wrote of the exquisite enjoyment two single women friends can feel for each other. The personal intimacy which existed in such a relationship allowed for complete knowledge and understanding of one another. 'This is seldom attained, even in the holiest and truest marriage.'

Emma and Hattie and Ned 'the great Cushman's nephew,' as Kate called him, visited Isa Blagden and Frances Power Cobbe at Bellosguardo. Kate reported to Aunt Corda that they laughed all night long, the way one always did when Hattie was present. 'Miss Cushman does not visit Florence *en route* to England, so they say. Miss Stebbins is at work upon her Lotus Eater, and has completed a "wonderful" bust of Miss Cushman.'

Kate tried to convince Charlotte to join them. 'Beloved Romeo,' she wrote. 'We've had a capital installment from Casa Cushman—and now we only need the head of the establishment—and her other half.'

But Charlotte's other half wanted to be alone with Charlotte in Rome, while she finished her *Lotus Eater*. And Charlotte too believed separation would allow a needed reprieve from the sexual tensions of the last three months. She believed Emma's nerves had stretched hers as well to the breaking point and things would be calmer when she was gone.

Yet after Emma left Rome, Charlotte found out that the girl's 'energy'— Faraday again—was still in the house. She could not sleep well and she could not herself disconnect from what she called the electricity of their attraction. 'Your will is great, your magnetic power is very extraordinary. You can control *my* spirits to a curious extent even at your absence at a great distance.' Once more she realized love was too subtle to be controlled.

Emma's letters must have been as passionate as she wished their lovemaking to be. For Charlotte urged her, almost begged her, to try to calm herself. Fires always frightened her, she reiterated. 'Temper the fire of your spirits my darling & I shall be better in mind & body.' They would meet soon again, she assured the girl.

'Our actual entire union shall not be far off—be patient, oh my darling.'

Ned returned home restless and miserable and good for nothing other than writing to Emma. Not that Charlotte was faring any better, for she now had to admit that she longed for Emma just as much as Emma longed for her. Distance had not calmed her. She found, to her deep distress, that she was not whole with Emma gone.

'Does *that* make you happy darling?' she asked with an uneasy, confused irony. 'Are you more content that I go about the world *un*whole, & that if fate interferes—as I fear it must & will—I am never to be an entirety again? Yes I know you will find a comfort in these thoughts, & I kiss you down deep into your soul's heart, for your love of me & its expression!'

Now it became imperative to Charlotte that she and Emma meet in a place where they could find privacy. Emma, in Brussels, must let her parents and sister and the Ass know that she wouldn't think of buying her summer wardrobe in any place other than Paris. Then Ned would write to Mary suggesting they all stay at the same hotel there—the suggestion should not originate with Emma.

'Yes, darling there are people in this world who could understand our love for each other, therefore it is necessary that we should keep our expression of it to ourselves, & not demonstrate too clearly.'

The plans for the Paris meeting were almost upset by the Ass—probably under orders from Mr. Crow. But Charlotte told Emma she wasn't doing justice to her father's confidence in her when she allowed her chaperone to interfere. Simply tell the Ass what Emma with Mary planned to do. 'You are not abroad for Miss Whitwell's pleasure, but *she is abroad for your convenience!*'

Charlotte came to Paris, sending Miss Stebbins on ahead to Scotland.

'She is very very dependent on your darling . . . & if she thought or dreamed *how* I love you—it would go near to kill her I believe. This makes me very very unhappy at times, & I wonder whether I ought not to school myself to her without such love!'

But Charlotte knew this was impossible. After she and Emma finally and fully consummated their love, she could not turn back:

'Ah how hard it would be now, now that I have tasted the sweet of such communion as is given to few to know. My darling love do you remember our last night in Paris, ah what delirium is in the memory . . . as I look back & feel you in my arms held to my heart so closely, so entirely mine in every sense as I was yours, ah it is very sweet, very precious, full full of ecstasy.'

In that hotel room in Paris, Emma sat on Charlotte's lap and vowed to help her 'ladie love' do her duty. Emma's influence over Ned was already making a better person of him, taking him from his wastrel ways and relieving his Auntie of her burden. It made sense in every way for Emma and Ned to marry.

'Darling mine. How glad I was Ned got your letter from Berne. The poor lad was becoming quite desperate. . . . I will not confess to you all I feel for it would make you very conceited I am afraid. Dear do you know you write very much nicer letters to Ned than you used to write to me . . . perhaps that was because you were not *engaged* to me. Are you engaged to me now?'

By becoming engaged to Ned Cushman, Emma committed herself to Charlotte.

Ned brought his fiancée to London to meet his grandmother and Uncle Charlie. Charlie took an immediate liking to the girl. And Charlotte was happy that Emma liked Charlie. What he lacked in polish he made up for by his gentle heart.

Emma liked the house Charlotte owned on 1 Bolton Row as well, which pleased the actress.

'Everybody says I have prettier homes than people generally & when I have made some more money . . . I shall hope to live in Bolton Row again & you shall be mistress there & have your own servants & I will take control of the Roman house & you of the London one—I must have more money first!'

It was a quick decision to return once more to the American stage. It would not do for Ned to press his suit with Wayman Crow without his aunt to watch over it all. It would be a terrible mistake if either of her dear children let Emma's father think for a moment that they were already engaged. They could be engaged in terms of affection, but that was all.

Mr. Crow was not a man to want a playboy for his daughter—particularly *this* playboy. Ned had to find something to do. More accurately, Auntie knew the something Ned should do.

When Charlotte adopted Ned, he wanted to enter the newly formed Naval Academy at Annapolis, not be educated in London, living with Auntie and Matilda Hays. The disappointed Charlotte, on her long American tour with Miss Hays at the time, traveled to Washington to pave Ned's way with the Senator from New York, William H. Seward. What a lucky meeting that had been. Not only was Ned accepted at the Naval Academy (he later left for the merchant marine), but the clever and politic statesman with his beaked nose and sophisticated wit and the actress who spoke horse sense became fast friends. Seward and Cushman shared the same vision for America, and the same political savvy.

Now, Charlotte was sure Abraham Lincoln would be elected president in November and that William Seward, who almost won the presidential nomination himself, would be in the new administration. Seward could help Ned get a diplomatic assignment to Rome. A position that would give him a semblance of responsibility, thus paving the way for his marriage and allowing them to all live together on Via Gregoriana.

No matter that Ned knew nothing of politics. Garibaldi was on the march, Italian unification was in the air, and in the States, there was the threat of the South seceding. Ned couldn't care less. Charlotte complained to Emma that he did not read newspapers and was so ignorant of current affairs that she was afraid well-informed Americans would consider him stupid when he returned home. She begged her lover to use her influence to convince him to take the *New York Times*.

Once more Miss Stebbins accompanied Charlotte home on short notice. In Liverpool she was as melancholy as a newly caged bird. She was not pleased when she learned Emma was coming from London to see them off. Charlotte was:

'I am so glad you are on your way to me, & I shall be so truly happy to see you again—ah—when the time comes for us to be separated no more! Will that time ever come? I pray God.'

But as for sleeping with her as Emma wished—despite what Emma promised her their night together would entail—that could not be. Miss Stebbins would certainly not have it, and Charlotte liked harmony so much that she would wait a little for her pleasure.

How long would she have to wait? Emma asked.

'You shall wander over England with me—you shall see all these places in their beauty with me—if you wish—but I must go to California & get some more money first.'

When Emma arrived in Liverpool, she surprised Charlotte by speaking strongly to her on Ned's behalf.

Ned did not want to be the American consul in Rome. He had absolutely no interest in such a position. He wanted to go into a business—not read the *Times.*

Did Emma have any idea of the difficulty of setting a young man up in business? Especially one like Ned who had not one single attribute for it?

It had been a terrible mistake, Charlotte now realized, letting him give up the sea. He might have gotten to be the master of a cotton ship.

But Emma was insistent. Business was what Ned wished. Her loyalty to her fiancé only made Charlotte love her more.

Ned was now visiting with his half sisters in Liverpool before sailing home with Auntie. He was neither ignorant of Charlotte and Emma's feelings for one another, nor was he exacting. That was not his nature.

He loved Emma and he loved having a good time. And he loved Auntie too, even though her endless advice drove him to distraction. Living in Rome under her roof? He must have told Emma it would not be the paradise she imagined. If Emma wanted to go to Auntie in the summers, travel with her, she could do as she wished. But if Mr. Crow needed to see his son-in-law work, why so be it. Ned rather fancied a business of his own. That should be easy.

Charlotte told Emma she would do as Ned wished, even though a position in Rome was the only way she and Emma could be *together* (she emphasized the word) as much as they wished.

Emma came aboard the ship, hoping for a last kiss. But that was not to be. The two women were surrounded by hungry, greedy eyes. Miss Stebbins was in a little fury of jealousy when she saw Charlotte holding Emma's hand. And another of Charlotte's friends was so jealous to see this display that she could not talk all day and sulked like a fool. When they sailed, Charlotte soon settled her spouse, who became as sweet as a summer morning. 'She knows how dearly I love her & allows me to smooth her ruffled feathers.'

On board, Ned complained to Auntie that he did not believe Emma loved him the way a woman should love the man she was about to marry.

The weather was dreadful on the sea. 'Ah, darling I am afraid you are mistaken in what you think of your father's consent being easily had, but we shall see.'

A Fashionable Wedding

NEW YORK, NEWPORT, WASHINGTON, D.C.,
BOSTON, ST. LOUIS
1860–1861

MISS STEBBINS had been suffering from abscesses in the face for some months and could not immediately join Charlotte when she visited the Crows that summer at Newport. But Charlotte acted as her agent, as always, collecting the hundred dollars each that Mr. Crow owed Miss Stebbins for the two crayons of Hattie which Charlotte convinced him to commission. They were marvelously rendered with Stebbins' strong line and were filled with lively verisimilitude, difficult enough to capture since Hattie was always on the run. Charlotte had hoped to be able to set the stage for Ned's first visit all by herself, and was disappointed to find Hattie beat her to Newport.

Hattie had come back to the States quite reluctantly, after receiving the news that her father had a stroke. By the time she arrived in Watertown, Dr. Hosmer was recuperating and Hattie was off to Newport to meet Cornie and to be with people who really were her second—if not her first—family. Mr. Crow could never do enough for the girl.

So Hattie, Cornie, and Cornie's baby daughter Hatty were there when Ned joined his Auntie by the sea. He was on his best behavior with Mr. Crow, and Charlotte could see Mrs. Crow warm up to the boy as women did, while Mr. Crow stayed polite. She advised Ned to pay particular attention to Emma's mother—to go through her, if possible, to advance his position.

By good luck, before Ned arrived, Mr. Crow advised Charlotte to make a will. She was more than happy to comply. Mr. Crow could see for himself that Ned would be a wealthy man. Naturally, he needed a position, but he did not have to make his fortune. Or as she put it to Emma, 'His fortune which he will never make for himself—is made for him.'

It was frustrating for Charlotte to leave Newport just as Emma was about to arrive home from her grand tour and her Parisian dressmakers, but she had to go to work:

'I must wait until the days are brighter for *our* union. But sweet, *it shall come.* I love you dearly, fondly, passionately and you *must* come to me even though the day be postponed, for you are my heart's core, the light of my eyes & I shall never have a peaceful *whole* hour without you.'

Hattie told Ned she would help him win Mr. Crow's consent to an engagement with Emma, but Charlotte didn't trust 'Hattie the Selfish.'

'I don't want your father to think you have *engaged* yourself to anybody without consulting him. He told Hattie in speaking to her about it that you had promised him you would come home untrammeled or something of the sort. Now for the world I would not have him think you engaged by any promise. Engaged in your affections yes, he *may* know that, but nothing more, for I have never felt that you could be engaged without your father's permission.'

She urged Emma to be guarded. 'I do love you very much, *as much as you love me*—though I am not young & my will is not so strong.' Emma must not hurt her father unnecessarily, for he loved her more than 'any other man ever can or will.'

The Crows were wonderful parents. They trusted in Emma's truth and loyalty to them and had been very good to Charlotte during her stay. 'What can I do to repay them?'

While appearing onstage in Boston, Charlotte made some provisional plans for Ned. If Ned wouldn't come to Rome, why, he'd work in Boston and each summer Charlotte and Emma would meet either in New England or in England. Charlotte's friends the publisher James Fields—who enthusiastically published Charlotte's poetry—and his wife Annie helped find a temporary spot for Ned where he could pick up some business skills.

After her husband's death, Annie Fields, a renowned Boston hostess, would form a lifelong relationship with one of Fields' authors, the novelist Sarah Orne Jewett, fifteen years her junior. They spent all their winters

Wayman Crow, left, and his wife Isabella Conn Crow, right, as they appeared in midlife. Wayman Crow became a respected St. Louis business leader, state senator, and patron of the arts. He early supported Harriet Hosmer's artistic ambitions, as well as becoming the financial advisor to Hosmer, Fanny Kemble, and Charlotte Cushman. This photograph was taken around 1853, when Mr. Crow became a trustee of the newly founded Washington University. His wife, Isabella, with forebears from Virginia and Kentucky, was a gracious, if reserved, hostess. She had her first child, Cornie, when she was nineteen, her last, Isabella, when she was forty-two. This photograph of her is in Charlotte Cushman's album.

together in Annie's house on the Charles River in Boston and often traveled to Europe in the spring. Annie became 'Fuff'; Sarah, 'Pinny.'

Henry James knew all of these people, and as a young man visited the Fields house at 148 Charles Street. He wrote that Mrs. Fields' relationship with Sarah Jewett was a second long chapter in her life, using such contorted language to say it that the hardest scroll embossed within the book seemed to be in Arabic.

The novelist, who was too young to go with his parents to see Cushman on her first return in 1849, and waited up to hear word of her performance, would come to know of her and her Italian circle. The only biography he ever wrote was of the married sculptor William Wetmore Story, keeping the same-sex relationships within that expatriate community as muted as an underpainted portrait. And in his late masterpiece *The Golden Bowl,* he eliminated any whisper of such love, while recasting much of Charlotte's psychology and story. He kept Charlotte's name, but as involved and sophisticated as his love intrigue was, he normalized the truth he could have told.

Our Charlotte was not five days out of Boston for her Montreal run before the Fieldses found Ned associating with disreputable fellows, rather than learning bookkeeping.

Charlotte meanwhile was finding it more difficult than she thought to go back to work at the age of forty-four. Her throat bothered her very much and made her miserably nervous. It was not a new affliction. Sallie had convinced her to have her throat burned out with nitric acid twice before she made her London debut as Bianca sixteen years earlier.

While Charlotte acted in New York, she and Miss Stebbins were living in and fixing up a house around Gramercy Park that belonged to the Stebbins family, and Miss Stebbins was also nervously getting ready for her first professional showing at the Goupil Gallery. John Gibson himself had commissioned the *Lotus Eater,* a standing male nude she would exhibit. She also showed the bust of Charlotte. And there was the *Commerce: The Sailor,* based on young Ned, and its equally virile counterpart, *Industry: The Miner.*

These were all tabletop marbles, measuring about twenty-eight to thirty inches, which, as her sister Mary Garland opined, in the long run limited their evocative power. Stebbins was a perfectionist and she was able to control all aspects of the small sculptures. She did not have them worked on, polished, or enlarged by the talented Italian artisans who performed such services for all sculptors. With her highly exacting nature and her frail health, she hurt herself physically and mentally as she fretted over the pieces in Rome, turning clay models into marble.

'She cannot be contented with anything she does and ever sighs for her ideal,' Charlotte reported to Emma earlier. But one wonders if Miss Stebbins' attitude to her work would have been more joyful if Emma Crow had not entered her life, if Emma and her sister and their chaperone hadn't invaded her home. Alone in her studio in the back gardens of Via Gregoriana, Miss Stebbins bore an invisible weight heavier than marble. She was denied even one season of untroubled love.

Sallie knew it. As Miss Stebbins, fretting, readied herself for her show in New York, Sallie went about with raised eyebrows making 'a sort of uncomfortable atmosphere' for Charlotte. When Charlotte was not working, she was entertaining.

'It seems to me you can never bear to be quiet, you always want company,' she told Charlotte, and not in a flattering way.

All this elaborate socializing, even among the extended Stebbins family itself, had little to do with Miss Stebbins, who never pushed herself forward. It was meant to pave a way among the right people for highborn Emma and for Ned. It was meant to indicate to Mr. Crow that he could do worse for his daughter.

When a visiting prince left a ball early, in his words, to see Miss Cushman act, Charlotte took it as a social, not an artistic, compliment. She was not thinking of her spouse's feelings or her health. Miss Stebbins was worried to distraction about Charlotte's preoccupation with Emma Crow and was miserable over the possibility of Ned marrying her. Sallie had known Ned since she was fourteen and he was six and was very loyal to him. She did not like what was going on either. Neither wished Emma Crow to be a permanent fixture in their lives. Both wanted their Charlotte back from what seemed to be a growing obsession.

In New York, after being so full of advice for Emma and Ned, Charlotte made her own faux pas with Mr. Crow. A stepnephew of Charlotte's had borrowed seven thousand dollars from her which he couldn't repay. He was ill now, and she had life insurance on him that she was transferring back to his wife and children. He wanted to take out a second policy so that she could reclaim her money at his death. She asked Mr. Crow what to do.

Mr. Crow was appalled. He wrote back in no uncertain terms that he considered this speculating or gambling on human life. She defended herself:

'The matter was presented to me . . . & I failed perhaps to see the dangers in my willingness to repay myself. However, I at once & willingly abandoned the idea. . . . I may not in the end be much poorer for this 10.000—but it was a temptation to repay myself—although I never dreamed of *gambling*—speculating is a less objectionable word—because it seems to me that all business in this country is more or less of a speculative character. I may be wrong—but such has been my opinion!'

She told Mr. Crow she would not take out a policy. But that didn't stop her from doing so—any more than preparing Ned for business in Boston stopped her from going to Washington and conferring with William Seward concerning the American consulship to Rome.

Abraham Lincoln was elected president of the United States, as Charlotte predicted. The preoccupation with the election and the large demon-

Sallie Mercer, Charlotte Cushman's faithful dresser, servant, critic, and friend, joined the actress when she was only fourteen and was by her side throughout the rest of Charlotte's life. Sallie knew the actress's secrets and understood her ways better than anyone else.

strations in New York afterwards were attractions that did not hurt her box office, though they might have. She was earning a thousand dollars a week. At her last benefit, there was such a crowd that she could hardly get out of the carriage. 'So you see your darling is worth something to her public yet—old as she is.'

The papers were referring to Cushman as 'legendary,' that chilling euphemism, giving her more reason to work as hard as she could to put more money in Mr. Crow's hands. Real estate looked interesting once more.

She heard Chicago was coming up again and she saw for herself that in Boston rents were high and property increasing in value.

Sending Wayman Crow fifty coupons to place as he wished, she told her financial advisor, 'It is a good time to invest in a state as strong & healthy as Missouri.'

No it wasn't, Mr. Crow responded. 'We should withhold any further instruments until we see if your Republican friends bring about a dissolution of the Union!' (Mr. Crow, apparently, unlike Lincoln and Seward, still considered himself a Whig.)

Charlotte would have none of it. 'I believe the Lincoln administration will be the most reputable, respectable, conservative & protective we have *ever* had.'

What did Mr. Crow think about a parcel of land her friends the Fieldses might sell, close to their house? 'A water lot, looking far over Charles River toward the Brookline hills.' For about seventeen thousand dollars. Was it too much?

'You see how I bother you. Spinsters are notoriously troublesome, if they get a foothold.'

Ned would be going to St. Louis for Christmas. Perhaps Hattie *had* paved a way. For the Crows now knew of their daughter's attachment and they were not objecting. Impulsive Ned told his Auntie he wanted to marry in the spring. Charlotte doubted Mr. Crow would allow it. Again, if Ned wanted to broach the idea, do it lightly and through Mrs. Crow.

She sent Ned off with a letter to bring to Emma: 'I am envious of him, but must go on my working ways, while my season lasts for making hay. I try not to work too hard for the sake of those who love me, but the temptation is too strong. When success is so full upon me as it has been in Boston & New York, I begin to fear—with the oncoming year—that it may change.'

Was Ned staying with the family or at the hotel? What did Emma's friends think of him? Had Ned gotten any promise from Mr. Crow that they might be married?

'At last I have found a helper, one who loves me well enough to take up my burthens & help me to bear them.' If her parents did agree to the marriage, 'you will be *my own,* more mine than any one *else's* will you not?' Auntie suggested Niagara Falls for the honeymoon.

Miss Stebbins' show opened in January 1861 to very good reviews. That such impressive, vital work was produced by a woman surprised the *New York Times.* The American spirit with which Stebbins infused her work was singled out. So was the Germanic 'inwardness' of the bust of Charlotte Cushman, which the critic attributed to 'a peculiar intimacy between the artist and the sitter.' Her first show was quite a success. Stebbins would go back to Rome with many orders for her work, as well as with a heavy heart.

Ned returned from St. Louis happier than he had ever been in his life. The engagement had been accepted by the Crows. And he loved Emma's mother, who was as good to him as his own mother could have been.

What about the marriage date? Charlotte asked.

Mr. Crow said he couldn't make definite arrangements with the country in such an unsettled state after Lincoln's election. He told Ned his aunt's Republican friends might see to it that neither he nor Auntie had the money to *do* for their children.

Charlotte looked at Ned and shook her head. Once more it was up to her to act. "Dear Friend," she began her letter to Mr. Crow. She would like to see her children married before she left the country, for she could not return again to the States for two or three years. (That should sweeten the pot.)

She assured Mr. Crow that she would keep his daughter free from any care at the expense of her own peace of mind if need be. 'No relation that Ned could have entered into could have been half so full of happy anticipation for me. I love Emma as though she were my own child. I feel very confident that her affection *for me* will grow with years.'

Her firm decision to back her children's wedding plans by cutting through Crow's procrastination (and her own) seemed to enrich her portrayal of the Danish prince. She added new dimension to her Hamlet at a time in her life when she could barely squeeze into the costume Edwin Booth lent her. 'I acted the part as much better than anything else I have done here, that I am really amazed at myself—& wonder whether the spirit of the Dane were not with me and around me last night.'

It had to have been a marvelous performance. She mentioned the work that consumed her so rarely in her letters, and she was never one to brag.

It was her personal life that concerned her. She settled with Mr. Crow on their children's marriage contract with dramatic flair. Should Ned die without children, she assigned to Emma not only half of his property, which was her widow's right, but *all* of it for herself and her legal heirs. 'I wished your father to see & know that when I gave, I gave without a reservation.'

Still, a reluctant Mr. Crow added a provision. Ned and Emma should be married on the third of April 1861, a month after Lincoln's inauguration, *if* by that time there was no civil war.

Emma Crow Cushman and Charlotte Cushman in 1861. After Emma married Charlotte's nephew, Charlotte wrote to the bride: 'Never more shall I stand alone darling. Never more will you be free from your auntie's loving spirit at your side.'

From New York Charlotte mailed Emma card designs from which to select for the wedding breakfast. The patterns themselves could be engraved in St. Louis quite well. 'Your wedding cards I will bring with me.' As for what they would wear: 'I have a lavender moire which I hope will please you, to have your Auntie decked in, & you, I hear will be in *white*, eh!'

'A Fashionable Wedding,' the papers called it. Charlotte clipped the notice for Mr. Crow:

'Dr. Eliot's Church was opened yesterday morning at eleven o'clock for the marriage ceremonies of the daughter of one of our oldest and most respected merchants, with a nephew of Miss Charlotte Cushman. The

Church was lighted up, and the organ pealed forth its sweetest tones, while the audience were waiting. The time was fixed at 11 o'clock, and notwithstanding the inclemency of the weather, the bridal party entered the Church at the precise hour. There were four bridesmaids . . . and of course an equal number of groomsmen. Miss Charlotte Cushman was present, escorted by the father of the fair bride. The nuptial ceremonies lasted about fifteen minutes, and were witnessed by about one hundred and fifty spectators; two-thirds of these were ladies. We understand that the young couple will remove to Boston, where they will permanently reside.'

Instead of Niagara Falls on their own, Emma and Ned chose to travel back east with Auntie. They picked up Sallie in Philadelphia, where she was visiting her family. Sallie was very needed as Emma's maid was undone by the hard journey. While in the city of brotherly love, the newlyweds got to Bailey & Ketchums, Charlotte reported to Mr. Crow, and Emma was delighted by their purchase of Electroware.

In New York Charlotte had to leave them dining with Miss Stebbins' brother Henry while she went on to Boston. She had arrived in St. Louis for the wedding on the third of April and was back acting in Boston on the night of the eighth. 'I am feeling the effects of my hurried journey & am suffering from nervous headache—else I am well,' she wrote to Mr. Crow.

In Boston Emma and Ned joined Charlotte at the Parker House, until the house she furnished for them on 70 Pinckney Street—a water lot—was ready. When it was, they urged her to move from the hotel and stay with them. 'As you can see by the address, I am now with the children,' she wrote to Mr. Crow. 'I have consented in spite of my judgment, which deemed it wiser for them to be by themselves with their household.'

Everybody (who was anybody) was charmed by Emma. 'My friends come to see *me* & go away perfectly delighted with *her.*' Annie Fields appeared to raise an eyebrow at times, however. She and her husband invited Emma to meet Ralph Waldo Emerson and Oliver Wendell Holmes, among other dignitaries, but Emma chose to go to the theatre with her aunt first, even though Mrs. Fields knew it was a play the girl had seen before. And she did not come to their party until Auntie was ready to accompany her, which was very late indeed. 'Miss Cushman and her niece' was the way the two entered the diaries of the time.

Not that Charlotte had forgotten Miss Stebbins back in New York, at least in terms of advancing her career. One of Charlotte's greatest friends in Boston was Elizabeth Peabody, the single-minded and rather eccentric educator who introduced kindergarten in America. Miss Peabody's sister Sophia was married to Nathaniel Hawthorne; her sister Mary was married to Miss Peabody's great friend and fellow educator Horace Mann, who had died unexpectedly a few years before. Horace Mann was the founder, in Massachusetts, of the Normal School system to train women teachers and was, at his death, the president of Antioch College, a coeducational institution. One of the early advocates of women's education, he was a true pioneer. Now the city of Boston planned to commission a commemorative statue of him and Charlotte wanted that commission for Miss Stebbins. Harriet Hosmer and another former Bostonian and expatriate sculptor, William Wetmore Story, wanted it as well.

Horace Mann must be sculpted by a woman, Charlotte determined. She would even roll up her sleeves and go on a fund-raising tour toward this end, if necessary. Mann, who had *raised* women, must be raised by a woman! she proclaimed among her friends. Miss Stebbins returned to Europe that summer with her first full-length commission—a monumental bronze of the educator.

Brother Henry was not to be outdone. As head of the Parks Commission in New York, he would soon help his sister, who never once promoted herself, to obtain what is perhaps the most well-known and beautiful work of the women sculptors in Rome—even though by now hardly anyone remembers it was by a woman, not to mention one named Emma Stebbins.

Miss Stebbins submitted drawings and received the commission for the fountain that would be a central focus of the new Central Park in New York. She created the Bethesda Fountain with its glorious swooping angel and its four graceful putti at the base representing 'healing' elements sorely missing in her life, such as Health, Temperance, Purity, and Peace. It must have seemed brutally ironic to her, as well as to Mr. Crow, that ten days after Emma became Emma Crow Cushman, on 13 April 1861, Fort Sumter was fired on.

Charlotte Cushman had an immediate, independent understanding of what the Civil War was going to be. Previously, in Washington, Seward, whom she respected mightily, and who was now secretary of state under Lincoln, told her that if the issue of secession did come to arms, it would be a sixty-day war. She knew better.

In Boston, after the outbreak, she predicted Missouri would not secede, telling Mr. Crow that she hoped when he found Missouri was going to remain sensible and true, he would not hold himself a prisoner in the West, but would come east for the summer as he planned. She did not mince words with that Whig. She copied out a quote from Colonel Henry Stebbins (he was in the National Guard): 'The North & West will place the flag of the Union in all elevated places . . . & establish the Supremacy of the Constitution & laws or perish.' It would be very bad business for Missouri to think otherwise.

Elizabeth Peabody remembered Charlotte asking her banker father to withdraw twenty-five thousand dollars from American securities at that time.

'Oh no,' Mr. Peabody replied, as her banker he could not in conscience do it. Why, gold was at 128. The businessmen of the world were not going to let this war go on.

'Mr. Peabody,' Charlotte told the banker, 'I saw that first Maine regiment that answered to Lincoln's call march down State Street in Boston with their chins in the air, singing "John Brown's soul is marching on," and believe me, this war will not end till slavery is abolished, whether it be in five years or thirty; and gold will be up to 225 before it is over.'

A loyal Unionist and shrewd businesswoman (especially when she took her own advice), Charlotte Cushman substantially increased her net worth during these tumultuous years. Had she not returned with Miss Stebbins to Europe that summer, she believed she could have become through speculation the richest woman America had ever seen. She would have made much more money in 1862 than Wayman Crow lost. As it was, she still did quite well.

While in America, she made hay while she might. And invested it. She left the newlyweds in Boston in order to act in Portland, Maine; New Bedford, Massachusetts; Providence, Rhode Island. She was worn out and her foot pained her. 'Romeo has tired it very much.'

At Providence, her train arrived at six in the evening. She disembarked and was about to go to her hotel when her arm was seized by a lady. She was startled. It took her some seconds to realize it was dear Miss Stebbins. A very thin, very anxious Miss Stebbins who hadn't seen her spouse in a month. They had been parted while Charlotte married her children in St. Louis and then settled them in Boston. Standing there, unsure, on the platform, Miss Stebbins was looking very ill, very poorly.

Once Charlotte recovered from the surprise, she was so glad to be with Miss Stebbins again that she was late to the theatre. And then it was so comforting not to have to go back to a lonely hotel room. It was gratifying as well to see how, with Charlotte once more, Miss Stebbins snapped back to life. But now there was a secret life between them.

'How strange it is dear one,' Charlotte wrote to Emma, 'that our own belongings know us less than almost strangers. I am sure it is so with her— & with me—& perhaps with you. Do *I* know you, my sweet darling? No!'

Emma was miffed by Miss Stebbins' appearance, and not a little jealous. She shouldn't be, Charlotte responded, emphasizing how unique their own relationship was. Emma was now a Cushman. Her lover had become her niece as well as her friend. 'Dont you see dear how the *"part is in the whole."'* By marrying her lover to her nephew, Charlotte bound Emma to her for life; she was the daughter of Charlotte's heart, the future mother of Charlotte's children.

Charlotte neglected to mention she had also become Emma's mother-in-law. When she came back to Boston and just walked into Emma's house as if she owned it (which she did) Emma was not amused. Nor was she amused by *Miss Stebbins'* arrival, or by the fact that Ned's grandmother, Mary Eliza, had been staying with them.

Charlotte apologized from New Haven for the way she had barged in on the girl, asking her wee lady if she still loved her 'auntie, mamma, Ladie dearly.' 'Does she forgive her all her shortcomings?'

Emma was now seeing those shortcomings up close. But just the thought of Charlotte returning to Europe with Miss Stebbins turned Emma into a bundle of nerves.

On the other hand, she was certainly ready for Mary Eliza's departure, and was annoyed when she stayed an extra day. If Emma thought her relationship with Charlotte granted her leave to speak against Charlotte's mother, she had better think again.

'Grandmother staid on a day extra for the sake of books & keys—always does her *duty*—what she considers her duty.' Emma must remember that Charlotte herself was who she was through early lessons in duty.

Emma had called Mary Eliza 'common,' not realizing how such a word struck Charlotte straight in the face.

'She has been a good & faithful mother—& though she has suffered herself to grow in & not expand, there are many fine traits in her character, which you might fail to find in many people who would seem less "common." I only wish God had given every child so good & faithful a mother. She has her faults, who has not? I only reproach myself that I cannot be as patient with her as she has too often been with me.'

Family was the only gold that did not fluctuate with the market. No one talked against Charlotte's mother.

All her life Charlotte had longed to be a mother herself, had longed for a child of her own. But time after time life taught her there would only be 'mind children' for her—her creative reproductions on the stage. Now God had blessed her for her hard life, her hard work. For she would have her own children by the woman she loved. Emma had already miscarried, early enough to make one wonder if she had attempted an alternative way to ensure her marriage had war erupted before her wedding day. '*White,* eh!'

Charlotte reassured her there would be others.

She was thinking of them even before she returned to Europe. She planned to write Emma a long journal letter each week, once the Atlantic Ocean was between them. Would Emma allow her to avoid all love words in her correspondence? Charlotte would like to substitute words that might meet *any* eye. Perhaps rather than the love word, she could put in a blank. Whenever Emma saw '————,' she could use her own imagination to fill it. Wouldn't that be even better? So much more evocative than a few concrete words.

If Charlotte used this system, Emma would not have to continue burning her letters. They could be kept as a record of Charlotte's life. Eventually they could be collected and put in a case by themselves, for her grandchildren to read after she died. 'What do you say to this plan my precious?'

Would Emma forget the love words for the sake of having her children know and love their grandmother after she passed away?

How Charlotte regretted she had not been able to keep the run of her letters since she left America for the first time: 'My letters were fresher then than now though perhaps not worth so much in their lack of experience. But I have been unfortunate. My first six months letters were written to my friend Miss Sully. My next were written to my friend Eliza Cook, the poetess—and they have been destroyed. Since then I have scarcely been separated from my friend & companion or whom that might be at the time, so my letters have not been worth much. . . . I shall be glad for my grandchildren to know how dearly I loved their Mother & this seems to me to be the best way of their knowing.'

But for Emma it was bad enough being separated from Charlotte. She refused to live without her love words. It certainly would have changed the texture of the correspondence had Emma allowed it. Charlotte herself knew that only in her letters to her lovers did she translate the hardest scroll embossed within the book into flowing, unencumbered narrative. Only in those letters condemned to be destroyed could she be who she was.

Up until then her letters to Emma were chronicles of passionate observation and spontaneous, absolutely uncensored truth. Sunlight and shadow, without moralistic excuses. Had young Emma agreed to forgo the love words, the letters after Emma's marriage would have lost their punch, given their wider audience. Addicted as Charlotte was to giving good advice neither her nephew or her new niece ever took, she would have become even more than occasionally insufferable writing reams of wisdom to her belongings still unborn. But Emma put her foot down. The love words had to be spelled out and Charlotte left for England assuming her intimate journal letters would continue to be destroyed.

There should be a big bronze neoclassical statue of Emma in St. Louis. Something on the order of Harriet Hosmer's monumental statue of Senator Benton that stands in that city. 'Emma Crow Cushman, daughter-in-law, friend, and lover of Charlotte Cushman,' the base should read. 'She Lied and Never Burnt a Letter.'

In Walked Jane Carlyle

A FTER MARRYING her nephew to the woman she loved, Charlotte sailed back to England with Miss Stebbins and her mother. On board Miss Stebbins gave her an earful. Was it true, Charlotte wrote to Emma Cushman, that she disliked Miss Stebbins? She would be sorry to hear she brought a visitor to her house in Boston whom she objected to or disliked. Writing to her little lover, she was able to articulate her feelings for Miss Stebbins quite clearly: 'I love her very very much.'

Charlotte lost patience with Ned and her mother on the subject. Ned had been brought up to believe that it was only right and natural that his Auntie should give everything, body and soul, to her own family and to nobody else. He had never entertained the thought that his Auntie had earned everything she had for herself and had chosen not to marry. If she had married, nothing would be left to them. It never crossed his mind that as an independent woman she had a perfect right to spend her money as she pleased. 'I love my friends—as he loves his.'

She wrote to Emma, 'It has made my blood boil with indignation to know how my mother (*and* Ned) have felt & spoken with regards to Miss Stebbins.' (*And* Emma?)

If it were not below Charlotte's dignity—and if it were not the trick of her family to disbelieve her in these matters—Charlotte would have come right out and told them that 'Miss Stebbins is under no more obligation to me than Hattie!' The exception being that Miss Stebbins was more dependent on Charlotte for affection than Hattie and could not bear to be separated from her. 'But let them think of me as weak & poor as they will. I love them! I have always done the utmost of my duty by them & ever shall. I am truly happy for Ned's happiness, though it may be only my duty to have contributed to it.'

She had done Ned a great favor. Was it wicked of her to admit she was a bit jealous of his good fortune?

Having done her duty, Charlotte was once more in harmony with Miss Stebbins, and, imitative animal that she knew herself to be, she was absorbed by the concerns of the friends she was with. That her spouse was greatly relieved by all this renewed attention shows in her *Memories* of Charlotte Cushman, where she highlighted the two of them together in London, at Islington, at the home of their friends Stavros and Sarah Dilberoglue. It was a time of repose, a time when their own marriage took center stage. As usual, Miss Stebbins hid behind her lover's skirts, and only expressed her own joy through Charlotte's.

The couple could be themselves with the former Sarah Anderton, who went onstage in Manchester through hero worship for Charlotte, and while an actress, according to Charlotte, 'worked out some (to me) curious problems.' They were equally at home with her husband, the charismatic Stavros, whose darkly striking, bearded face combined masculine fierceness with a feminine sensitivity of brow and lip. George Lewes, living with George Eliot and attempting a novel himself, likened Stavros' Titianesque head to that of 'a vulture fed on milk,' so excitingly contrasted were the male and female of his nature. Stavros had originally emigrated from Corfu to Manchester as a boy of fourteen and got his start as a merchant there through Frank Jewsbury, the novelist Geraldine's youngest brother. Both Sarah and Stavros were also close friends of Jane Welsh Carlyle, who met them in Manchester through Geraldine during a very stormy time in Mrs. Carlyle's very stormy marriage.

Miss Stebbins reflected her happiness at having Charlotte all to herself in a sympathetic environment by quoting Charlotte's words to an unnamed correspondent: 'I have never known three more soul-satisfying days.'

'You don't know how we two grow and thrive in this atmosphere,' she continued, 'how much as one's own individualities are respected and loved we are forced by atmosphere to love and respect theirs. They were three perfect days.'

And those days were made even more perfect when on Sunday the person Charlotte had wished to know for fifteen years came self-invited to meet her. It was quite a dramatic entrance. In walked Jane Welsh Carlyle! She was the wife of the historian and philosopher Thomas Carlyle, Charlotte explained to her daughter-in-law, in a letter from which Miss Stebbins did not quote.

WHEN THE young American actress Charlotte Cushman took London by storm in 1845, the Scottish Jane Welsh Carlyle would not meet her. Jane was forty-four at the time; Charlotte was twenty-nine. London had been Mecca for both of these women. However, Jane, in her younger days, had girlish illusions that Charlotte would never have shared, and in her forties she was experiencing the results of the choices she made long before she knew the world. She had many reasons for being angry. But not at Charlotte Cushman.

It has been assumed that Jane and Charlotte did meet during the heyday of Charlotte's British career, and they may have bumped into each other once, but if so, it was unintentional on Jane's part. They shared significant friends—the novelist Geraldine Jewsbury, Ralph Waldo Emerson, the Brownings—and they knew many of the same people, the intellectual crème de la crème in both Britain and America. But the two women did not meet until those halcyon days in 1861 when Miss Stebbins was momentarily freed from her chronic concern. And Charlotte, having accomplished her missions—marrying her nephew to the woman she loved, securing the important monumental Horace Mann commission for Stebbins—was ready to resume her Italian life.

That Jane Carlyle had actively snubbed her, and at a time when everyone who was anyone in London only wanted to meet her, was an insult that Charlotte could not abide. It made her only more determined to meet Jane. But in this case, her American brand of determination was matched by Jane's Scottish resolve.

That a triumph deferred was hardly a triumph uncelebrated can be seen in Charlotte's unbridled exaltations to Emma:

'I wish you my darling could have seen this unhandsome, clever, keen, witty, scathing Scotch woman, come entirely down from her proud Eminence to sit at Auntie's side—with her hand entering hers & occasionally giving it a nervous clutch—as though she had found some warmth and nature there, which she failed to find among the proud intellectualizers which surround Carlyle to gather up his crumbs—but who invariably come away glamoured by her! I confess darling to being pretty flattered.' Flattered enough to tell Emma, 'Well dear *she* came—*she* saw and *I* conquered!'

Why Jane would not meet Charlotte tells much about the friendship between women as it was practiced in those days. Charlotte was correct in intuiting that by the time Jane, at the age of sixty, came to meet her, Jane Welsh Carlyle was certainly, perhaps desperately, looking for warmth and comfort in her women friends.

Jane was a woman who had long since said goodbye to the romantic girl she had once been. Yet only as a brilliant, wrongheaded, and valiant girl had she, in her own opinion, ever really lived. She so clearly saw the ironies of her life that they expressed themselves overtly in the cutting edge of her wit and her ridicule of the cant and half-truths of others. Her wicked tongue was her knight in shining armor, keeping the enemy from her heart. That she had once been Jane Baillie Welsh was her only claim to self-respect. Mrs. Carlyle was a completely different animal. That was what she thought, but on the surface you would never know it.

Both Charlotte's and Hattie's childhoods are interesting in themselves, but what the two were born to be, they also became. Jane Baillie Welsh and Mrs. Carlyle were diametrically opposed. Jane became painfully aware of what she willfully squandered.

Hattie Hosmer had traveled to Rome bringing with her her certificate of proficiency in anatomy from Missouri, two daguerreotypes of her *one* sculpture bust, and an exuberant self-confidence. How different from the young Jane Baillie Welsh, born at the very beginning of the nineteenth century, on 14 June 1801, who wrote so much, had so many accomplishments accrued in early days. Yet Jane never believed in her own genius; she believed in the genius of the men in her life. Whereas Charlotte and Hattie took little pleasure in their fathers, Jane adored her father, a man widely respected as a surgeon and healer. She had a prickly relationship with her very beautiful and conventional mother, Grace Baillie Welsh, with her old-fashioned eighteenth-century ideals as dainty as her china and with her abrupt, capricious, not-so-pretty changes of mood.

Dr. and Mrs. Welsh knew early on that Jane, born the first year of their marriage, would be an only child. And as much as she was the apple of her father's eye, it was not lost on Jane that Dr. Welsh wished his only child had been a boy.

She was as brave as a boy, so why wasn't she one? When she was perhaps seven or eight, she wrestled a fearsome turkey cock that always ran up to her, gobbling and clucking, blocking her on the road to school. Jane was afraid of the bird, but more by the thought of living in fear. So in front of a group of workingmen and schoolboys who were enjoying the show, she went right up to the turkey, grabbed him by the throat, and swung him around, clearing a path for herself.

"Well done, little Jeannie Welsh!" the men and boys cheered.

This took place in Haddington, Scotland, eighteen miles east of Edinburgh. Even today in Scotland, pasture begins exactly where road ends, so it is not difficult to imagine the crooked road and the cocky turkey. Or the slim, well-dressed child who had no idea why she was not a boy.

Jane, like the boys, did what they dared each other to do. On all fours, she climbed up to the steep peak of the Nungate bridge in Haddington and then down the other side. Once in a fight in the schoolyard, she decked a boy, giving him a black eye and a bloody nose. When the schoolmaster assembled them to ask who the culprit was, and promised to punish them all if no one answered, this elegant little girl, so simply and finely turned out by her mother, broke ranks and confessed.

You? He could not keep a stern face.

The only two classes boys and girls took together were algebra and mathematics, and Jane was the best girl in algebra. But then, when Jane was eight, the boys went on to Latin, a subject the girls did not take at all. So this was the difference between the sexes, the little girl opined. She begged her father for a tutor in Latin, but her mother was against it. Grace was what Grace wanted for her daughter. Social Grace. Gentility. A daughter should be her mother's companion. She should learn music, a bit of French, and how to sew an elegant stitch, appropriate accomplishments that would lead to a good—perhaps a brilliant—marriage.

But Jane knew her father had different ideas. He wanted his daughter to be educated. An education was something no one could ever take away from a person. Wealth could be, land could be, as the doctor's birthplace, Craigenputtock—a remote farm—had been for a time, but *not* an education. He wanted his only child and heir to have one. Though Dr. Welsh was clearly the head of the household, Grace was against having her overly bright daughter's head cluttered with Latin.

Jane found a Latin grammar and began teaching herself with the aid of a boy she was friendly with at school, an intelligent boy from a background humbler than hers. She had great status in Haddington as the good doctor's daughter. One night, as her parents were talking after dinner, she hid herself under the heavy crimson tablecloth and heard yet one more conversation not meant for her ears. Her parents were talking about her education, having their usual difference of opinion, this time on the subject of Jane's learning Latin.

She waited for a pause in the conversation. She must have been frightened by her own temerity, because when she spoke out from under their legs, her voice was small and breathless: '*Penna,* a pen, *pennae,* of a pen . . .' She declined the entire Latin noun. Her parents were speechless, giving her time to scramble out from under the cloth and run into her father's arms. 'I want to learn Latin. Please let me be a boy!'

Her father smothered his exceptional child in kisses and got her the best Latin tutor in town.

That was how Edward Irving entered her life. The eighteen-year-old Edward stood over six feet four, perhaps six feet five, with long black hair and ruddily masculine good looks. The only discernible flaw in his singular vision was a perennial squint in one eye. Edward had completed university (which began for Scottish boys at the age of thirteen) and was teaching and directing a school while he studied for the ministry. In those days he wore a flowing cape and used his splendid oratorial voice for poetry as well as for the pulpit.

He was delighted by his small young charge, who would wake up every day before dawn so that he could tutor her for two hours before school began for both of them. Some mornings she would still be sleepily in her nightclothes when he arrived. He'd sweep her up in his arms and bring her to the windows in the drawing room that faced the back gardens of her pretty home and point out the stars and constellations to her.

It did make Edward uncomfortable that, as versed in Latin as she was by the age of ten, she still played with dolls.

Dolls. Charlotte Cushman remembered having no facility when it came to dolls. 'I was born a Tomboy.' She was no good at all in making dolls' dresses, though she could make their furniture. She could do anything with tools. But her poor dolls! 'My earliest recollections are of dolls' heads cracked open to see what they were thinking of—possessed with the idea that dolls could and did think.' No matter how her mother admonished her, she kept looking for their brains.

Hattie, motherless since the age of four, did not play with dolls. She snuck into her father's office whenever she could and played house with the skeleton the doctor kept there, just as he forbade her.

Jane had no ordinary doll. Grace made many sumptuous dresses for it—and it had a lovely four-posted bed. Jane decided that if she were to give up her doll, the proper end for it was to commit suicide the way Dido did in Virgil's *Aeneid*. So Jane made a Roman funeral pyre under the doll's bed, composed of its clothing, some cedar chips, a few sticks of cinnamon, cloves, and a nutmeg. Then she put her doll in its bed and, excellent classic scholar that she was, helped it recite Dido's last words in Latin—which Jane knew as well as she did her ABC's. That done, she had her doll stab herself to death, providing a penknife as a sword. Once the doll was dead, Jane lit the pyre. Later in life she recorded her feelings at that moment, giving as well a good example of her literary power:

'Seeing my poor doll blaze up—for being stuffed with bran she took fire and was all over in no time—in that supreme moment my affection for her blazed up also, and I shrieked, and would have saved her and could not, and went on shrieking till everybody within hearing flew to me, and bore me off in a plunge of tears—an epitome of most of one's "heroic sacrifices" it strikes me, magnanimously resolved on, ostentatiously gone about, repented of at the last moment, and bewailed in an outcry.'

Jane was a different kind of tomboy than Charlotte or Hattie. She wished to be a boy, but her reasons were those of a girl. She wanted to please a man.

Edward, between the ages of eighteen and twenty, and Jane, between the ages of nine and eleven, developed a deep affection for one another. For Jane, there was nothing her tutor did not know. Edward was amazed and delighted with the dark-haired, hazel-eyed, precocious Jane, with her Gypsy looks and clever tongue. In the good weather they could be seen walking the roads and roaming the meadows together. He had taken her under his abundant wing.

When Edward left Haddington for a better-paying position in Kirkcaldy, another prominent scholar, James Brown, tutored the eleven-year-old Jane, and she continued her studies in school. There was too much of a rough male influence around her daughter, Grace complained to the doctor. And finally her parents reached a compromise: Jane could continue her studies if, at the same time, she went to board in Haddington at a finishing school just started by a Mrs. Hemming, married to a former military man from the West Indies.

Rather than the refinement and manners her mother thought she would receive there, Jane found abuse. The only mention of these eight months was an account written down a half century later by Thomas Carlyle, who called them the little cup of bitter in her happy years at home. 'She was fixed down, for a good few months, and suffered . . . manifold disgust, even hardships, even want of proper food; wholly without complaining (too proud and loyal for that); till it was, by some accident, found out, and instantly put an end to.'

She had stonily and stoically submitted herself to the consequences of her mother's way.

Not until Jane was almost sixteen did Grace once more have an influence. Jane was sent to Edinburgh to finishing school, and she spent her weekends with her cousin there. But by then Jane had developed into a young woman, and it was obvious even to herself that she was never going to be a boy. She was over five foot four, slender, big-breasted. She hadn't her mother's classic beauty; she had a rather irregular wide mouth and a strong nose. But she was exciting to look at, the Gypsy blood from her mother's side of the family shone in her animated face. She had an animated spirit as well, and the sharpest, wittiest tongue. As the doctor's daughter, she held an elevated position in the hearts of her neighbors, and when she walked the streets, dressed with such simple elegance, such authentic style, the townsfolk turned as she passed and said, There goes the Rose of Haddington.

Dr. Welsh was not pleased by Jane's popularity when she returned from finishing school in Edinburgh, or by her complaining to him about the narrowness of her world and of how she wanted to travel. The doctor did not want her head turned by all this attention she was receiving. It was not on looks and charm alone that she should rely, but on her own study and wit and wisdom. There were so many young men attracted to her, but he personally didn't think any of them worthy of her. When it came to choosing a partner for life, she must choose wisely and well.

Jane, at first, thought him severe, for she was only playing with those absurd, egocentric fellows who kept proclaiming their love. They did not interest her. She wanted to see the world. She'd like to go to Glasgow!

When her handsome father saw that she was annoyed, he took her hand and, with an unusual emphasis she would never forget, told her that someday she would be thankful for his words and for his wanting her to stay in Haddington, for 'you will not always be at home with me.'

Soon enough that turned prophetic. She was still eighteen when Dr. Welsh contracted cholera from a cottager he saved from the disease: 'I was forced away from him—but I sat by the door of his room, and heard his voice—and when it was opened I saw his face—and sometimes I stood an instant by his bed in spite of their efforts to remove me—and then he looked so anxious, and said to my Mother, "Will you not send her away?" Oh my God! the recollection of that short awful period of my life will darken my being to the grave.'

He seemed to be reviving, he was forty-two, at the height of his powers, but then he succumbed, perhaps more a result of the bleedings his inexperienced younger brother gave him than from the disease.

For a good half hour there was silence in the house. Jane sat in front of the locked door to his room, until she suddenly rose crying and screaming, 'I must see my father!'

Her father's partner, Dr. Howden, took her in his arms and she fainted. He carried her through the drawing room to the little bedroom off of it and laid her down in bed next to her poor mother, who was in a dead swoon as well. The thirty-six-year-old widow and her eighteen-year-old daughter, unconscious in the same bed, like two stone effigies on a Scottish kirk's floor, united in an unsparing grief.

Betty Braid, a young servant Jane's age, who would remain close to her heart through her whole life, remembered the scene, the mother and daughter lying there 'like twa deid corpses! Eh, but it was waeful!' '

There is hardly a whisper of Elkanah Cushman in Charlotte's letters, except for the notice of her father's death while she was in Philadelphia. When Dr. Hosmer died a few years after his stroke, Charlotte did not even see *one tear in Hattie's eye*! 'I do not think she cared for him. He had not done as he aught during the years of her life when she was making her name. They had nothing in common. He had bred her to the largest individuality—nay selfishness—& he reaps the consequences in her not regretting his death. She is no hypocrite. She does not profess what she does not feel—& therein lies her only title to respect in this matter.'

Jane was too distraught to attend her father's funeral. When she did rise from her bed, she put on black, which she planned to wear until the day she was lowered into the grave that held her father's remains. When she was well enough, she was told he was buried in the ruins of the medieval apse of their church. She wished to visit it in moonlight. 'Those Ruins appear to me now to possess a sublimity with which my fancy never before vested them—I feel that I can never leave this place.'

She became closer to her mother during these months, but unknown to everyone, at the time of her father's death, there was another man in her life, a secret love, that comforted her through letters.

Edward Irving, Scottish preacher and orator, pictured in London in the 1820s.

She remet her former tutor Edward Irving in Edinburgh, preparing to take his vows and to go off to Glasgow as a minister's assistant. She was sixteen, he twenty-five. Edward was promised to a minister's eldest daughter, Isabella Martin, whom he taught right after he left Haddington. Certainly there was no harm in seeing his former pupil Jeannie Welsh. Being rather obliquely engaged for five years allowed Edward, an expansive man who got along easily with women, a certain freedom. He could go far, but no further. And Edward was a manly, loving man, with a glint in his good eye.

Before they consciously admitted it, Edward and Jane fell in love and kept it a deep secret. The world of books and romance Jane lived in, combined with the constant adoration she received from family, friends, and admirers, set her imagination on fire.

Charlotte Cushman said most women knew little of the world as they lived indoor lives and all they discerned of reality was through books and their parents. Jane lived an indoor life surrounded by book learning. Yes, she told Edward, she would marry him, but only on the condition Reverend Martin and his daughter agreed to release him from his engagement. In Scotland that was the way things were done. And Jane, beyond her romantic fantasies, was Scottish to the bone.

Edward, nine years older, was by then so deeply in love with Jane that he would have married her whether or not the Martins released him honorably. But when Reverend Martin did not agree to breaking the engagement, Jane told Edward that he must fulfill his duty to the woman he did not love. He and Jane would share instead something more exalted and nobler than marriage: Platonic Love. In her innocence—and in her vanity—she saw no threat in Edward having a silly wife. They would continue their *conversazione.*

It would all be just like Jean-Jacques Rousseau's *Julie; or, The New Héloïse,* an epistolary novel about two secret lovers from a small town at the foot of the Alps: a poor brilliant tutor and his student, Julie, the beautiful, talented only child of a rich family, who is adored by her parents, friends, townspeople—everybody! The only difference between the Scottish pair and the French is Edward and Jane never shared a night of illicit love. In fact, the Scottish maiden skipped over that Frenchified lapse.

That fatal book! That was what she called it. Rousseau had given her an ideal of romantic friendship no man could come up to, she wrote to her cousin Eliza (as Julie writes to hers). But of course Edward secretly had fulfilled her ideal. She was resigned to being a virtuous old maid, she told her cousin, in the offhanded jovial style she most often used to hide her heart. It was all Rousseau's fault.

In the novel Julie is forced to marry the man her father has chosen for her. In life it was Edward who was forced to be true to his word. But Julie's marriage turns out all right. Her husband is wise and passionless and eventually her former tutor comes to live with them on the highest Platonic level (though secretly, of course, he never loses his mad, passionate feelings for Julie). He even tutors Julie's children as a sacred privilege. That fatal book. When Julie contracts smallpox, she longs only for her tutor, who would love her no matter how she looked. Of course she recuperates with nary a scar. From this book of imaginary letters, a self-centered and spirited young woman of genius who knew nothing of the world read her life.

Jane gave it to Edward to read. But Edward returned it, telling her he received consolation from Jane's words, not from what he called *Rousseau's* letters.

Condemned by Jane to Rousseau's concept of romantic friendship, Edward introduced his best friend Thomas Carlyle to her. He was too jealous to bring men friends before then. Once he had done so in Edinburgh and exploded when she paid attention to the friend. Jane did not respond to his outburst, just left the room. Immediately he collected himself and, never afraid of self-examination, followed after her to ask her forgiveness: 'The truth is, I was piqued. I have always been accustomed to fancy that *I* stood highest in your good opinion, and I was jealous to hear you praise another man.'

Now he half hoped to bring his two friends together. Thomas did not know anything of their love, only that Jane was Edward's dear former 'Pupil,' whose education still concerned him. She was a brilliant girl stuck in a small town, whose father was the great love of her life. His death had been her great tragedy. She could not bear to mention his name and wore perpetual black in his memory.

That was all Edward told him as he walked from Edinburgh to Haddington with his brilliant, irascible friend three years his junior by his side. Grace and Jane watched the two approach one May evening. Thomas Carlyle was only three or four inches shorter than Edward. He had straw-colored hair, deep purple-blue eyes, a pronounced jaw, and a protruding underbite. He was good-looking in a tall, lanky, unkempt sort of way, despite the stubborn chin which announced the stubborn man, pouting, inward, proud, relentless, shy. He looked something of a hayseed.

Sunshine and shadow. Thomas, a violent-tempered farmer's son, was as ungainly and withdrawn and awkward socially as Edward, a violent-tempered tanner's son, was outgoing, loving, and graceful.

On daily visits to the Welshes—Carlyle had never seen such a pretty and tasteful house—Edward drew his shy and gloomy friend out. Carlyle—that's what Jane would always call him, once she learned how to spell his name. Carlyle or Mr. Carlyle or Mr. C., never Thomas, talked of the Germans, of Goethe and Schiller, as if he were speaking of a new world. How Carlyle reminded Jane of her father. She herself had done some tutoring in recent months, but for the first time since her father's death, her enthusiasm to study and to learn was renewed. Here was another man of genius who was impressed by her intellectual potential, who wanted to teach her, who told her she must study German. Why, Carlyle even promised her a reading list!

For Carlyle, women existed on a separate planet. And the higher they soared above his head, the more pleasure he took in bowing, submitting, at least inwardly, to their ideal presence. He considered himself the dark son of earth; he called Jane his sun. He had none of Edward's ease with the fair sex—and knew it. This young woman, so brilliant, so beautiful, so devoted to her father's memory, captured his imagination—the place in his constitution where women lived. He could swear she held his hand a moment longer than necessary when they parted. He wrote to her with a sweaty palm.

It was thrilling for Jane to let Edward see how easy it was for her to turn the difficult and suspicious genius's head. This ability of hers to capture on contact did not in fact fade with her youth or with the loss of her looks. For many men and some women, she was irresistible.

She knew from that first encounter that Carlyle was a genius—even more of a genius than Edward. Both of them would be famous, she knew and predicted—and both told her she took too much stock in fame.

But love Carlyle as a husband? Never, never, she told Carlyle. 'I will be to you a true, a constant, a devoted *friend*—but not a Mistress—a Sister—but not a Wife—*Falling in love* and marrying like other Misses is quite out of the question—I have too *little* romance in my disposition ever to be in love with you or any other man; and too *much* ever to marry without love.' Her devotions were filial. She had never known passion. And in many ways, that suited Carlyle just fine.

Meanwhile Edward and Jane still hoped. After all, he was not married yet. And his ministerial assistantship had not been such a success in Glasgow. He might have to go to the West Indies, to Jamaica, for a ministry.

At the last moment, he was given a trial to preach for a few weeks at the humble Scottish church in London at Hattan Gardens. What would have happened to Edward Irving if he had been five feet tall, the poet William Hazlitt wondered. But he wasn't tiny as a sugar tong—Jane's later description of the writer Thomas De Quincey. He was a towering giant of a man, Christ-like in appearance, with a spellbinding oratorical style, and with a burning belief in the message of Jesus at a time when belief was crumbling all around.

He preached on Christmas Eve, and among the congregation were distinguished Scottish guests and their English friends, who came back to hear him again. It is said that in Parliament at the time, a bill for increasing monetary compensation for clergy of the Church of England was being discussed—in order to attract more ecclesiastical talent. The statesman George

Canning stood up and said that, on the contrary, he had just experienced the most eloquent sermon he ever heard given in a humble chapel by a poorly paid minister of the Scottish Church.

This inflamed the imagination of the rich and powerful. Fashionable England flocked to hear Edward Irving preach. The papers would soon be calling him 'the Spanish Adonis.' Though in Glasgow his congregation was suspicious of his expressive oratory, Edward was not too overdone for London. No less than Charlotte Cushman twenty-four years later, he was famous within a fortnight. But hadn't Jane Welsh always told him he would be?

For a moment fame did what it was famed for doing—gave Edward hopes of reclaiming what he could not have without it. Perhaps he could now marry Jane. But it actually gave him a ministry and money enough to fulfill the pledge he had avoided for over ten years.

Two years later, he spent the long weekend before his wedding day in Haddington with Jane and preached there that Sunday. During that time, the two of them built their castle in Spain.

'I am almost out of my wits with joy—I think, in my life, I was never so glad before,' Jane wrote to Carlyle on the heels of Edward's wedding day, 13 October 1823, with an élan unique in her letters. She was not dissembling. 'You and I are going to London! You and I! We are to live a whole summer beside each other, and beside the One whom next to each other we love most—We are to see magnificence of Art as we have never seen, and to get acquainted with such excellence of Man and Woman as we have never known—in short, we are to lead, for three months, the happiest, happiest life that my imagination hath ever conceived—In the same house for months!'

'Tell me how he gets on with a wife,' Jane continued. Carlyle was traveling with the couple for part of their wedding trip. 'It must be very laughable.'

Carlyle reported back that he had seen the 'great Divine' and studied him: 'He loves you as a sister & will treat you as one. His wife you will hardly like.' A dull, pimply, pretentious woman, he considered her.

Edward spoke to Thomas about coming to London with Jane: 'He seemed to think that if set down on London streets some strange development of genius would take place in me, that by conversing with Coleridge and the Opium eater [De Quincey], I should find out new channels for speculation and soon learn to speak in tongues.' Strange that Carlyle used the term 'speak in tongues,' for in a matter of years Edward would believe

God was speaking directly through members of his congregation, who were allowed to interrupt the service when the spirit seized them and 'speak in tongues'—or rave and rant, as Carlyle described it.

Already Thomas was suspicious of this popularity of Edward's which he believed his friend mistook for fame: 'The popularity of a pulpit orator is like a tar-barrel set up in the middle of the street to blaze with a fierce but very tarnished flame, for a few hours, and then go out in a cloud of sparkles and thick smoke offensive to the lungs and noses of the whole neighborhood.'

He had no idea why Edward wished Jane, when in London, to meet Mrs. Basil Montagu, the stately woman who was Edward's confidante. What advantage did Edward contemplate 'from submitting you to the example and kindly influences of this seraphic Mrs Montagu'? Still, Jane should accept Edward's invitation and go to London, where she would meet cultivated men and see new forms of life—not that Carlyle, even given the inducement of spending three months with the woman he claimed to love, would be tempted to join them for the season.

'Indeed unless our friend doth greatly amend his ways there is little likelihood of my seeking happiness under his roof with or without you,' Jane responded. 'He has not written me a single line since he was here for all the lecture I gave him on the subject and for all his promises of good behavior in time to come—I do not under him—sometimes I think he loves me almost half as well as you do and then again that I am nothing at all to him.' (She meant to write 'I do not understand him'; however, 'I do not under him' is an interesting slip.)

The married One did not invite the woman he loved to live with him and his wife in Rousseau-like bliss in London. He only invited Carlyle in the long run. Tortured by his undiminished feelings (marriage, it would appear, was not a magic wand), Edward realized he could not balance his two loves the way he thought he could. He confessed his passion to his wife, and the two of them knelt together and prayed for his healing. The year after next he would be ready to receive Jane, Edward wrote to her. But Jane realized it would never be. As she phrased it, she had done his wife too great a favor.

Jane had a nervous collapse, more severe than her breakdown after her father's death. It was only then that she told her frightened mother of her and Edward Irving's love. It hadn't been Thomas Carlyle, as her mother feared, but Edward Irving, whom her mother trusted. *Edward* had caused her child such secret distress.

Of course, in a small town like Haddington, everyone else already knew. Edward Irving had let the minister in him loose, forthrightly stating on the eve of his wedding that Isabella Martin was the love of his youth, Jane the love of his intellect. That intellect again. When Jane broke down, the whole town said it was a result of Edward's jilting her.

Have you ever heard of such a thing, Jane wrote to Carlyle. 'Do you know that they are giving out that I am dreadfully disappointed at his marriage!!! and that he has used me very ill—*me* ill! was there ever any thing so insufferable?' *She* jilted. Why, it was Jane who convinced Edward to go ahead with his marriage.

Why should idle gossip bother her? Carlyle replied, it wasn't true. What did it matter what people said? What mattered was the absolute honesty that existed between himself and Jane. That blunt, uncompromising severity was the golden cord that bound them.

'How comes it that I have such a Friend as you?' Jane at times wondered out loud to Carlyle. 'That I deceive you without seeking to deceive you? I am so different from the idea in your mind! stript of the veil of poetry which your imagination spread around me I am so undeserving of your love! But I *shall* deserve it—*shall* be a noble woman.' Those at least were her aspirations.

Carlyle, in these first years of their correspondence, urged Jane to write, to translate. He definitely encouraged her literary ambitions. He wanted to collaborate with her on an epistolary novel, on a book of translations. Her letters themselves revealed her extraordinary talent. Write for *him*, he pleaded, vigorously encouraging his 'Friend' to become a bluestocking. She could become the bluest in the planet of the Blues, he told her.

But Jane had lost her appetite for such projects. She explained to Carlyle that since her father's death (she often folded her disappointments about Edward into her grief for her father), she had neither the same pleasures nor the same motives. 'I am *alone,* and no one loves me better for my industry.'

And that was it. Neither her father nor Edward was there to love her for her genius, so she had no reason for furthering it. Unlike Charlotte or Hattie, she never entertained the idea that her own talent, her own intellect, might be what held her together when life got rough. It did not matter that her beloved father had schooled her in the idea that no one could take an education away from a person, or that Thomas Carlyle encouraged her literary pursuits. The men she loved were gone. She was *alone;* her intellect no longer brought her love.

Essentially, Jane did not believe in herself on the deepest level, the way both Charlotte and Hattie did. That was something her friend Geraldine Jewsbury would one day discern. As Jane wrote to Carlyle, if she only had *his* genius melded to *her* ambition. 'Oh for your head!' She still sought fame and would not think of marrying a man unless he was a genius. But genius or not, she would never marry Carlyle. Married or not, she would love Carlyle the same: calmly, delightfully, 'but so unimpassioned.' Their epistolary friendship would continue.

'I know very well you will never be my wife. Never! Never!' Carlyle mocked by return mail. But should she marry another, 'I shall of course cease to correspond with you.' Though he would always love the memory of Jane Baillie Welsh, the married woman he could not love.

He did not mean it as a threat, but to Jane it was. How could she live without his letters? He was a genius who would be a famous man in his lifetime and immortal after his death—she predicted in these years before anyone knew his name. If he would not be her friend after she married, she would never marry. She could not give this genius up—unless she met another. Which she didn't. Some of her beaux had money, some charm, some good looks. But none had Carlyle's head.

Two years after that letter, she burned her four unfinished novels and her finished play and her drawings and paintings—all of them—the way she burned her doll. But this time no regrets. She had a plan. At twenty-four, she cleared the decks. Carlyle would be proud of her as he would see she was *completing* all her new projects. It was her 1825 New Year's resolution.

But by then Carlyle was staying with Edward Irving in London and was sick of literary men and women. Through Edward's supporter and confidante Mrs. Montagu, that regal woman, tall, aloof, her once fabled beauty fading, he met them all. Edward called Mrs. Montagu the Noble Lady, and so did Carlyle at times. He used an ironic tone, though he was secretly in awe of her as well. Dorothea Montagu and her husband Basil (the natural son of the Earl of Sandwich) gathered all of literary London to them at their beautiful home at 25 Bedford Square. Both were identified with the Romantic poets: Basil had gone to school with William Wordsworth, and Dorothea once had roamed the Lowlands of Scotland the intimate of Robert Burns. Edward believed there was much Jane could learn from his Noble Lady, and very much wanted them to meet when Jane—in the future—came to London.

Carlyle was not impressed by their circle: Coleridge spit as he spoke and was 'sunk inextricably in the depths of putrescent indolence. Southey and Wordsworth have retired far from the din of this monstrous city. So has Thomas Moore. Whom have we left? The dwarf Opium-Eater [De Quincey]. . . . Hazlitt is *writing* his way thro' France and Italy: the ginshops and pawnbrokers bewail his absence.'

And the literary women were as bad. 'Depend on it, Jane, this literature . . . will *not* constitute the sole nourishment of any true human spirit. . . . What is it that makes Blue-stockings of women, Magazine hacks of men? They neglect household and social duties, they have no household. . . . They despise or overlook the common blessedness which Providence has laid out for *all* his creatures.' Mrs. Montagu had made it quite plain how peculiar it was for a man of his talents not to have a helpmate,

Samuel Taylor Coleridge in the early 1830s by Daniel Maclise. 'Figure a fat flabby incurvated personage,' Thomas Carlyle wrote to Jane from London after meeting the ailing and addicted Romantic poet. 'I reckon him a man of great and useless genius—a strange not at all a great man.'

not to have a home. Even his great love for his mother and reliance on her affection seemed a bit excessive. She influenced his thinking on domesticity. Thomas Carlyle did not need a genius, he needed a good wife.

'Do you know, I heartily rejoice that you *cannot* write a book at present!' he told Jane.

The bluestocking years were over: 'Gifts like yours are fit for something else than scribbling.' An hour with Coleridge or the poet 'Barry Cornwall' (Mrs. Montagu's son-in-law, Bryan Waller Procter) would make her 'forswear *fame* forever and a day!' He wished to have a farm, a quiet place away from the madding crowd, where he could write in peace.

If Carlyle wanted a place to farm, why not farm *her* land, Jane replied. A fatal joke about that moor of a farm, silent, high, and remote, a square mile of land near the English border, yet a universe away from London: Craigenputtock, her father's folly. Dr. Welsh sunk his money into reclaiming his desolate birthplace, one of the reasons her mother was secretly in debt. As Dr. Welsh died intestate, Jane, his daughter, not Grace, his wife, inherited the burden of his meager estate, including the harsh, and at times unleasable, farm.

Carlyle took Jane seriously and in delight purposed going to Craigenputtock immediately. Where was it, by the way? His brother Alick would work the farm, they would both get things ready for her, and then Carlyle would marry Jane and carry her over the threshold to his new life.

Carlyle a farmer? Please. She was only joking. Herself, she would not survive a month in that horrid place with an angel. If Carlyle wanted to marry her—by now they *were* circling around marriage—he had better find a more practical way of raising money.

In a sense, that was it for Carlyle. He was angry with himself for having an unaccustomed moment of optimism and building his plans around a landed woman's joke. After all, he was a peasant from Ecclefechan, a stretch of southern Scotland about as big as its name, and she was a doctor's daughter. What did she know about necessity, about leasing farms? All his class sensitivity kicked in. Her love was more fit for a book than for life, he told her.

He didn't write again and he didn't even come to see her once he came back to Scotland, until he and his brother had leased a farm of their own without telling her a thing about it beforehand. He could get on without the Welshes' land! When he did visit, he confessed his first love—unrequited—to Jane. One Margaret Gordon, a pupil of Edward Irving's he met through his friend. From Jane, not a word about her love of Edward.

They had a terrible fight. If not before, Jane's mother now witnessed Carlyle's violent temper. Like his pious father James, like the men of the Carlyle clan, Thomas Carlyle had moments when he could not contain his rage. That was why his mother Margaret, the love of his life, made him promise not to fight when she first sent him to school. He kept his word for a good four years, taking his beatings and slinking into the isolation and sullen contempt that marked his young life.

Some months after his display of temper with Jane, Carlyle told her flat out he could never marry an heiress.

So Jane made a will, as she should have done earlier. When she was sick unto death after Edward's marriage, she was warned that should she die without one, her mother would be left with nothing. But she couldn't bear to talk to a lawyer of such things. Even now she handled the matter by letter, writing to the mother she lived with that she was giving everything over to her immediately, because Mr. Carlyle was too proud to associate with an heiress—and she proudly announced her accomplishment to Carlyle as well.

It would take almost a year before Carlyle's rage boiled over. When he said he would not marry an heiress, he did not mean *that*.

'I asked of you no less than yourself and all that you had and were, your heart your hand and your worldly resources; *you* were to have the happiness of snatching the immortal Mr Carlyle from the jaws of perdition . . . to you he was to owe a home, and the peace and kind ministrations of a home.'

But that was not to be: 'These things you could not do, your fortune was called from you by a higher duty; from you I was not to receive a home.'

Jane hardly noticed the change in his letters, as she pondered life after Edward. There were so many other suitors. But even her dazzling dandy of a cousin, James Baillie, as well as sober Dr. Bell lacked—genius. Why couldn't she love Carlyle as she should, she wondered out loud. If only she were his sister. If only she could '*love those I have, when I have not those I love.*'

She railed against her own perversity to Carlyle.

In a quandary concerning her future, she asked Carlyle if Mrs. Montagu would write to her. He had previously let her read a letter from Mrs. Montagu, one filled with news of their Edward. It was the remarkable style of the letter that impressed her, she said. Wouldn't Carlyle ask the Noble Lady to write?

Writing to Jane put her in a difficult position, Mrs. Montagu told

Thomas. The Noble Lady did not want to stir the embers of love which were still burning between Edward and Jane, and there was Mrs. Irving to consider as well. . . .

How could she even imagine that Thomas knew nothing of his best friend and Jane's love? Still, on the same day she fretted to Thomas, Dorothea Benson Montagu made an entrance into Jane's life like a grand dame in an epistolary novel:

'My dear Young Lady, If your servant were at this moment to announce "*Mrs Montagu*" we should both feel something of that natural Embarrassment with which stranger meets stranger, tho' the conventional forms of good breeding in all cases, and a desire to please in our case, would teach us to hide it, but now, living as I do in your mind's eye and associated with the friends you love best, I approach you without reserve, and I feel that I am welcomed. . . . And rely upon this, you will know me best by my letters.'

She intuited both Jane's main reason for wanting her to write and Thomas' reason for pushing it—so that she could be his intermediary: 'I could say much to you of our dear friend Edward Irving whom I love for himself alone. . . . His Wife, but for her great piety, must be wretched, for he cannot (with every desire to do so) give her any part of his time except in the hours of refreshment & sleep—and she must live among persons whom you could not endure for a moment. As for Thomas Carlyle! but he deserves a whole letter to himself.'

Jane was thrilled with the letter and answered in a burst of enthusiasm, swearing eternal friendship with the Noble Lady. She was superior to any woman Jane had ever known. So frank, so kind, so motherly, so high-souled. 'I have never met with any thing like this from Woman before—I purpose loving Mrs Montagu all my life.'

Whereas Charlotte adored Fanny Kemble and the younger Hattie had Charlotte Cushman to emulate, Jane now found her first woman guide. Here was the only woman outside of her cousin Elisa who did not shy away from the intellect revealed in her letters or by her sharp tongue.

'I am glad that you have answered Mrs Montagu, and liked her,' Carlyle wrote. 'She labours under some delusion, I believe, about your secret history. . . . I have had a letter from her, full of eloquence, in which she tells me that "your heart is in England your heart is not here."' He attributed it to the Noble Lady's *romance* of real life.

Her heart was not in England with Edward, but in Scotland with Carlyle, Jane told him.

And she quickly explained the situation to Mrs. Montagu. Carlyle knew nothing of her relationship with Edward Irving. Jane's own mother had told her it would be better to keep this secret, and Mrs. Montagu must keep the secret too. In fact it might have been at that moment, with the fear of discovery lurking, that a wavering Jane decided she definitely *was* engaged to Carlyle, would indeed marry him. Perhaps this passionless regard and friendship she felt for him was best in a wife. It had been for Rousseau's Julie.

How could her dear Jane Welsh consider herself engaged while she concealed such information, Mrs. Montagu replied. Jane was acting as if she were free, while she was in prison, and she expected to lock Mrs. Montagu in prison with her. Only a few weeks before, Jane had told her she was not in love with Carlyle and realized that 'there was no loving by logick.'

Jane had confided to her grand friend that there was a fearful void aching at her breast. Wasn't Jane now attempting to transfer her feelings for Edward to Thomas Carlyle, the way an uprooted plant might try to cling to another tree?

'Examine yourself well, my dear friend,' Mrs. Montagu warned her, for to fill that void, Jane had even been glad to cling to Mrs. Montagu herself, a woman who was just a name, a shadow, to Jane.

And as far as being *engaged* without telling Thomas about Edward: 'I must honor your Mother for her most liberal views,—but I again charge you look well to yourself—shall I . . . put a case to you; If any accident set our friend Edward free, if you felt that his love had been like all well founded love, indestructible, and only in abeyance to his duty . . . how would my dear Jane's pulse beat then? If with truth and frankness I expect from you, you can lay your hand upon your heart and say "*calmly as before*" I will say Marry then in heaven's name and the sooner the better.'

Jane received that letter at her grandfather's house at Templand, outside Dumfries and not far from the Carlyles. She was soon to visit Carlyle and meet his family at the farm Carlyle and his brother had leased at Hoddam Hill. How could she look him in the eye?

'I have deceived you *I* whose truth and frankness you have so often praised have deceived my bosom friend!' Jane wrote. 'I told you that I did not care for Edward Irving, took pains to make you believe this—It was false.'

She could not even claim merit for disclosing this to him voluntarily. It was Mrs. Montagu who had moved her to honesty. She enclosed the Noble Lady's letter.

'I loved him—must I say it—*once* passionately loved him—'

What was worse, she had made a *conscious deception* year after year by disguising her feelings.

'The Ass,' 'the Orator' 'the Stupendous Ass,' she called Edward, ridiculing him to Carlyle and at the same time digging for information in letter after letter.

'What a wicked creature you are to make me laugh so!' Carlyle responded to one of her essays against Edward. How often he ended up acting as mediator between his two friends, finally wondering why he was spending so much time writing to Jane about Edward when they had their own lives to resolve. Jane had so cleverly dissembled that *no* reader of her letters could unearth her true feelings without her forthright confession. She had passionately loved Edward and consciously kept it from Carlyle for over five years.

Carlyle's response to her was delayed in the mail and she was devastated by the silence. 'Mr Carlyle do you mean to kill me? . . . Oh I do love you my own Friend, above the whole earth—no human being was ever half so dear to me—none, none—and will you break my heart?'

They had to put leeches on her temples to keep her quiet.

The doctors thought the trip to Templand had made her ill again. Once more, just as when Edward did not write and the town of Haddington whispered of his abandonment, as when her father died in the prime of his life, she became psychologically as well as physically unhinged.

She had destroyed herself by changing how she looked in Carlyle's eyes.

Carlyle had as great a desire to ignore his feelings as Jane hers, but he answered her with true tenderness. She did not know the world outside of Haddington. There were many men she would one day meet who were more worthy than either himself or Edward. And as for her loving Edward and deceiving him about it: 'You exaggerate this matter greatly; it is an evil, but it may be borne; we must bear it *together;* what else can we do? Much of the annoyance it occasions to me proceeds from selfish sources, of a poor enough description; this is unworthy of our notice.'

So he overlooked it all. Margaret Gordon, his first love, and Jane, his second, had both been Edward's pupils. Edward introduced both to him. Carlyle fell in love with both. They both loved Edward better. Happiness was fool's gold. He always knew that. The sepia tones of his moral landscape simply deepened. What else was there to say?

This. Did it really matter? More and more he became convinced of his impotence. While out of Scotland, he had attempted a cure for his chronic dyspepsia, through one of Mrs. Montagu's friends, Dr. Badams. It may have been an attempt to deal with this sexual misfunctioning as well, as he always connected his bad stomach with his inability to love. The dyspepsia had worsened after Margaret Gordon rejected him. It was one thing to die romantically of a broken heart, he would write in his semiautobiographical *Sartor Resartus*. Quite another, like the book's Germanic hero Teufels-dröckh (Devil's Shit in English), to live with churned bowels and ghastly indigestion.

Plied with castor oil and mercury and whatever else could by chance purge the tormenting fire of his dyspepsia, this man who had little confidence in his body was in constant contact with his excrement. No wonder he called himself the man of earth, of dirt; the woman he wrote to lived on a different planet he called the sun.

The sun was flickering now and it was time to be as truthful to Jane as she had been to him: 'I can no longer love,' he responded. 'Think of it, Jane! I can never make you happy. Leave me, then! Why should I destroy you?'

Leave him? Never.

Once more she became the heroine of her own epistolary novel: 'Too late to think of obeying reason when I love! Yes! you have said rightly I will save you, or we perish *together*. . . . You can no longer love, you say; I hear but believe not. This is a mere delusion my Darling: you *can* love,—will, shall love; not Jane Welsh, perhaps, but your Wife you will love.'

Carlyle ached to believe her. 'My dearest little Ruth!' he responded. 'The evil is deep and dark, but it is *one*, and I see it clearly. If this accursed burden of disease were cast away, nine tenths of my faults and incapacities would pass away with it.' He pictured his youth as one spent in a 'deathlike cold eclipse.'

Jane's mother, who read all his letters, read this one and developed a new caprice: 'Now *sighs* and looks terribly cross, at the least allusion to you.'

Grace Welsh was in a fright that her daughter actually would marry this excuse for a man who she believed bewitched and poisoned Jane's mind. What did her mother know? She didn't read books. And Grace had the nerve to complain of Jane's friendship with Mrs. Montagu as well, calling her a woman Jane had never met, knew nothing about, and for whom nevertheless she had the most unbounded love and admiration.

Grace was so upset that she retired to her room for an entire twenty-four hours. During that time she wrote her intellectual daughter a letter, trying to explain her objections to Thomas Carlyle rationally, not capriciously.

Her objections to Jane marrying him went far beyond the fact that he came from a family of farmers and masons and had no wealth or position. It was his contemptuous attitude and its effect on Jane. Grace's soul was *torn* after experiencing Carlyle's violent temper.

Carlyle's terrible temper? Its effect on Jane? 'A pack of damned non-sense, the whole of it!' Jane retorted, using Carlyle's idiom and foolishly revealing the contents of Grace's letter to a man Mrs. Montagu had accurately assessed as oversensitive to even the most unintentional slight. Her mother's temper had a hundred times worse effect on her than Carlyle's temper, Jane reassured him, and without such tender solicitude as Carlyle displayed once the eruption subsided.

Carlyle's irritability was a result of his sufferings. Jane was confident that after their marriage, when he was well and happy, he would become 'the best humoured man alive.'

The Noble Lady did not believe in or trust in long engagements, and now that there were no secrets between Jane and Carlyle, she urged Jane on to what she termed the fifth act of her drama, while Jane's mother watched a tragedy unfold.

Soon Mrs. Montagu, who had been married twice (her husband three times), schooled Jane in—and warned Jane about—what it meant to be a good wife. She emphasized all through the correspondence that marriage meant different things for a man and a woman. She portrayed for Jane her own daughter, Anne Procter, in labor, looking to her mother's eyes more than to her own pain, to see how bad her situation was: 'My daughter had a difficult and tedious labour, and I had to control my feelings lest I should alarm her.' And then the birth of that pretty little granddaughter, followed by worries for her fragile health. Childbearing was a physical danger, marriage an emotional one. For a devoted wife was not a self-centered maiden.

A wife exchanged her will for willing submission to her husband, her 'King.' However, by so doing, Jane would establish a 'magical circle' of duties in which she remained even more the 'sole enchantress.' The Noble Lady spelled it out: 'The wealth our friend wants, you have, you have more polish, more elegance, a higher acquaintance with the conventional forms of society, so far all is right—but you have literature which he does not want, and poetry which he does not want, and you must barter all this for something which you both want, a knowledge of domestic detail, and the art of making home delightful.'

Jane's *entire* life *must* of necessity change once she marries.

'Never reply to a hasty or an apparently unkind observation at the time it is made; tho' the observation is alike unjust and unwise,' the Noble Lady counseled her.

'Swallow your vexation.'

Wait for the first cool and tranquil moment to state your thoughts truly and fairly on the matter and say no more. 'Mr Carlyle would brood for a year upon hasty words forgotten by you in a minute.'

And never forget, to mere worldlings, Jane, the daughter of a skilled surgeon, was giving up more than she was receiving by marrying the son of a farmer and mason. She must always keep this in mind and be even *more* dutiful and humble.

'Do not resort to the common notion of perfect equality. There is no equality.'

A woman who was highborn before marriage only had further to stoop. While the man is the monarch of all he surveys.

'But you have the freedom of love, which makes light spring out of darkness.'

Unfortunately, Jane and Thomas did not have the freedom of love that leads to the type of intimacy and understanding and sexual fulfillment that marked the marriage of their future friends Robert and Elizabeth Barrett Browning. They were both relying on the institution of marriage to change them, to save them, to make them suddenly happy when they were together. No matter that Thomas gave Jane fair warning that she was choosing a 'barren and perplexed destiny.' If she became his 'life partner,' he emphasized, he would not change.

'These are hard sayings, my beloved child, but I cannot spare them.' He had lately gotten into the habit of referring to her in the diminutive.

When Jane told her mother she wanted Grace to come live with them after the wedding, the poor woman burst into tears, threw her arms around her daughter's neck, and said, 'Why have you never said as much before?' But Carlyle would have none of it.

'*The Man should bear rule in the house and not the Woman.* This is an eternal axiom, the Law of Nature.'

Grace Welsh became ill, but made no further objections to her daughter's marriage, or any objection to living apart from what Jane called Carlyle's *Fatherland.*

'She thinks it all things considered the best I can do.'

But there were constant arguments between Jane and Carlyle—by post—on their way to the altar. Carlyle had to remind himself they were negotiating for an eternal union, not an armed neutrality.

All dreams of a literary collaboration between the two turned into a dream of humble, economical domesticity—which they both shared. Jane would faithfully take care of the household duties while Carlyle wrote his allotted pages a day. They would meet over frugal meals.

For more than five years their relationship was basically epistolary. Engaged, they did not see each other for over a year, though they were within easy traveling distance. Their letters dwindled down to one or two a month.

'I know not what in all the world to say to you,' Jane confessed. 'This marriage, I find, is like death; so long as it is uncertain in its approach, one can expect it with a surprising indifference; but certain, looked in the face within a definite term, it becomes a matter of tremendous interest.'

They sent many kisses by letter, and once Carlyle even spoke of pressing her bosom to his chest, but Jane remembered very few actual kisses. In the last letter before their marriage, Jane wrote, 'But indeed Dear these kisses on paper are scarce worth keeping—You gave me one on my neck that night you were in good humor, and one on my lips on some forgotten occasion, that I would not part with for a hundred thousand paper ones. Perhaps some day or other I shall get none of any sort.'

That day was soon approaching.

They married on 17 October 1826 at the charming low and wide white house at Templand overlooking the undulating hills of the Scottish Lowlands where Grace would now live. Jane and her mother took care of all the arrangements, Carlyle asked only the permission to smoke three cigars on their nine-hour voyage to Edinburgh that they made the same day they wed. When they finally arrived at their new home at Comely Banks, there was a welcoming fire and flowers to greet them. Carlyle saw for the first time how Jane and her mother had arranged everything modestly yet with unerring taste. The furniture was from the Haddington house Grace had sold, against Carlyle's wishes. Another secret kept from him—till after the marriage—was that Grace needed money.

Carlyle appeared strange, out of sorts, very nervous once they were alone. They had supper together and about eleven o'clock Jane said she would go to bed, that she was very tired. She put her hands on his shoulder as she passed and said, 'Dear, do you know that you haven't kissed me once, all day—this day of days!'

She bent down and laid her cheek against his and he kissed her begrudgingly. 'You women are always kissing—I'll be up soon!'

She went upstairs, undressed, and got into bed.

He came up a little later, undressed, and got into bed beside her. Jane expected him to take her in his arms.

But nothing like that happened. He lay next to her jiggling. Jiggling. She lay next to him, not knowing what to do. 'One moment I wanted to kiss and caress him; the next moment I felt indignant.'

In all her hopes and imaginings of a first night, she had never envisioned a silent man lying there jiggling, jiggling. It was too wretched, too absurd. Suddenly, she burst out laughing.

'Woman!' Carlyle got out of bed and left the room.

'He never came back to my bed.'

The barren destiny that Carlyle warned her of, would be. There was not going to be physical consummation. There was not going to be any mother living with her. There were not going to be any children.

Thomas wrote his beloved mother two days after the wedding, just as he had promised. Pious, devoted, hardworking Margaret Carlyle, who learned to write in order to communicate with her firstborn genius of a son, was justifiably worried about his adjustment to married life.

She must not worry, he reassured her, though he was still 'dreadfully confused.' He had been sullen all day, 'sick with sleeplessness, quite nervous, *billus,* splenetic and all the rest of it.' But Jane had been a wonderful nurse; not even his own mother could have been kinder. 'She seems happy enough if she can but see me and minister to me.' His mother should not fear about his sleep. His wife was taking care of that. 'She herself (the good soul!) has ordered another bed to be made for me in the adjoining room, to which I may retire whenever I shall see good.'

A month later he wrote to his mother: 'Tho' this is now the fourth week of my marriage, I am by no means "come to" as you would say, or yet "hefted" to my new *gang.*' He had not found himself or risen to his new life. He was still too sick and could not survive without drugs for his stomach. 'I adopt resolutions of living which are beyond my power of executing, and am forced to abandon them in mortification and chagrin. Give me time, I say still, give me time.'

His wife was the best of all wives: 'In *every* thing great and little she gives me entirely my own way; asking, as it seems, nothing more whatever of her destiny, but that in any way she could make me happy. Good little girl! Sometimes too, we *are* very happy.'

Jane Baillie Welsh, left, and Thomas Carlyle, right. Jane as she looked at the age of twenty-five, in 1826, the year of her marriage, and Thomas as he looked at the age of thirty-seven, the earliest image of him, London, 1832, by Daniel Maclise. 'Ah! when she was young, she was a fleein', dancin', light-heartit thing, Jeannie Welsh, that naething would have dauntit,' a devoted Scottish servant remembered. 'But she grew grave a' at once. There was Maester Irving ye ken, that had been her teacher; and he cam aboot her . . . then there was Maester Carlyle himsel'; and he came to finish her off likee.'

The good little girl added a postscript to her mother-in-law. 'We love each other; have done ill to no one, and one of us at least is full of hope.'

After two years in Edinburgh, during which time Jane established quite a salon, her monarch deigned to move. Where? To Craigenputtock. That place with the 'hard name,' Mrs. Montagu called it—thinking such a move was *Jane's* idea—and advising her against it. The unmarried Jane Baillie Welsh said she would not be able to live a month in the godforsaken place even with an angel. But Jane Welsh Carlyle lived there for six years with a husband so distracted by his writing that she could hardly even talk with him, except while he was shaving. Brother Alick, housed in a separate building, farmed. Jane swore she could hear the cattle breathing in the distance.

In 1832, while Charlotte Cushman was still singing in the choir of the Second Church of Boston, Ralph Waldo Emerson gave up his ministry there and traveled to Europe. He had tragically lost his beautiful young wife, and before he left Boston he did the strangest thing: 'I visited Ellen's tomb and opened the coffin.' In those days of religious doubt and confusion, what did Emerson expect to find? Some confirmation beyond moldering flesh and dry bones?

In Europe Emerson put a name to the anonymous essays that had so impressed him in the *Edinburgh Review.* This 'Germanick new-light' was actually one Thomas Carlyle, who was redefining the religious experience, saying that whether or not God existed, we must still act morally, as if He did exist. We must respond to our individual inner man, the God within.

Earnest American seeker that he was, Waldo, as he was called, actually located the place with the hard name and showed up. 'No public coach passed near it, so I took a private carriage from the inn. I found the house amid desolate heathery hills, where the lonely scholar nourished his mighty heart. . . . He was tall and gaunt, with a cliff-like brow, self-possessed and holding his extraordinary powers of conversation in easy command; clinging to his northern accent with evident relish; full of lively anecdote, and with streaming humor, which floated everything he looked upon. . . .'

Carlyle and Emerson took a long walk, across the hills, into the Lake District of England, Wordsworth's country, Emerson called it. 'There we sat down and talked of the immortality of the soul. It was not Carlyle's fault that we talked on that topic, for he had the natural disinclination of every nimble spirit to bruise itself against walls. . . . But he was honest and true, and cognizant of the subtle links that bind ages together, and saw how every event affects all the future.'

Craigenputtock. This 1829 engraving of the stone house the Carlyles lived in for six years in the remote moors outside of Dumfries was one of two personally requested by Carlyle's hero the poet Goethe for publication in the German translation of Carlyle's *Life of Schiller*. The six years of harsh isolation on the farm, where Carlyle, absorbed in his work, hardly talked to Jane and would neither take his daily rides nor go on walks with her, took a toll on her physical and mental health.

Carlyle told Emerson, 'Christ died on the tree; that built Dunscore kirk yonder: that brought you and me together.'

He told him, 'Time has only a relative existence.'

Jane quipped, We have met Emerson, '(over) soul to (over) soul.'

She never liked the man, saw him literally as two-faced—one young and open, the other strangely old and sinister. She thought Carlyle would tire of him, but they remained lifelong friends. It was Emerson who realized Carlyle's dream of bringing his semiautobiographical *Sartor Resartus,* being printed as a series of articles, out as a book. The title, 'Tailor Retailored,' referred to the old forms of Christianity that had to be retailored to suit new times. *Sartor Resartus* was published first in America with Emerson's introduction. Then the British followed suit.

The book, which was so influential in its time, was written in those years of isolation, in the small stone house where Carlyle was freed from his most pressing nemesis after dyspepsia—his hypersensitivity to any kind of noise.

After six years on the farm, during which time Jane got to visit London once, it seemed as if the days of isolation would end. Carlyle pondered the possibility of a move, and Jane held her tongue, as Mrs. Montagu advised.

When Carlyle decided they would try London, she was silently gratified. As they planned to leave, at just the right moment, she said, 'Let us Burn our Ships!'

Did she mean close up the farmhouse and take their furniture with them? She did.

At the age of thirty-three, Jane Welsh Carlyle arrived, furniture and all, in London. It was Mecca for her, just as it would be ten years later for the twenty-eight-year-old Charlotte Cushman.

Before Jane married, Mrs. Montagu sang a chant, a requiem she called it, to Jane's departing liberty:

"Oh Woman, Woman, must thou still be subjugated to the will of some master, still offering thyself in generous devotions a victim at some shrine, can none be found exempt from their destiny, sailing smoothly at their own sweet will, in still waters, in their little one-oared boats!'

Past the middle of the century, when Jane Carlyle and Charlotte Cushman finally met, there was a flotilla of the one-oared boats Mrs. Montagu envisioned. But for those unmarried women, there were often two hands on deck.

Mrs. Montagu's own granddaughter, whose difficult birth she described in one of her letters to Jane Baillie Welsh, never married. It was she who became the famous mid-Victorian poet Adelaide Anne Procter and replaced Charlotte Cushman in Matilda Hays' life.

Swearing Eternal Friendship:
Charlotte and Geraldine and Jane

LONDON, SEAFORTH, MANCHESTER

1840–1846

MRS. CARLYLE took a true womanly antagonism to me & would not know me,' Charlotte wrote to the newly married Emma, explaining why Jane had avoided her for so many years. It had been the novelist Geraldine Jewsbury's fault for constantly overpraising Charlotte. Mrs. Carlyle thought Geraldine was trying to make her jealous by swearing eternal friendship with Charlotte Cushman on the spot.

This fashion of women swearing eternal friendship came from Germany, just as blood brotherhood had. Victorian women, however, did not have to nick their veins in order to embrace one another. In the decades before Havelock Ellis and Sigmund Freud, before there was a name for women who loved women, there was an absolute lack of self-consciousness between women who loved each other as friends.

Geraldine Jewsbury seemed to realize early on that she loved Jane Carlyle in a way that might make her self-conscious. Her passion for Jane echoed the passion she felt for her male lovers—and then some. She hardly knew how to explain it.

When she was in her late twenties, Geraldine initiated a correspondence with Thomas Carlyle on spiritual matters, writing to him from Manchester, using only her initials. She thought of converting to Roman Catholicism, she told him, but on studying with a priest she was close to, she found herself realizing the shaky foundations on which *all* religion was based. Could Thomas Carlyle offer advice?

Carlyle immediately intuited 'GEJ' was a young woman, and she became 'Miss Jewsbury' to him while he remained 'Dear Sir' to her. Soon after, Geraldine's old and ailing father died, and seeing his physical deterioration made Geraldine even more despairing of the conventional religious solace of life after death. Again she turned to the Sage of Chelsea, who could console her only by telling her how miserable life would be if there was no death to end it, and tracing the history of religion in the East and the West. He kindly invited her to visit him in London.

Geraldine subsequently came to London to the Carlyles' home in Chelsea at 5 Cheyne Row and met the tall, sober seer in his upstairs drawing room. With admiration and awe, she listened to him talk, his broad Lowlands accent, his breadth of knowledge, the sweep of his wit. Robert Browning told Hattie Hosmer that *listening* to Thomas Carlyle was one of the three great pleasures he had revisiting England. (The other two were Alfred Lord Tennyson reciting *Maud* and Fanny Kemble's sister, the actress Mrs. Sartoris, singing to John Ruskin.)

One did not *converse* with Carlyle. It was, from all contemporary accounts, absolutely impossible to get a word in edgewise. But he must have been the most brilliant, diverse, outlandish, and entertaining of talkers. Because all one got—and all one wanted—when one visited the Sage of Chelsea was his talk—and perhaps, just perhaps, a bit of tea.

Geraldine listened carefully.

Her first novel, *Zoe: A History of Two Lives,* was filled with Carlyle's belief that one was obligated to negate one's self and all selfish desires, that one must act morally—as if God existed—even if one no longer had conventional religious faith.

Carlyle did not take *Zoe* as an homage to his thought, however. In fact, he threw *Zoe* across the room. 'George Sandism,' he proclaimed. 'Phallus worship,' he spit out—to a very quiet Jane.

At Jane's salon in the ground-level drawing room, one had conversation. If in her unmarried days at Haddington she was Penelope to a roomful of suitors, in London in her forties, she was surrounded by an intellectual elite—geniuses galore—who did not have to dress to come to Cheyne Row. Mrs. Montagu had advised Jane when a bride in Edinburgh that literary men found life too short for buttoning and unbuttoning, but would gladly come to entertain and be entertained if they were not forced to dress.

In Edinburgh before the barren years at the farm with the 'hard name,' as Mrs. Montagu called it, and in London after them, Jane's coterie was masculine. Her salon included close friends such as the exiled Italian revolutionary Giuseppe Mazzini; Lord Advocate Francis Jeffrey, who as editor of the *Edinburgh Review*—and admirer of Jane—had published her husband; the man-about-town Erasmus Darwin, the brother of Charles; John Sterling, once the thundering editor of *The Times,* and both his sons: John, the ex-cleric and writer, and his younger brother, the darkly handsome Captain Anthony, who did not get along with his bombastic father. Jane was often the glue that bound them. She was quite close to the journalist and publisher John Forster, who coedited the *Daily News* with Charles Dickens and became his biographer, the actor William Macready—she was godmother to one of his children—and a French revolutionary to balance the Italian, Godefroy Cavaignac—for whom, in her early days in London, she seemed to have felt a stirring of passion she negated by leaving London and visiting her mother during one of Carlyle's absences. Carlyle constantly left her alone amid this circle of male devotees. A Scottish Madame de Staël, she was called. Very Scottish, quipped William Wordsworth.

Jane was no longer the Gypsy girl of her youth. Her color faded soon after her marriage, during the years on the Scottish farm, when her health failed as well. She was thin, with a pale face, very dark hair, and intense, haunted, burning eyes. Yet everyone who met her seemed to experience in her conversation and her wit a freshness that is often associated with youth and health. When she complained of a big red pimple that made her uncomfortable while a houseguest of fashionable people, Captain Anthony Sterling immediately put her at ease. 'Damn your nose! For a sensible woman you really have the *oddest* ideas. As if anybody *really attached* to you could love you an atom less if you were all covered over with smallpox!!!'

While Carlyle wrote, he was always miserable (and he was always writing). Jane saw him through *Sartor Resartus* during the years on the farm. Published first in America through Emerson's intervention, and in England in 1838, four years after the Carlyles arrived in London, it established his reputation: a prophet of the future to some, a dangerous iconoclast to others.

In London Jane saw her husband through all the hell of *The French Revolution.* He gave the first volume of it to their friend the philosopher John Stuart Mill to read in manuscript. Both the Carlyles looked askance at Mill's soulful love of Mrs. Harriet Taylor, an intellectual from the planet of the Blues, whom he would marry after her husband's death. Imagine being influenced by a woman!

One day in 1836 Mill and Mrs. Taylor appeared at Cheyne Row as white as death. Carlyle and Jane brought them inside with trepidation, anxious about their condition. Mill's maid had mistaken Carlyle's bulky manuscript for waste and thrown it into the fire. The entire first volume of *The French Revolution,* sole copy, was gone. The Carlyles had to spend the next hours consoling Mill and Taylor, and hiding their own despair, until the two finally left, and Jane comforted Carlyle. In the following stressful six months, Carlyle rewrote.

During these years Carlyle also gave series of well-received lectures on German literature, The History of Literature, Revolutions of Modern Europe, and Heroes and Hero-Worship. These lectures introduced him to many of the fashionable who came to hear his spontaneous overflow of ideas. At present he was working on the life and letters of the Puritan Protector of the Commonwealth, Oliver Cromwell.

Jane spent her days taking care of the household, going through dramas with the servants, opening and scouring the mattresses to get rid of bed-bugs, not only directing but doing carpentry work. She decorated cabinets and screens. She sewed her own imaginative, fashionable clothes with amazing skill. She not only darned Carlyle's socks, she mended his boots and knitted his caps. And then went to tax court to argue his bill. She found ingenious ways to keep her neighbors' dogs and cocks quiet. The slightest noise unhinged Carlyle, another peculiarity of his temperament, as he warned her before they married. His reactions to sound could be violent. Some nights she lay in her bedroom directly under his, trembling when she heard the stir of his feet, indicating he had been awakened.

Chelsea in those days was a secluded, shaded, hushed outskirt of London. The Carlyles' home, close to the banks of the Thames, was quite idyllic—and silent. Oh, there were the fishermen crying out 'Shrimps as large as prawns!' others hawking 'Cowslips, primroses!' or 'Hot cross buns!'

That was not *noise* but local color to Carlyle's friend the poet and editor Leigh Hunt, who suggested the area to him. But then again, Hunt was a poet, no Carlyle. When Jane kissed *him,* he did not run for a cigar, but to his neighboring house to write his best-remembered lyric, 'Jenny Kissed Me.'

The girl who had learned Latin like a boy and lit her doll's funeral pyre beneath its elegant bed now had made her own bed and was lying in it. I married for ambition, she'd say in self-deprecation. She would only marry a genius—and now the world knew Carlyle was one. For all of her mistakes and marital problems, she knew she, only she, could provide the difficult genius with the home life he needed to accomplish his important work. She sacrificed herself for the benefit of unborn generations. Her husband was Mrs. Carlyle's meaningful work—and she did it brilliantly. With the taste and flair she inherited from her mother, she provided Carlyle with cozy and original surroundings. Still today the Carlyle House, 5 (renumbered 24) Cheyne Row, maintains the intimate glow of home. She delighted in giving everyone in her male coterie, in literary London, a good look at a no-nonsense, frugal Scottish wife.

When her closest friend, really her 'buddy,' the Italian revolutionary Giuseppe Mazzini, a political exile in England, teased her for the efforts she was making while Carlyle was away by trying to find an attractive solution for the heavy blinds that hung on the lower windows in his study, she responded: 'To be sure the rehabilitating of ones house was not so *grand* an employment as the revolutionizing of *Italy*—but the one thing I *could do* and the other could *not* do—and it would be a prettier world if every one would keep within his sphere of *possibility.*'

Jane kidded Mr. Carlyle—he was still Carlyle or Mr. C. to her, never Thomas—that the reason *she* found enjoyment with some of the people who bored *him* was that people felt they had to tiptoe around the great man. When they were with her, they could be themselves.

Not that she didn't frighten some people. When Browning was at tea one day, he lifted the steaming kettle and filled the teapot for her in the middle of one of Carlyle's monologues. Mrs. Carlyle certainly wasn't used to helpful men: 'Can't you put it down?' she snapped.

Browning got confused and put the hot kettle right down on the carpet, scorching it. The poet was even more confused as he saw Jane's horror and he quickly picked the kettle up again.

Carlyle interrupted his own talk for a moment to tell his wife, with dry humor: 'Ye should have been more explicit.'

Jane scared Browning, but many people fell in love, as Carlyle had witnessed time and again. He made a real attempt to keep Geraldine to himself during their correspondence, telling her, 'It is always with me you correspond, not with her and me. . . . Write always as to me alone.' But once Geraldine met Jane, Carlyle's attempt proved useless.

'I think of you very often,' Geraldine wrote to Jane, soon after leaving

Jane Welsh Carlyle from a painting by Gambardella in 1843, when Jane was forty-two. In her forties, Jane had a young masculine coterie in London. Among the many men who sought her company: her best friend Giuseppe Mazzini (top), one of the architects of Italy's march toward unity, and a political exile in England; John Forster (middle), the young editor and future biographer; and John Sterling (bottom), writer and ex-cleric.

Cheyne Row. 'You are scarcely ever out of mind.' There was not a day that Geraldine did not most sadly want her. She had vague, undefined yearnings. 'You will let me be yours, and think of me as such, will you not?'

Now that she had found Jane, 'I wonder how I ever lived without you.'

There was something dazzling in bearing the name Mrs. Carlyle. Geraldine admitted to a flash of envy. 'Every thought, feeling, and power of intellect is called into perfection, in order that it may be an offering to the one she has made her idol!'

That sounded enough like one of Jane's own idiotic ideas before she married for her to disabuse the silly girl of that notion as soon as possible. She was not a genius's muse, she was a genius's Wife, needed to keep Mr. Carlyle free from everyday practicalities so he could write. That was her mission in life. A mission she chose for herself.

Her mother Grace Welsh came on occasion to visit—usually when Carlyle was out of town. Soon, the women thought, the railroad would bring them even closer. During one visit, her mother went out and shopped for a party Jane was giving that evening. She bought candles and sweets and came home quietly to set a fine table, light the room beautifully, and then call Jane in to surprise her with the splendid effect. Jane looked about and was appalled. What was her mother trying to do? Show all London that Mrs. Carlyle was extravagant and wasted her husband's money? It must never look as if Mrs. Carlyle was too highborn for him! Jane snuffed out the candles, rewrapped them, tucked them away.

Grace only wanted to please her, Jane realized once her anger subsided. The look on Grace's face! That small, sharp act of cruelty, daughter to mother, did what such acts are famed for doing, grew in magnitude as time passed. Then it was too late. Grace suffered a stroke, and though it was made light of by post, Jane set out immediately, stopping at her cousin Babbie's in Liverpool on the way. There she found out, 'All is over at Templand, cousin, gone, gone!'

Jane was undone. Carlyle came to her in Liverpool and then traveled on alone to Scotland to settle his mother-in-law's affairs. At Templand, as he reluctantly got ready to auction the household effects, he hinted that they should think of keeping the house for themselves—as a summer place. He further hinted that if Jane was not so against it, they might live in Craigenputtock again. After all, now that it was his, they could do with it as they wished. The very name 'Craigenputtock,' his biographer J. A. Froude recorded, awakened a kind of horror in Jane's debilitated state.

'I cannot deliberately mean anything that is harmful to you, unjust, or painful,' Carlyle responded. Yet after such hints, Jane could not bear the thought of even visiting Scotland again.

Geraldine, who had lost her mother so young, wrote letters full of sympathy and compassion. But Jane had not been there to comfort her mother in her last illness or to receive a last blessing. She had not given her mother a home. She had not given her mother grandchildren. She had not given her mother respect. She had turned to Mrs. Montagu when Grace had only attempted to save her. Her mother's last words were only of her: 'I am dying. . . . Oh my poor Jeannie!'

Geraldine persisted, 'I love you, my darling, more than I can express, more than I am conscious of myself, and yet I can do nothing for you, not even help you to sew up one of your interminable seams!'

It had been—quite uncharacteristically—Carlyle's idea for Geraldine to come to visit the winter after Grace Welsh's death.

'I am afraid that having her beside me from morning till night would be dreadfully *wearing*.' Jane said at first.

'You had cousin Babbie beside you from morning to night—what would be the difference?'

'Babbie! Babbie was not always in a state of emotion! dropping hot tears on my hands, and watching me and fussing me as Geraldine does!'

'Oh as you like! Only I think it would be a kindness to the poor lonely girl—and that her company might be useful to yourself when you have so little of mine.'

Geraldine arrived—and was scandalized. When Carlyle was not writing, he was not at home. That was why he suggested Geraldine's visit—as a buffer. After seventeen years of marriage, life handed Jane an irony greater than six years on the harsh Scottish farm with the hard name. Carlyle, the champion of the workingman, the upholder of the sturdy peasant values of his birthplace Ecclefechan, had been taken up by the queen of London society, the very highborn, haughty, and brilliant Lady Harriet Baring, who on her father-in-law's death would become Lady Harriet Ashburton. Jane had never even met the woman, but in her characteristic way, she laughed this attachment away.

She breezily told her Liverpool cousin Babbie that Geraldine was shocked by the one *new female* friend in which Carlyle took a vast pleasure. Jane herself was immune to jealousy and was rather pleased that Carlyle found that he liked to go to Bath House, the heavy yellow Ashburton house in London, at least once a week and then to go to Addiscombe, their 'Farm' outside London, on Sundays.

Just as Jane understated the many nights Carlyle spent with Lady Harriet and joked about *philosophic* titillation, she made a parody of Geraldine's long visit. She pictured the effusive redheaded Geraldine for Babbie with '*her* Sunday's bare neck—and *grande toilette*' vamping in front of Carlyle's younger brother, Dr. John, not to mention Jane's great friends Giuseppe Mazzini and Erasmus Darwin. 'Carlyle made a grand mistake when he held this Geraldine up to me as something superlative—she is sharp as a meat axe—but as narrow.'

Virginia Woolf in her essay 'Geraldine and Jane' portrayed this visit and Geraldine's effusive love of Jane with great insight and élan. With it, as T. S. Eliot phrased it tongue in cheek in a letter to Leonard Woolf, Virginia became the greatest authority on Jewsbury—a woman novelist who was no longer read in the twentieth century. 'Geraldine Jewsbury would certainly not have expected anybody at this time of day to bother themselves about her novels' is the way Virginia began her review in 1929.

'The odd thing about Geraldine Jewsbury,' Woolf wrote, 'was the way in which she combined oaths and endearments, sense and effervescence, daring and gush.'

While Mrs. Carlyle was 'so metropolitan, so brilliant, so deeply versed in life and scornful of its humbugs.'

What a contrast to the overenthusiastic novelist. 'Jane was the most caustic, the most concrete, the most clear-sighted of women.'

Of course one would have had to know that other Jane, that long-lost Jane Baillie Welsh, to realize that the persona Jane created for herself in her letters—and in her life—defended against her secret fragility and her endless sense of loss. Before they married, while Carlyle was in London living with Edward Irving and his wife, he found a cutout of a heart mixed in with his papers. He opened the heart to find half a heart within it and, in Jane's handwriting, one word: 'homeless.' It drove him to tears though he did not know quite why.

Jane needed Geraldine's grand devotion, whether she admitted to it or not. This was female friendship in all its Victorian complexity, kept in check by Jane's biting tongue, running wild in Geraldine—necessary to both.

Usually kept in check by Jane. By the end of Geraldine's long visit, which Carlyle instigated, Jane realized she had sworn eternal friendship with Geraldine too impulsively and had told the girl too much. She hoped it would not be a 'memorable folly,' she wrote to her cousin Babbie in her offhanded, unflappable manner.

It was probably as early as that visit that she let Geraldine know she need not be so shocked by Carlyle's attentions to Lady Harriet. After all, Mr. Carlyle was indifferent to '*all* women *as women.*'

Her marriage to Mr. Carlyle had not been consummated. On their wedding night he became so enraged by his failure that he went outside and tore the front flower garden to shreds. It was his chronic dyspepsia, his burning stomach, his renegade bowels, that kept him from loving women the way men usually did. (Once when complimented that in a world of philandering men, she did not have to worry about the conduct of her own upright husband, Jane responded, it might have been quite different had Mr. Carlyle's stomach not been bad.)

Geraldine, a romantic to her core, developed a compassion for Jane that equaled her passion. Through the years, no matter how often Jane slighted or mocked her, Geraldine refused to budge in her love and respect. If one knew what Mrs. Carlyle suffered, she would say, one would forgive her anything. In Geraldine's words, Mrs. Carlyle never tasted the wine of life.

Carlyle, Geraldine continued to believe, was magnificent—when seen from the right perspective. It was simply that a sphinx did not fit into our living rooms.

But Geraldine no longer envied Jane her lot. It made her wonder about women's lives per se. Jane's life was an emotional kaleidoscope, shifting daily as she anticipated her husband's needs.

'That unwearied girl has fairly *conquered* me into a hot correspondence with her again,' Jane wrote to Babbie. After telling Geraldine too much, Jane attempted to cut her off—to no avail. 'I am almost over-persuaded back into my old illusion that she *has* some sort of strange, passionate—incomprehensible *attraction* towards me that leads her thro . . . *the miry puddle*—of tearing and *begging*—to do me pleasure.'

'Do, my dear love, come! Leave the things at home to find their own level,' Geraldine counseled a desolate Jane almost a year and a half after the shocking visit.

But Jane was not going anywhere until she finally took a look at this Lady Harriet. She still had not met her. Mutual friends arranged to have them both to tea.

Carlyle was furious. Why, they had Americans coming that day. Eliza-

Lady Harriet Ashburton, the brilliant eldest daughter of the sixth Earl of Sandwich. Aristocratic and imperious, Lady Harriet was the queen of London society and drew an adoring Thomas Carlyle into her conservative political circle and further away from his wife. With a tongue sharper than even Jane's, she lorded her superior lineage over her immensely wealthy—and docile—husband, Mr. William Bingham Baring, who became, on his well-liked father's death, the second Baron Ashburton.

beth Peabody and the Horace Manns and Julia Ward Howe. Jane did not back down. She could not remember when she had done such a spirited thing, or one she so little repented. Mrs. Howe poured tea to a red-faced and preoccupied Carlyle. No wonder he had a bad stomach. All the tea he drank! And he talked as if he were reading from one of his books. Horace Mann was very disappointed.

'Lady Harriet!—I liked her on the whole,' Jane told cousin Babbie. 'She is immensely *large*—might easily have been one of the *ugliest* women living—but almost beautiful—simply thro the intelligence and cordiality of her expression.'

Jane was not exaggerating. The queen of London society was indeed immensely fat and immensely homely, just as she was unquestionably the most clever and witty woman Jane had ever seen—'and I have seen all our "distinguished Authoresses."'

The tea lasted until eleven at night, during which time Jane attempted to estimate the fat Lady's seductive powers. That she had been able to fascinate Carlyle proved her to be the most masterly coquette of Modern Times! Jane quipped. She caught the Lady giving her prodigious looks as well.

Mrs. Carlyle was a *reality* Carlyle had hitherto *quite suppressed,* Lady Harriet subsequently told him.

Carlyle's female friend was a very lovable, spoiled Child of Fortune, Jane opined. A little judicious *whipping* would have shaped her into a first-rate woman. But she would find out it was the imperious Lady who held the whip. Carlyle jumped to it. He still took pleasure at the feet of an idealized, disdainful woman.

Jane was living in what she called the valley of the shadow of Oliver Cromwell—the subject of Carlyle's latest book. But she was also living in the shadow of a woman who could describe the glimmerings of someone's teeth as reminiscent of the diamonds one's grandmothers used to wear in their hair. Lady Harriet with her cutting wit, her salon, her intelligence, her high birth, and her scorn was Mrs. Carlyle—enlarged! Mrs. Carlyle—replaced!

It was hell on Cheyne Row. Carlyle wrote to his best friend John Sterling (who was quietly dying of tuberculosis) that he was walking hand in hand with madness, that he was plunging through Chaos.

'Send him to Chaos!' was Carlyle's 'Send him to Hell!'

'You can't,' Lady Harriet once replied.

'Why?'

'It's full.'

And Jane wrote to cousin Babbie in Liverpool that the Reign of Terror was raging at home and that it seemed stupid rather than heroic to stay till her life was crushed out of her. She would visit them, she would visit Geraldine. Her uncle's telling her to come sounded '*in the ears of my heart.*' A few weeks away from Carlyle would restore the philosophic frame of mind needed to endure her lot as *Man-of-Genius's wife.*

She wouldn't ask Carlyle if she could go, she would wait until she had made all her plans and could tell him she *was* going. Then he saw a letter from a friend, Elizabeth Paulet, inviting Jane and Geraldine to visit her and her husband at their beautiful seaside estate outside of Liverpool.

'What is it about, what does *she* want?'

'She wants *me.*'

'Oh, to visit her?'

'Yes.'

'And you are thinking to accept?'

'Why, I should hardly think of going off simply to visit Mrs Paulet—but I do mean to go to see her when I *am* in Liverpool and I really purpose going to Liverpool.'

'Very well,' Carlyle answered shortly. 'There is nothing in the world to hinder you going when you please, and there is no use in *looking so tragic* about it.'

He hadn't mentioned it since. Did he remember? Jane secretly took money out of her savings account. She gave her Liverpool relatives a frothy explanation for what she called the whimsical delicacy of using her own money rather than her spouse's. Her actions, however, were those of a woman ready to make a run for it.

Yet as soon as she left Cheyne Row, it was as if Chaos never happened. Carlyle felt wonderfully calmed after not speaking to anyone for almost a day. He was better off by himself—at least till the weekend at the Ashburton farm. 'Goodykin,' he called Jane.

Jane responded with a happy, coquettish bounce, hoping he wouldn't find the silence too delicious. 'I wish you to be neither quite miserable nor quite content in my absence.'

'*How* unhappy am I to be, you little gypsy?' he answered.

Their true intimacy was epistolary. The rule was one letter every day or two when separated—and they were often separated—full of understanding, full of hope that things would be better between them the next time they met. They called themselves life companions, life partners. He was 'the Good,' she was 'the Goody.' Sometimes he used a more monkish term for a wife, calling her his 'Necessary Evil.' Their letters were full of their shared history, replete with familiar images and notable turns of speech which evoked Scottish family and funny friends. Powerful, beautiful, pathetic, tragic, these letters. They were fine together, as long as they stayed apart.

Geraldine was on tenterhooks waiting for Jane to visit her in Manchester. Like an eager young lover, she listed all the disasters that might prevent the visit, except the one that did.

'I am looking forward to having you here so much, but it seems fated we are to meet in a crowd first,' Geraldine wrote. For Jane informed her that she would see her at Seaforth House, the Paulets' estate.

However, 'Provided I get my fair share of you, I will promise not to torment you, which is promising a great deal, for I am as Jealous as a Turk,' Geraldine continued. 'When one loves either man or woman it rouses all the ferocity that was calmly slumbering till then.'

But at Seaforth House, recuperating from a bad cold, Jane, in the privacy of her comfortable bedroom, told the girl, 'Since we are together *here* Geraldine—the going to Manchester does not seem to be any longer necessary.'

'If you *wish* to *sacrifice* me,' Geraldine answered, 'in God's name do so!'

For three days Geraldine seemed under the weather. Imagine seeing the ebullient Geraldine *cross,* Jane wrote wickedly to Carlyle. It was a sight for sore eyes!

But on Jane's forty-third birthday, the thirty-two-year-old Geraldine went on a rampage. She turned tranquil Seaforth upside down on that July day. 'Her vagaries exceeded my reminiscences of Mrs Jordan in *The Jealous Wife!*' Jane wrote to Carlyle.

'Nothing but outbursts of impertinence and hysterics from morning till night—which finished off with a grand *scene* in my room after I had gone up to bed. . . . It was a *revelation* to me not only of Geraldine but of human nature!—such mad *lover-like* jealousy on the part of one woman towards another it had never entered into my heart to conceive.'

Finally, Jane got Geraldine to laugh at the absurdity of another *woman* being the object of such incomprehensible passion, and promised her she'd go to Manchester with her if she behaved reasonably. At that, with her hair all disheveled and her face all bewept, Geraldine sat down at Jane's feet 'and—smoked a cigaritto!! with all the placidity in life!—She keeps a regular supply of these little things—and smokes them before all the world. In fact I am not at all sure that she is not *going mad*!'

That night out at dinner with friends, Jane watched Geraldine flirting with a gentleman and set everyone in a fit of laughter by asking the girl how she expected Jane to behave decently to her after Geraldine had spent a whole evening making love before Jane's very face to *another man*!

Jane had calmed Geraldine, but at the very last moment did not return to Manchester with her. Geraldine was too shocked to realize the extent of her sudden loss until she walked through her own front door. 'The house was looking so nice, and tea all set out, like a wedding breakfast with the principal character absent.'

In London, the drink Jane was given by mistake one evening after she almost took a fall made her quite leaden and half drunk at one fancy party. She was physically ill, mentally depressed. And she certainly did not drink *only* by accident. For those sleepless nights and those illnesses there was morphia prescribed.

Carlyle stubbornly refused to understand Jane's jealousy of Lady Harriet. What could she possibly be jealous about? He was not an unfaithful husband; Jane knew he did not love women the way men usually do. With that, he left her alone when his day's writing was over, and went his own way.

This time it was not the small town of Haddington but all of London town that whispered, and there was no escape. The blow to Jane's self-esteem was brutal. She did not tell her husband or anyone else what she swallowed down. 'The fact is I have been in a sad way for a long while, and was not saying anything about it to any one,' she confided to cousin Babbie. 'Indeed I was ashamed to talk of illness which had taken the form chiefly of frightful depression.'

'Swallow your vexation.'

For the next year she swallowed and swallowed until right in front of Carlyle, in an uncontrollable fit of crying, she exposed everything she had been thinking and feeling. Every demon came out. 'He was not a little horrified at my revelations and immediately declared that I must get away into the country as fast as possible.' But not before she suffered four days at the Lady's farm outside London. Her first visit, though by then Carlyle kept a small permanent wardrobe there.

She, the conversationalist, was uncomfortable among the aristocrats. Her stories seemed longer than they did in Chelsea. She went on like a Wife.

Only in August, once more with Geraldine at the Paulets' seaside estate, did she begin to repair her shattered nerves.

It was a different moral atmosphere at Seaforth House than anywhere else Geraldine had ever been. Jane wrote to Carlyle of the 'unformal speculative, civilized-gipsey manner of life.'

Servants were treated as human beings at Seaforth. One could walk on the grass rather than the gravel if one wished, one could *pick* the flowers, one could eat the fruit right from the garden, grapes right from the hot-house—and as many as one wished. One was able to lie about on all the different sofas, in all the different rooms. 'Every where there is a *freedom* and a great big fire.'

Here, by the sea, women made much of Jane. Such attention agreed with her constitution, she said. Why, she had not had a headache or any illness at all since she arrived. Yesterday a woman visitor sang delightful songs from Mozart's *Don Giovanni* while both Mrs. Paulet and Geraldine rubbed Jane's feet!

'My dear,' she wrote to her husband, 'I wish YOU would *take a notion* to rub my feet! it is so soothing to the feelings.'

She felt '*happy.*' Hardly a Carlylean virtue—especially after the way she left Cheyne Row. She had to underline the word and put it in quotes and qualify it as well. '*To a certain extent*' she was '*happy.*'

Among these women, she became aware of the condescension in her husband's letters. 'Always my "bits of letters" and "bits of letters" as if I were some nice little Child writing in half-text on ruled paper to its Godpapa!' She made a joke of it, naturally: '*Monsieur le President!*' was her greeting. She would not have her '"*rights of WOMAN*" so trifled with!'

'Pray, my Goody, let me call your Letters by any name I like,—grant me freedom in that,' Carlyle responded, as if he were a hopelessly henpecked husband.

Harriet Martineau visited (from the planet of the Blues) and this must have added to the ensuing conversation about the *rights of WOMAN*. Jane's youngest Liverpool cousin, Maggie, came and by a stroke of genius Mrs. Paulet invited a sweet, pretty girl from the neighborhood as well and the women watched as the two girls swore everlasting friendship within ten minutes and then ran off to eat grapes.

The women walked together along the shore or went out driving in a gig. They had their main meal served at one-thirty, and after it, 'we—*speculate*! (Geraldine being still here) and I get my feet rubbed.'

It was an idyllic retreat until Geraldine's jealousy flared up again.

'Geraldine until you can behave like a *gentlewoman*—if not like a woman of commonsense, I cannot possibly remain in the same room with you.'

It didn't take a half hour for Geraldine to come to Jane drenched in tears. She had been so nasty because Jane hurt her feelings that morning.

How?

She would not tell her, and even if she did, Jane would not understand. Jane's manner had grated on her soul.

Jane was so upset that for the first night since she had been at Seaforth, she could not sleep well.

The next morning, Geraldine came to her in tears and confessed: She had treated Jane so badly only because she loved her better than all the rest of the world put together.

That explanation for hurting a person entered Jane's repertoire of favorite sayings.

Jane had other reasons for disturbed rest. Buoyed by her women friends, she made it clear she wanted to see her husband at Seaforth House on his way to Scotland or she would come to see him at Chelsea before he left. He chose Seaforth: 'I rejoice in the prospect of sea-bathing; in the prospect of cigars! Could you, however, procure me a good tobacco-pipe or two, and lay them in some greenhouse, they also would be welcome.'

His book on Oliver Cromwell completed, he finally arrived. She wrote to John Forster, the editor and writer who admired her wholeheartedly: 'Only think of his bringing me *old trowsers* to repair at Seaforth House!!'

From Scotland, Carlyle sent Lady Harriet a more fulsome offering: 'Accept my salutations from the *Shore of the Departed,* whither I am now at last come! Full of distractions, regrets, distresses and astonishments, as my way is when I get hither; but looking still (you see) across the great gulph; begging still to be remembered there. Indeed I think you seem beautifuller to me here from Hades then you ever did before.'

To his immense Lady, Carlyle bowed low.

Jane returned to London, to her male coterie and to getting the house in shape during Carlyle's absence. She made sure to let Carlyle know that Mazzini was so devoted that as soon as he heard she was home, he rushed to her through a rainstorm, soaking his good Italian doeskin boots.

Earlier that year, when Jane showed Mazzini Geraldine's latest long letter, holding it up in her hand, he was amazed.

'But my Dear, this is *goodness!* That is *more clever* than *Zoe!* for upon *my* honour I have sent her last week work enough to leave her not time to eat— and it is all done!'

With the success of *Zoe* (Mazzini sent a copy to George Sand; here was 'an English' who understood her) and the difficult translations from the Italian Geraldine was doing of his political tracts, not to mention her prodigious book reviewing, Geraldine still found time for such long letters to Jane. What *an English!* Mazzini extolled in the Italo-English Jane loved to parody.

Yes, she wrote a journal letter to Jane every Sunday without fail, and was delighted if she got back one letter for her five. No matter how offhandedly she treated Geraldine, the girl stuck to her like destiny. When Geraldine came back from a trip to Paris she took with the Paulets and her brother Frank, spending time there with Ralph Waldo Emerson as well, she appeared at Jane's door flushed with her new success. Ushered in coolly, she sat on the floor and unlaced Jane's shoes.

Whatever are you doing? Jane asked, still annoyed at Geraldine's long absence.

'Why my dear I am merely going to rub your Feet—you look starved— I am sure your feet have not got well rubbed since I did it myself last year.'

Jane, her feet warmed, realized she had never seen Geraldine looking so well. 'She actually looked like a *woman*—not as formerly like a little boy in petticoats.' Jane could not say whether it had been her latest love affair in France with Lambert Bey—a man she called 'the Egyptian' (he was a convert to Islam)—but there was 'now and then a gleam on her face that was *attractive*—I could now fancy a *man* marrying her!'

Witty Jane. So cosmopolitan, so urbane. But perhaps 'no English' at the time would even think to attribute such a glow to the success of a woman's first novel.

Then, suddenly, Charlotte Cushman appeared on the scene in Manchester and from Geraldine all Jane heard was Charlotte Cushman this, Charlotte Cushman that. Jane's close friend William Macready, who had played against Charlotte in the States, told her that Charlotte Cushman was 'not only a woman who *lied,* but a woman who *spoke no truth.*' What in goodness' name was Geraldine up to? Why had she sworn eternal friendship with Charlotte? Because Jane had not put up with her scenes of last summer? Was this Geraldine's retaliation?

What a screed of her mind she wrote to Geraldine. It would probably terminate their correspondence—at least till the 'finale' of Geraldine's friendship for Miss Cushman. She imagined Geraldine had never received such a letter. Could Geraldine not live her life for five minutes without finding another new and insane enthusiasm? Was she swayed by Charlotte Cushman's sudden rise to fame?

Jane's jealousy was not unprovoked. She might have intuited from all of Geraldine's unbridled enthusiasm that Geraldine was acting toward Miss Cushman as she acted toward Mrs. Carlyle.

Which was true. When a letter arrived from Charlotte Cushman, Geraldine read it twice before she opened the one from her most recent male lover—the Egyptian.

Charlotte too caused her new friend pain. 'The thought of you is always in my heart. You said a very cruel thing yesterday to me. . . . You have the power to *torment me* in a way I wd be sorry for you to know the length and breadth of.'

The friendship was as necessary: 'Do my darling love me as long as you can & as much as you can for I am superstitious about my friends & if I lose *one* it wd be a breaking of the magic ring.'

The demands were as great. If Charlotte failed to visit her on her way to Leeds, Geraldine would scratch her like a wild cat.

The jealousy was more directed. Why didn't Eliza Cook realize other women had the right to love Charlotte as much as she did?

Charlotte, new to England, was not sure how to react. She hinted to Geraldine, asking her if she should continue to see two women who were talked about. Were these women sweethearts? Geraldine asked her, saying she knew something of such things and advising her to hold fast. 'I don't think that "*society*" ever thanked any body yet for minding its clamour.'

When Geraldine kept insisting she had as much right to Charlotte's love as Eliza Cook had, and when she blamed Miss Cook for her excessive possessiveness, Charlotte sent Geraldine some of Eliza's poems and letters, perhaps as a subtle explanation of Miss Cook's rights—which extended beyond swearing eternal friendship.

Whatever Geraldine believed she knew of women who were sweethearts, Eliza Cook's love of Charlotte was a revelation to her—a shocking one. Geraldine wrote on returning the material: "This time last year I cd have written passionate things *myself* to another—& to see that poem & read E.C.'s letters seems like meeting my own ghost—& I am frightened of it.'

This mirror image of her own behavior toward Mrs. Carlyle now alarmed her.

So when Jane wrote her that angry long letter, that screed of her mind about Miss Cushman, Geraldine assured her that the angry letter would strengthen their friendship, not end it.

There would be a new honesty between them from now on. Jane's dislike of Miss Cushman was Geraldine's fault—she hadn't the skill to describe the extraordinary woman. But more importantly, Jane no longer had reason to fear Geraldine's jealousy.

For instance, Jane wrote that she and Lady Harriet were now bosom friends, and that she had not wished to *bore* Geraldine with that news earlier, the way Geraldine bored her about Miss Cushman. But Jane was not being truthful. She was frightened of Geraldine's temper and jealousy; that was why she had said nothing.

Jane needn't worry any longer. Geraldine now realized her outbursts had been the result of her confusing her own fancies with real things. There would be no more scenes to horrify Jane, Geraldine assured her. All this after she had read Eliza Cook's letters.

'I do really feel pleased that you have someone near at hand to love, and who desires to be loved by you. . . . Tell me a great deal how you go on with her, and don't fear making an explosion of jealousy.' Geraldine was quite certain that Lady Harriet cared for Jane much more than she would admit.

So was Jane.

After all, she was used to captivating Carlyle's friends. When the Lady took a sudden interest in her, she was surprised but not suspicious. At first she believed that as much as the Lady wanted to, she really did not love her, but that changed after a while. When she had Jane on a long visit at one of her many country estates, she could not do enough for her. And then when they were both back in London, the Lady sent her carriage at least two evenings a week. At Bath House they'd study German together—Jane acting as 'Dictionary'—or they'd play chess.

Lady Harriet had such integrity. 'What a contrast I often think betwixt that woman and Geraldine! the opposite poles of woman-nature!' The Lady despised sentiment and never put what she felt in words, but Jane could see her warm feelings 'peeping out' in her actions. Her letters were stiff and formal, but she remembered the flowers one liked and enclosed petals from them. At times she sent Jane no words at all, just an envelope filled with violet petals. Recently, she sent Jane a gift, a splendid Indian scarf, a facsimile of a cashmere she had herself. It was the best thing that had happened to Jane all season. Actions, not words.

'She goes upon *the silent system* as to all the thoughts of her *heart*.' Just the mere fact that she *kissed* Jane when they met and when they parted proved more authentic affection 'than twenty reams of protestations from a Geraldine.'

But the queen of London society, who never said what she did not mean, had said nothing. Her reaching out to Jane, coming on unannounced visits while Carlyle was away, her taking her to the opera, her sending her carriage, her wordless affection, had been a cruel mockery. All of it came after Jane's outbursts to Carlyle the summer before. The Lady was securing her house-philosopher's peace. That was why there had been no words. Jane had been played for a fool.

Better to die young, before all one's illusions as well as one's rational hopes were shattered. She knew there were physical causes for her depression, she was in terrible health and was going through menopause. But still she felt as if she were going insane. And she had *moral* as well as material problems, she confided rather enigmatically to her Liverpool cousins.

There was a torturous visit to the farm during which the two women avoided each other. Back at Cheyne Row, on Saturday, the fourth of July, Jane had a violent scene with Carlyle. The year before as she left she berated him for trying to kiss her goodbye without taking the cigar out of his mouth. But never had there been a scene like this. There were dreadful recriminations against him, against Lady Harriet. He had to end his relationship with her. The Lady was up to no good. Then she walked out on him. Just left him standing there. Not a word of reconciliation.

'Certainly we never before parted in such a manner! And all for— literally,—Nothing!' Carlyle wrote to her. Perhaps she thought he was happy at the Ashburton farm that Sunday. Far from it!

Jane was so unhinged that she couldn't even bear to show herself to her relatives in Liverpool. 'Mrs. Carlyle is going to Seaforth on *Saturday*,' Geraldine wrote to Charlotte Cushman. 'She is *ill*, something is not right—tho God only knows what.'

But even Seaforth House, with Geraldine and Mrs. Paulet in attendance, could not calm her during these days. When she thought Carlyle had not sent her a birthday greeting, she went to pieces, though she soon found out it was due to an error at the post office.

'My poor little Goody,' Carlyle wrote to her, 'you are still very unwell!' How could her entire well-being depend on the vagaries of the postal system?

He would end his relationship with Lady Harriet, if it came to that.

'Her intents towards you and towards me, so far as I can read them, *are* charitable and *not* wicked: my relation to her is a very *small* element of her position, but a very just and laudable one; and I wish to retain that if I can, and give it up if I cannot.'

Give it up was what Jane expected him to do.

When he came to Seaforth House that summer on his way to Scotland, he brought no old trousers for her to mend. But Jane realized he would not give up his Lady, no matter how he phrased it, any more than he gave up his idea of living on Jane's remote farm years ago. Matter-of-factly, he told his wife that he would meet the Lady and her husband in the Lowlands in August.

More hotly, he wrote to Lady Harriet from Seaforth House telling her he would walk as far as he needed to in Scotland for one blink of her bonny face. 'You are full of charity to me—for which the Supreme Destinies will certainly reward you. I, if I could ever reward you, Oh, would I not! But it is a vain hope that. Adieu dear Lady mine,—*mine* yes, and yet forever no!'

Jane was so unwell, so unhinged mentally and physically after Carlyle's visit, that she could no longer bear Seaforth. Mrs. Paulet made tactless remarks about her wild insane looks. 'That great echoing, disorganised place had got to look to me a perfect madhouse.'

She broke away—to Geraldine, who was back in Manchester. And it was then, six years into their relationship, that Geraldine proved herself the best of friends. Geraldine received Jane at her garden gate with a quiet kindness that boded well. 'The stillness, the good order, the modest elegance of this bright little half-town half-country house feels like a sort of *cradle* into which my good angel has laid me for a little while to lie still and make-believe to sleep.'

'No word from Jane yet?' Carlyle's mother asked.

'None.'

Geraldine brought Jane out of her depression and her serious thoughts of attempting suicide by doing in practice what she and Jane *speculated* about summer after summer at Seaforth House. She gave Jane a good dose of meaningful work.

Jane showed interest in the industrial city and Geraldine immediately got her admission into all sorts of factories in Manchester. Day after day Jane viewed the working life and workingmen, she went up and down on hoists, she saw what she called forests of machinery for every conceivable purpose. 'I have seen more of the condition of my fellow-creatures in these two weeks than in any dozen years of my previous existence.'

In Manchester Geraldine made Jane take vigorous exercise walking the fields and exploring the city. Jane joked she now knew enough to write a guidebook. They would go home at night and Geraldine would rub her feet. Or her brother Frank would invite their Greek friend Stavros Dilberoglue over. Jane liked the young merchant a lot. He had a metaphysical fervor that exceeded Geraldine's. Stavros admired Carlyle, but Jane feared he admired Emerson even more. Geraldine wrote to Charlotte Cushman that Stavros had many good things to say of women. Perhaps Charlotte passed that on to her young protégée Sarah Anderton, who became his wife.

In Manchester, soothed by Geraldine's calm friendship, Jane slowly came back to what was left of her self. And when Lady Harriet wrote—no violet petals this time—Jane made her decision. She would respond, as her husband wished, though the letter did not require an answer. She was and would remain Mrs. Carlyle. 'Resignated,' as Mazzini sternly advised her, she would do her duty.

MRS. CARLYLE, Geraldine wrote to Charlotte Cushman, was a woman who perplexed all the social issues of the last thousand years. No sooner do you speak of her than you begin to misstate. 'I have sat quietly down over it & will at least *hold my tongue* for some years.'

As a good friend, Geraldine most certainly did hold her tongue and then some. When a former lover of Geraldine's came to Manchester after visiting Jane in London, he declared that no matter how many men circled around, 'Carlyle was the only man she cared for.'

Geraldine told Jane she encouraged the man's perception, 'telling him with a most confidential air he was quite right in that surmise, and that as to all the men about you they just were obliged to live together like Austen's "happy family," and that you were the innocent little lamb in the midst, to tempt them to death, but which they were none of them to touch!'

But that was not the truth. There was a man in Jane's circle that touched her heart and who loved her deeply. He was a man of Scottish blood who did not get along with his father, the former 'roaring' editorial voice of *The Times,* a man four years younger than the woman he loved. He left England for a while in hopes of ameliorating his wife's insanity. She had a manic obsession that he was in love with Jane Welsh Carlyle. When reminded of Jane in the smallest way, she would fly off into outbursts of hysteria. This man returned to England and loved Jane, exactly the way Rousseau's Julie was loved by a man she could not marry—even if she were covered all over with smallpox. He was Captain Anthony Coningham Sterling, knighted after the Crimean War. He had integrity, earnestness, his own heart, and his own genius.

What is it about these Sterlings, Jane would ponder in one letter. All three of them so loved her. The father, Edward Sterling, the once powerful editor, became entirely dependent on her after his wife died. He uttered her name with his last breath. Carlyle's best friend, dear John, who died of tuberculosis so young, would have married her if they both hadn't been married, she once wrote merrily to Carlyle. And Captain Anthony Sterling.

Anthony, soon after his brother's death, brought one of his orphaned nephews to Manchester to put him under the guardianship of the scholar and vegetarian Francis William Newman, estranged brother of the converted John Henry, future cardinal of the Roman Catholic Church.

'He is a curious man this Anthony Sterling, worth some *making out*,' Jane wrote to Geraldine. 'Externally he is hard and angular—but I who thro the late distresses in his family have had opportunity of getting to know him intimately am persuaded that at the bottom of all his disagreeableness there lies a good and clever man—his coldness and sharpness of manner being merely the very natural *reaction* produced in him by his abhorrence, from youth upwards, of his own Father's humbug and *fine sentimentalities*.'

She told Sterling that she was writing to Geraldine to warn her to act as ladylike as she could stand to be when he came to see her.

'Why on earth should you do *that*?' Anthony responded.

'Because sent by *me* she will naturally fall into the mistake of fancying you are one of *my* sort of people, with whom it is unnecessary to make-believe *respectability* and *conventionalism*—and so good Heavens she would talk to you in a way to make the hair of your head stand on end!'

'Now *don't* write pray!' he said very earnestly. 'Pray leave her to her own inspirations—I am less easy to shock than you seem to think.'

'Humph!' was Jane's response. 'I have seen you occasionally dreadfully shocked with *me*.'

But their relaxed and easy intimacy as well as their no-nonsense repartee belies this. Off Captain Sterling went to Manchester, to be scrutinized by Geraldine Jewsbury's very weak, chronically inflamed, but quite observing eyes, and to be turned into the character of Conrad Percy in her new novel.

For Geraldine would soon give Jane Carlyle another, and stronger, reason to avoid contact with Charlotte Cushman. She paired Jane and Charlotte as the secret half sisters in her second, very popular novel.

As a friend, she held her tongue; as a novelist, she wrote.

The Meeting of the Half Sisters

LONDON

1848–1861

J ANE WAS frightened. She wrote to the editor John Forster, a man who
would do much to please her, with a 'delicate embarrassment.' Leave it
to Geraldine to dedicate *The Half Sisters* to her. Jane informed Forster
she was so scandalized by the end sections of the novel that she told Geraldine she would not write to her again until she revised them. She fully
expected Geraldine to send the revisions of this second novel to her; instead
she sent them on for publication.

Was the novel still dedicated to her and Mrs. Paulet? she asked Forster.
She neither agreed nor objected to the dedication and planned to read the
revised work first and be guided by her husband's feelings, for she knew Mr.
Carlyle would dislike being connected in people's minds, by even the
slightest spider-thread, with what he called 'George Sandism and all that
accursed sort of thing.' Well, 'if *anything* of the last Chapters I read be left
in it, not only would he detest dedication to *his* wife but his wife herself
would detest it.'

As so often, Jane's real motives lay buried in her letter to Forster. It was
not the dedication per se she objected to, but that her name in bold capital
letters might alert the reader to the fact that 'Alice Bryant,' the unhappily
married woman in the novel, was based on JANE WELSH CARLYLE.

Without revealing this to Forster, Jane wrote, 'What I want *you* to do is, if there *be* a dedication to erase *my* name and leave it all to Mrs. Paulet.' She explained, 'You see how I am situated—wishing *not* to give pain to Geraldine—still less to give offense to my Husband and least of all to promenade myself as an "emancipated" woman.'

John Forster was not able to serve Jane in this instance and *The Half Sisters* was published with Geraldine's Valentine's Day, 1848, dedication intact. Jane was furious with Geraldine, telling anyone who would listen that she did not approve of that scandalous book.

On the surface, the respectable housewife in *The Half Sisters* and her husband were quite unlike the Carlyles in one crucial aspect, and this might be the reason no one, Jane's anxiety aside, ever did make the connection between them. Geraldine, quite cleverly, stripped away the couple's genius and placed them in the provinces, where they could be Mr. and Mrs. Anybody. The husband, 'Mr. Bryant,' rather than leaving the wife in the valley of the shadow of Oliver Cromwell and Lady Harriet, left her in the valley of the shadow of his extensive ironworks.

But the housewife was obviously based on Jane. When we meet her, she is an only child, living with her mother in the provinces; her father is dead. She has advanced ideas which her mother does not understand. She meets a man who is some years older than she, and is knowledgeable, paternal, and passionless. How can she live among such provincial people, he asks her. As soon as they marry, he is called to his business. They cancel their honeymoon—permanently, it would appear.

In the ten years of the marriage, the cold husband has less and less time to devote to his wife, nor will he share his business concerns with her, though she begs him to. He retreats into his work and is often out of town. They do not have children, nor, apparently—it seems a given of the novel—will they.

The married woman turns from a brilliant, literarily inclined girl into a consummate housewife, though she is seized by ennui and the realization that she has no meaningful work. Her husband does not like her rather silly mother with her genteel aspirations and avoids inviting her to visit until a time when he will be going away. The mother catches a chill and dies, leaving the daughter alone in the world.

Morbidly afraid of blame, the lonely wife is haunted by a sense of self-reproach which divides her against herself. She does not have the confidence needed to make a way for herself in the world, as does the foreign actress Bianca, whom she meets and helps without knowing they have the same British father and that the actress, raised in Italy, is her illegitimate half sister.

Why wouldn't the reader expect a real-life prototype for the married woman when her illegitimate half sister, Bianca, was so obviously based on Charlotte Cushman? Why, even the name 'Bianca' was instantly recognizable as the character Cushman played in her heralded debut on the London stage, little more than two years before. The foreign actress in the novel at times strikes a 'strong bass note,' for she has more knowledge of society and life than women usually do and is as a result a bit coarser than her proper, ornamental sisters. Still, she has gone on the stage only out of unselfish duty to her family, to support her feeble mother, and this motive, the narrator tells us, elevates the acting profession itself.

What made the possibility of people identifying Bianca's half sister as Mrs. Carlyle even more horrifying to Jane was that in the last chapters of the novel, the married woman is in love with and almost runs away with a man.

At first the character based on Anthony Sterling considers the married woman a provincial housewife. He is forced by the father he did not get along with to leave England in order to end his love affair with the actress Bianca, but when he returns he finds in the married woman the British modesty and utter selflessness he has learned to love in women. While away, the character grew even more like Anthony Sterling, joining the army in Vienna and returning a debonair mustached soldier. He is dark and handsome and a bit younger than the married woman.

Her husband is delighted that their returned friend will entertain his wife while he travels on business. The relationship between the wife and the military man deepens. They spend their days together, they shop together, they buy a lamp, and he becomes even more enamored realizing the perfect dove-like modesty of her emotions. Although she is a married woman, she seems to have the 'purity' of a virgin. She 'had never witnessed strong passionate emotion. All her life her soul had been athirst for words of love.'

When the young man impulsively lies down next to her on a sofa and declares his love, she sends him away.

Alone once more, the housewife is left feeling just as Jane felt as Carlyle abandoned her more and more for Lady Harriet and her circle: 'Her health failed, her temper failed; it became unequal, passionate, morose. She was in misery; misery that no words could express; and, at times, she was near suicide, as the only escape from her intolerable suffering.'

She tells no one the cause of her depression; she swallows it. 'Oh, that I had any one to counsel me, to tell me what I ought to do.' She begs her husband, 'Do not leave me alone. . . . You care not what comes to me. You would never miss me. You would live equally contented if I were dead.'

Then she rationalizes to herself: 'I am nothing, or at best of secondary importance. Well, be it so, be it so; I need feel no more remorse; he has lost me by his own fault.'

Enter the lover: 'Neither of them spoke. A passionate, guilty joy was in their hearts; they were interpenetrated with each other's presence.'

They decide to run off together: 'She would shrink from no blame or scandal, or loss of reputation, so long as she could to her own conscience throw the least varnish of rectitude over her crime.'

In Mazzini's letters to Jane at that time, he constantly pleaded with her to think of her mother in heaven and do nothing that would shame her parents. He, like Geraldine, knew what Jane was contemplating. Geraldine later told Carlyle's biographer, 'When the intimacy with the Ashburton house became established, she had definitely made up her mind to go away, and even to marry another person. She told him afterwards on how narrow a chance it had turned.'

In the same way, in *The Half Sisters:* 'By one of those coincidences that occur so often in real life, and which sound so unreal in books,' the husband comes home unexpectedly at the very moment his wife is writing a farewell letter to him.

The shock is too much for the wife's system. Consumed by a severe attack of hysteria, she has to be put to bed. Only as she lies prostrate does the husband realize the truth—and he blames *himself.*

She tells him: 'One thing I want you to know: you are not dishonoured—in that one sense, at least, I have been faithful to you.' Her illicit love had not been physically consummated. 'Do you believe me?'

He does.

'It is more than I deserve.' That evening the wife falls into a stupor and dies of guilt.

Her lover—sounding just like Geraldine—blames the husband for her death: 'Had you taken her away when she entreated you, she had been saved; but your business, your money, your time, your cursed convenience, made you refuse her harshly,—blind fool that you were! . . . Oh, when you refused either to remain with her, or to take her away, to whom else could she go but to me who loved her?'

Beyond the melodrama of the novel (which imitated life more closely than one might care to admit) lay the tragedy of Jane's situation. 'You left her, you left her.'

Not only Jane but Carlyle himself was inflamed by *The Half Sisters*. He wanted to contradict Geraldine's point of view in an article he began but never completed on phallus worship and George Sandism. Could he even use a term like 'phallus worship' in print, he wondered. Geraldine had cut too close to the core—and both the Carlyles knew it.

Geraldine considered *The Half Sisters* the one novel in which she most successfully explored the woman's question, and it was a question she saw vividly personified in the lives of the two friends she loved the most and could not bring together. The most radical element of the novel was that the independent actress Bianca does not die of heartbreak when her lover leaves her—the usual fate of women abandoned in novels. This professional woman through meaningful Work finds a way to survive the loss of love, whereas her half sister, the proper British wife, with nothing to occupy her mind or legitimately assuage her loneliness, dies of heartbreak and shame.

Charlotte Cushman's life offered Geraldine a new model of womanhood. And if one believes the author made up Bianca's loss of her lover and her dedication to work, it should be noted this melodrama came straight from Charlotte's girlhood.

Charlotte made the mistake of confiding to the novelist that when she was young and acting in Albany, a very wealthy, socially prominent man lied to her about his intentions. She and her mother had been treated with great respect in Albany because of their own social connections, which they made sure to advertise. Charlotte was a distant cousin of Governor Marcy on her mother's side. It was not surprising that as a young and socially conscious girl, she contemplated supporting her family in the way her mother approved—by marrying a rich and prominent man. And of course, and much more importantly, Charlotte always yearned for children of her own.

Once Charlotte realized the unnamed man did not mean his proposal of marriage, she told Geraldine, she broke off the relationship at once and did not succumb to his advances.

'You were strong!' Geraldine replied.

'I, strong! Child! I was as weak as water, but I was kept from harm.'

Work saved her.

'I *believe* a true lover is a *possibility*,' Geraldine wrote to Charlotte, as if to reassure her. 'And yet nine times out of ten marrying a man only obliges one to keep for life what was not worth having for a month—so now all I ask of the Gods is to let me think well of a man as long as I can. I shut my eyes so willingly that if I open them it is because . . . a light *forces* me!'

She seemed to be advising Charlotte to do the same, without realizing that since those early days, Charlotte dealt with men with her eyes wide open. She had no need to force them closed.

'There was a time in my life of girlhood when I thought I had been called upon to bear the very hardest thing that can come to a woman,' Charlotte wrote to Emma of the Albany man, confiding and confirming the incident. She seemed to be telling Emma she was spared bearing a child out of wedlock. Again, Work saved her.

One would expect, given the praise of the professional woman in *The Half Sisters,* that Work would triumph. Yet after staunchly defending women's role in the theatre, at the very end of the novel, at the last possible moment, the actress Bianca marries an unselfish aristocrat of liberal views. His sister asks Bianca one favor—that she not fulfill her contractual obligations that season, but give up the stage immediately. Without so much as a murmur or a frown or a blink of an eye, the actress says yes. And she and her lord and their future offspring live happily ever after.

Reviewers noticed the extremely sudden last-minute shift. Geraldine was ahead of her times, but she was not beyond them. The novelist was not above turning Charlotte Cushman into Susan Cushman at the proper moment. The most meaningful work for a woman begins—when all is said and done—at home, satisfying her husband and raising her children. Revolutions always go beyond revolutionaries; that is why revolutionaries—and Geraldine was one—are so dangerous.

Geraldine Jewsbury was a woman who '*speculated*,' as Jane put it; a thinker who was very much influenced by the most unlikely of bedfellows: Thomas Carlyle in the arms of George Sand. Geraldine 'used' the novel form, but unlike Charlotte Brontë and George Eliot, some propriety or reserve she had about the form, perhaps inspired by Carlyle himself, seemed to separate her from it. The novel was not an organic mode of expression for her; it was a vehicle, a platform—it was 'only' a novel. With great passion, she wished to explore certain issues: What was the meaning of a woman's life, what was the nature of romantic love?

Jewsbury the *speculator* might well have realized that in an effort to satisfy society and publisher, she relied too heavily on contrivance. The novel, like the acting profession, has its 'business.' Jewsbury had a great deal of talent and insight concerning love relationships, but not the genius to light a fire under the 'business,' a fire magical and intense enough to turn, not dross certainly, but silver, to gold.

Yet one cannot help wondering what if? Although Geraldine knew something of women who were sweethearts, none of this appears on the page. What if the strong bass note in the actress's character was played out? What if Geraldine's Bianca played Romeo, not Juliet? Geraldine *does* picture a retreat for women where they could go and think about their lives and possibilities. A teaching retreat modeled on the Seaforth House speculations. If *only* somebody got jealous. If *only* somebody got her feet rubbed.

Geraldine avoided that realism at the same time her enthusiastic nature made her prone to handle the melodrama so prevalent in life too melodramatically—adding a flourish rather than calming it down. 'Life does not end in a catastrophe like a book or a play,' Geraldine wrote toward the end of *The Half Sisters*.

When Jane told Carlyle she had almost left him for another man, he answered he had been so busy with *Oliver Cromwell* that he might not have noticed. Nothing had ever hurt her as much, she confided to Geraldine. But was Carlyle telling the truth?

The year after the novel was published, Carlyle, quite atypically, invited himself to visit Captain Anthony Sterling. Anthony's wife was under constant supervision, having gone mad again, and Anthony retired to the countryside by himself for a while.

Carlyle planned to visit alone. 'But Anthony had no notion of having *him* without me.'

Just as well, Carlyle replied. Jane would keep Anthony off him and let him enjoy '*the perfect* silence.'

After a week in the country, Jane and Anthony returned to town together on a Friday and Carlyle said it was bliss to be left alone. Jane had linens to change. Anthony had to speak to the 'Mad-doctors' about his wife.

Jane and Anthony returned to the country on Saturday with fresh linens and food from town and Jane recorded that it was the most successful visit she had made in a long time. She and Anthony laid the table and set out wax candles. The old cook prepared what food was not brought ready-made from London. 'And Mr. C. let himself be *waited upon* by us with an amiability!!'

If there was a moment when the Carlyles sat out in their back garden

Captain Anthony Coningham Sterling, the older brother of Thomas Carlyle's best friend John. He was very much in love with Jane and might well have been the man she thought of running away with when Carlyle's relationship with Lady Harriet overshadowed Jane's wifely role. In the 1850s Anthony fought in the Crimean War and Jane never read the war lists without terror she would see his name. When he returned, they had a bitter falling-out and she commented to his niece Kate that in Anthony's anger, as earlier in his love, he could not get her out of his head.

together or looked at a view holding hands, or enjoyed a lovely breakfast at an inn tête-à-tête, or petted either side of the neck of a fine horse, it is not recorded in all of their volumes of letters. But here, at Captain Anthony's country estate, we find the most relaxed and intimate moment between passionless husband, dutiful wife, and loving friend. It was as if for one moment Jane claimed Rousseau again.

Certainly Jane had a pressing reason to stay away from Charlotte after the publication of *The Half Sisters*.

While Jane recognized herself in the book and feared that her domestic situation would be discovered, Charlotte recognized a version of herself that was in a certain sense normalized—playing Juliet, being pretty like sister Susan, marrying like Susan and Sarah Anderton.

If putting her in a novel was not in itself the severing blow to Charlotte's eternal friendship with Geraldine Jewsbury, some of the details were. One could assume from the book that Charlotte's way in the theatre was paved by a man. Never was an actress's rise more an act of self-determination and less a result of the casting couch. One could assume Charlotte was not a virgin. (She probably wasn't.) But beyond any of that, the character based on Charlotte was illegitimate. In Edinburgh a few years before *The Half Sisters* was published, they whispered dear Ned was illegitimate, that Susan had not been married to Nelson Merriman. Charlotte sent divorce papers on to disprove the calumny. But to suggest, even in fiction, that Charlotte's mother, Mary Elizabeth Babbitt Cushman, bore a child out of wedlock! Years later Geraldine told Miss Stebbins that she and Charlotte just naturally drifted apart, but Charlotte would never trust Geraldine again.

However, Jane's vocal contempt for *The Half Sisters* was bogus to the core. Some later critics did wonder why she made such a fuss about a book that was much less scandalous than *Zoe*. Fuss and fume she did. But no one ever did make the connection between Mrs. Carlyle and Geraldine's 'almost' unfaithful wife, and Jane's fears died down.

Eight years later, when the book was in the second of its three editions, Jane sent it to a close Scottish friend and wrote to her in quiet pride that *The Half Sisters* was the novel of Geraldine's that she liked best. The reason she gave was that it had bona fide arguments in it, between Geraldine and her, written down almost word for word as they spoke on their walks together.

Women writers wrote of women's lives. And women's lives were filled with thoughts of romantic love—because they had nothing else with which to fill their minds, Geraldine wrote to Jane. 'I mean I would not on any account take up a woman's novel at a venture, unless I knew something about the writer.'

The heart of Geraldine's novel was that women must be educated to do useful work, must come together to find a way to have society open such work to them. These were the same ideas that Eliza Cook would soon propagate in *Eliza Cook's Journal*. Toward this end Adelaide Anne Procter would in the next decade edit a beautiful compilation of literature produced by the first all-women printing press.

What were Jane Carlyle's options at the age of forty-five, when she ran distraught from Seaforth to Geraldine in Manchester? To leave Cheyne Row with another man? To commit suicide, as she almost did? Legally she had the right to leave; Carlyle himself left that door open to her. Her marriage was no more consummated than her friend Ruskin's. Leave to do what? Become a governess? Teach or direct a girls' school? These more than summed up a woman's 'respectable' options at the time.

Write a novel? When Charlotte Brontë's novels came out under a pseudonym, many believed and circulated that they were written by Jane Carlyle—the same brilliant, caustic sensibility. People who heard Jane speak or received her letters expected a novel from her. But she did not write the epistolary novel with Carlyle that he suggested when they were young. She began to write such a novel with Geraldine, but soon dropped out—and *Zoe* was born. An intellectual Jane was. But from her earliest years, when she was her father's darling, she used that intellect for the purpose of garnering admiration and love. Her self-love was dependent on the men in her life—Dr. Welsh, Edward Irving, Thomas Carlyle. Her inner woman, to use Carlyle's phrase, was not strong.

But it was proudly Scottish. Even when Jane, in her forties, realized that the sacrifices she made so that Carlyle could write were not essential to his genius, that she was not the indispensable factor in his life, she stayed the dutiful wife. And for the next decade, Jane's role in the Ashburton household became a constant humiliation to a proud and fragile woman who in her secret heart lost her self-respect, what she called her 'original Self.'

'It is only in connection with the Past that I can get up a sentiment for myself,' she wrote in her journal. 'The Present Mrs Carlyle is what shall I say?—'

She paused and then answered herself in Mazzini-speak: '*Detestable*—upon *my* honour!'

JANE WAS so lonely and suffered so much physical as well as mental agony that she asked Geraldine to move to London. Geraldine was suspicious of the big city, she replied. Why didn't Jane move into a cottage in the country with her? Jane would do the housekeeping and keep the accounts and encourage Geraldine in her daily writing. At night they would have each other's company when they wished. Though she had earlier urged Jane to write, she now offered Jane a gentler Carlyle and a kinder Craigenputtock—easy to refuse. After Geraldine's brother Frank married and had his first child—Stavros Jewsbury—Geraldine reconsidered, and moved around the corner from her friend on Cheyne Row.

Geraldine Jewsbury and Jane Welsh Carlyle in April 1855. Jane stands behind the seated Geraldine, just as the bridegroom stands behind the bride in the standard pose of the time. Geraldine put together the album in which this photograph appears in order to cheer the lonely and ailing Jane—dedicating the album to 'Mrs Carlyle' and placing a picture of Jane's dog Nero on the cover.

In the winter, with her colds and neuralgia, Jane was a veritable recluse. Geraldine would manage to get to her on the most savage winter days. 'Dear Geraldine, as if she would contend with the very elements on my behalf, brought me a bunch of violets and a bouquet of the loveliest most fragrant flowers.' They would talk. Geraldine would rub her aching shoulders, her 'hungry' feet. But Jane was left alone at night. Carlyle was with Lady Harriet—now Lady Ashburton, after her father-in-law's death. Jane wrote in her journal:

> When I think of what I is
> And what I used to was,
> I gin to think I've sold myself
> For very little cas.

Always the joke—when possible, that is.

'The chief interest of to-day expressed by blue marks on my wrists.' Carlyle's 'extraordinary temper' became more violent and overbearing as he grew older and more famous, Geraldine explained to her friend and Carlyle's future biographer, Froude. But then again, Jane could be 'extremely provoking.'

'Oh, my mother! nobody sees when I am suffering now,' Jane called out to Grace Welsh.

> Oh, little did my mother think,
> The day she cradled me,
> The lands I was to travel in,
> The death I was to dee.

In earlier days, men hung on to Jane's every word. In her fifties, Jane noted sharply, they talked on and on, blandly assuming her to be simply delighted and flattered to *listen*! Women seemed to have gained a romantic appeal that they never had for Jane when she was younger. They had become an emotional necessity.

When she met the author Madame de Winton at a tea party Geraldine gave, Jane confided in her diary: 'I have not for years seen a woman who so captivated me at first sight, or indeed at any number of sights. There is a charm of perfect naturalness about her that is irresistible. When she went out of the room, I felt quite *lost*,—like to cry!'

When Geraldine returned from seeing her off, Jane said, 'What an adorable woman!'

Geraldine burst out laughing, for Madame de Winton had just said, 'I could adore that woman!'

Jane wrote, 'I must see her again; tho', *chi sa*. But perhaps it were better not!'

'But perhaps it were better not!' was the only full sentence Carlyle's nephew deleted when he published this diary of Jane's. What can such a deletion do but suggest there were reasons for it?

Jane's female friendships had taken on a highly charged quality.

Ironically, it was Lady Harriet Ashburton's sudden death in Paris on May 4, 1857, that set the stage for Jane's most intense female friendship and for her later wish to meet her fictional half sister. Fashionable London, to Jane's amazement, came straight to Cheyne Row. It was sheer curiosity to see how Mrs. Carlyle, who did not blink an eye, and Mr. Carlyle, who dared not blink an eye, took the death. Carlyle attended the funeral by himself.

A year and a half after the Lady's death, her mother Lady Sandwich handed Jane a letter and said, 'Read that, I thought you would like best to hear of it from *me*.'

Jane recognized Lord Ashburton's handwriting immediately and the first words to catch her eye were 'I have proposed to Miss Stewart-Mackenzie and she has accepted me.'

Like many widowers of strong wives, Lord Ashburton did not know what to do with himself. Jane quipped she could see Ashburton marrying again to take himself off his own hands. He had wealth, land, and no heirs. He was ripe for the fortune hunters. Still, Jane was deeply offended. The only good Lady Ashburton, it would appear, was a dead one.

Louisa Stewart-Mackenzie had come to London ten years earlier, a beautiful, daring twenty-year-old, on the lookout for a grand match. Loo, as she was called, had a face that could have been carved by the ancients, a wonderfully strong jaw, good nose, and brilliant dark eyes. Lively, intelligent, willful, evangelical, capricious, Loo was always attracted to artists and to art. The art historian Anna Jameson had been her governess, getting her best-selling *Diary of an Ennuyée* from early travels with her young charge.

Loo came from an ancient Highland family—albeit with an extremely eccentric grandfather who was a Sephardic Jew. With her father dead, Loo and her mother, herself once adored by Sir Walter Scott, had fallen on hard

William Bingham Baring became the second Baron
Ashburton in 1848. He was one of Thomas Carlyle's
closest friends and was very much in the shadow of
his first wife, Lady Harriet. Etching after Edwin
Landseer around 1860.

times. Her mother in fact had sold their wonderful hunting lodge in the
Highlands, Loch Luichart, to the Ashburtons.

Not six weeks after the Lady's death, Loo set her cap for Lord Ashburton. Imagine her showing up at Loch Luichart, where the widower was
grieving, on the pretense of offering him condolences. Carlyle wrote his
close friend a warning. Louisa Stewart-Mackenzie was said to be a
coquette—not that *he* had personal knowledge of that fact. But he did
know she was a bright and vivacious damsel, struggling fitfully about, like a
rambling sweetbrier, with thorny hooks under *her* flowers as well.

If, as an unmarried woman, Louisa was sure of her aims and willing to
pursue the right man more openly than most women, she was aided by the
fact that she had less emotional investiture than most. For Loo was a lover
of women. Her very early letters to women were excruciatingly overt and
lavish, according to her twentieth-century biographer, Virginia Surtees—

and others who have seen them. She had an early passionate attachment to Florence Nightingale, whom she called her 'beloved Zoe.' Nightingale signed her letters 'Ever your dearest life.'

When Florence Nightingale heard that one of those 'female ink-bottles' she so dreaded was collecting material for a life of her, she wrote to Loo that she wanted every letter written in her hand burned. Nervously she asked, 'You have not left any such maiden stores . . . have you?'

As with all women who loved women, there was the inevitable man who got away. As her biographer put it, Loo lavished a yearning heart on this man of letters, 'at the same time evincing an emotional tenderness for his aunt.'

Loo was as devoted to her mother as Charlotte Cushman was to hers. She *needed* a great match, and had the wiles to win her man. She could not save her mother, or herself, by the sweat of her brow.

Ashburton came along just as Loo reached thirty. What a godsend. He was a gentle man, passive, in his late fifties. He had such kind eyes. No man's eyes moved Loo as his did. How he reminded her of her own father.

When Loo was preparing to visit Egypt on her honeymoon, she wrote to Florence Nightingale for a reading list: 'No one can ever occupy Zoe's niche in my heart.'

On her honeymoon she had plenty of time to read what Nightingale recommended, for Loo had married without any idea of 'how completely *unoccupied*' Ashburton's health made him. The man was fifty-nine years old and suffering terribly with the gout. 'I wish there was any hope of a small chick, but that I much fear can *never* be,' she wrote to her mother from the Nile. This was a dreadful disappointment, but she suspected all married people were unhappy *at first*.

Jane and Carlyle did not rush to see the newlyweds after they returned from their honeymoon. Jane had her mind made up. She would never like yet another Lady Ashburton. Not even a Scottish one.

But the second Lady Ashburton knew how badly the aristocratic first Lady Ashburton treated Jane, and when the Carlyles made their first reluctant visit, Loo did everything she could to honor Carlyle and his wife. She could never fill the shoes of the first Lady Ashburton, she said, with a sincerity that touched them. Then they dined.

Jane had to confess that this French cooking introduced by Lady Loo agreed with her remarkably well and that she could easily get accustomed to drinking champagne every night. The loving and trusting feelings Loo exhibited toward Jane that night came as a wonderful surprise, Jane told Loo in her letter of thanks.

Soon cases of champagne began to arrive at Cheyne Row.

Lady Loo was kindness herself. Largesse was her married name.

Ten years before, Stavros Dilberoglue, sympathetic to Jane's loneliness, had bought her a little dog. When Jane named him Nero, the first Lady Ashburton quickly dubbed Jane Agrippina. Now Nero was gone. He had his neck run over by a butcher's cart, was the way Jane phrased it. Though he survived that dreadful accident, within a year her faithful companion died. The second Lady Ashburton wrote a sincere letter of sympathy to Jane. And she reprimanded her for being such a bad correspondent. She did not want them to be passing shadows.

The relationship between Jane and Loo developed into what Loo's biographer called a frenetic friendship, full of impulse and exaggeration. It was a full-blown female friendship with an exuberant underlying emotional pull. Letters between the two abounded in exclamation points. Jane felt a tremendous identification with the younger woman. The friendship became so strong that when Louisa, either miraculously or with considerable foresight, gave birth to her daughter Mary Florence (named after Florence Nightingale), Jane was uncharacteristically beside herself with joy. It was as if she too, finally, had a child of her own. 'Oh my Lady! I should *so* like to see Her! Lord Ashburton's own wee bairn!'

She *rushed* to the newborn, whom Loo called 'my wee Brown Beauty,' against doctor's orders. Jane came away from little Maysie 'vowing inwardly a life-long interest in her and a loyal affection to Her—the first human child that has ever, so to speak, come home to my business and my bosom! and awakened what is called *the maternal instinct* in me—me whose lines have always been cast in Babyless Places!'

Both women had impotent husbands, yet Lady Loo had given birth. Jane rejoiced with Lady Loo, blurring the lines between them as she blurred, as well, brown little Maysie's parentage. When it came to such things, Jane Carlyle was far from the sophisticate Virginia Woolf imagined. She was a woman who did not know the sex of her own cat. The way she doted on the child well substantiates something Geraldine told Carlyle's biographer privately, that Jane could never forgive Carlyle for her childlessness and had grown bitter over it.

Now her dearest friend, in a comparable situation, had given her little Maysie. The way Jane acted, it could have been both the women's child.

It was Jane's undying friendship with the second Lady Ashburton that opened her up to meeting Charlotte Cushman. Loo had a special place in her heart for women artists. Charlotte was known for her generosity to women. From early in her career, when Charlotte heard a woman street singer, she would send Sallie out to give her money. There but for the grace of God was Charlotte. Jane heard of Charlotte's charity to one particular woman, and it became the pretext on which she came to meet her at their mutual friends' home in Islington.

Geraldine, with a novelist's instinct, preshadowed reality in *The Half Sisters*—what she wrote finally did happen. By the time they did meet, the sixty-year-old married woman hungered for the comfort of her friends, and the forty-five-year-old actress, having just married her nephew to the woman she loved, was on top of the world. They were secret half sisters after all, their relationship playing itself out in the rhetoric of an intense female friendship.

To Miss Stebbins, Charlotte's joy at finally meeting Mrs. Carlyle added to their homecoming. She highlighted the moment in her biography of Charlotte, quoting Charlotte's words to an unnamed friend:

'She [Mrs. Carlyle] came at one o'clock and stayed until eight. And such a day I have not known! Clever, witty, calm, cool, unsmiling, unsparing, a *raconteur* unparalleled, a manner *un*imitable, a behavior scrupulous, and a power invincible,—a combination rare and strange exists in that plain, keen, unattractive, yet unescapable woman! O, I must *tell* you of that day, for I cannot write it! After she left, of course we talked *her* until the small hours of the day.'

The two women swore eternal friendship on the spot.

Once more Charlotte had triumphed over adversity, and brought circumstances under her control. What a visit she and Miss Stebbins had with the Dilberoglues. For that moment, life itself was in the palm of Charlotte's hand.

On Cheyne Row the next day, Jane's maid entered with a glorious bouquet of flowers: '*Not* from Mr Ruskin, I think ma'am!—at least it isn't *his* man that brought them.'

'No,' Jane said. And even though Charlotte had already sent her grapes that morning, she knew immediately: 'They are from Miss Cushman.'

'I have the strangest thing to tell you about your flowers!' Jane wrote in her first letter to Charlotte in a blaze of exclamation marks reminiscent of her letters to Lady Loo: 'The moment I set my eyes on them, and before

'Lady Ashburton with her little Mary,' Carlyle labeled this photograph of Lady Loo and her daughter taken in the early 1860s.

setting my eyes on the note, and in face of the glaring improbability that grapes and flowers should be sent from the same person, on the same day by *two different messengers*!!! I *knew* somehow—knew as assuredly as if I had taken them out of your hand, that those flowers were from *you!*'

Jane began this letter without salutation, by answering a question of Charlotte's in a sweep of warmth, as if continuing a conversation they had been having for years. Certainly it continued a conversation Charlotte was having with herself. Did Mrs. Carlyle believe one human will could have power over another?

'If I believe in one human will having power over another . . . if I believe in spiritual magnetism?—Most assuredly! I believe in it absolutely and

entirely! It is the Great Central Fact of the Universe for me!—The concentrated Essence of Life!—I would not say as much in "mixed company" . . .
but it suits my humour to begin my correspondence with *you* by a *confidence!*'

Jane was about to leave for Windsor Forest as a guest of the first Lady
Ashburton's mother:

'I *do* wish to see you, *do* wish to hear from you; *do* love you (You *know*
that; why make me *say* it?),' Jane reassured her. 'And further I mean, deliberately and imperatively that we two should be friends for the rest of our
lives,—and *good* ones! to make up for lost time.'

But for the present: 'I *must* stop—I have to go up to Piccadilly to
arrange about—about— . . . something much above my capacity! viz *placing Mr. C's horse out at grass* for a few weeks!! He had gone and got himself
bitten (the horse not Mr C) on the neck by another horse, and Mr C who
calls himself or is called a *Philosopher* is so ashamed of the trifling disfigure-
ment to his Horse's beauty, that he declines taking him on a visit to an aristocratic stable! and *I*(!) must find him a month's grazing somewhere!'

And she ends that paragraph in a way to show that she had, by her later
years, a firmer understanding of the hidden scroll between certain women
friends: 'My Dear! Men are—what shall I say?—*strange* upon *my* honour!'

ON THEIR way back to Rome, Charlotte and Miss Stebbins stopped at
the Forest of Fontainebleau at the invitation of the celebrated painter of
animals, the extraordinary French artist Rosa Bonheur, another independent woman who built her own house with her own money. Robert Browning had written to Hattie Hosmer from Paris, 'I don't think any new friend
of mine would please you like Rosa Bonheur . . . with a touch of Hattie
about her that makes one start.'

Small, plump, witty Bonheur openly lived with the woman she had
been with since school days, and was famous all through Europe for her art
and for the élan with which she dressed as a man, and at times tricked people into thinking she was a man. Queen Victoria was quite disappointed
when Rosa presented herself to her in female garb.

Bonheur was extremely popular in England for her unique understanding and rendering of horses. One can comprehend the decline in Harriet
Hosmer's reputation after her death, as her form of art went out of favor
and, as good an artist as she was, she was no better than her form. But Rosa
Bonheur! She understood animals from the inside out: dogs, horses, her pet

Thomas Carlyle on his horse Fritz, in Hyde Park, August 2, 1861. While writing his eight-volume biography of Frederick the Great, Carlyle said his horse was his only companion. 'He is the most careless, most reckless of riders and has often brought his horse down and been pitched over its head,' Jane wrote. 'In general he comes out of these adventures perfectly scratchless.'

lion who had free rein of her house. Her work renders an animal's essential nature, the animal's fierce soul. But it seems that while a woman artist's 'peculiarities' were quite marketable in the nineteenth century, they diminished her value in the next.

When Bonheur's lifelong love died, an earnest American painter appeared at her door, a young woman who devoted herself entirely to the aging French woman, and who wrote a fine biography of their life together which did not disguise their love, so proud she was of being Rosa Bonheur's mistress-daughter. 'You have made me very happy,' Bonheur wrote to her toward the end of the nineteenth century: 'When you are a famous old thing like me, it's hard to believe anyone loves you for yourself. I hope you will never be sorry you gave up marriage for your old Rosa Bonheur.'

A good thirty years before that letter, Miss Stebbins must have felt Emma Crow Cushman fading into the distance as she and Charlotte wended their way to Rome, stopping at another retreat in which their marriage was honored. How Charlotte wished she could describe Bonheur's house to Jane Carlyle, who was so house-proud herself. 'It was so pretty, & she was so beautiful & natural & took me up to her platform—without any ceremony! I was so pleased & contented with this day. *When I see you*—I must describe her studio to you, a new one, which she has just been building down in the forest among all sorts of wild things.'

POSTSCRIPT

CHARLOTTE'S BRAVADO to Emma about her great victory over Mrs. Carlyle—'Well dear *she* came—*she* saw and *I* conquered'—melted away as soon as she got back to Rome. When she received one of Jane's extraordinary letters, she reacted as many women had before her. 'I love you but I fear you.'

'What have I to do in communion with such! What though I *am* kindly bidden—what can I offer in exchange?' she asked Jane, then questioned herself. 'Can I not accept the bounty and be thankful . . . without this miserable *self* rising up to refuse an obligation? There is but one of you, none other in the world like you! I cannot hope to speak or think or write like you. Why should I consider myself . . . ? Because I want your consideration for me, I want your respect.'

Her soul 'blushed' when she realized her self-consciousness.

'You are so wonderful to me, I think of you . . . of all that you said and did in that first & only day I saw you, when a new heaven & new earth was revealed to me. I remember . . . all your looks, all your tones—all your unchecked flow of marvellously fitting words—all your far seeings—all your subtle fancies—your facile dissections—your graphic descriptions—your inimitable behavior—your perfect knowledge . . . all, all, all stamped upon my memory—with an electric fire which burns me yet! I find you marvellous!'

Miss Stebbins, working on a sketch of Horace Mann, called out, 'Com-

Rosa Bonheur, the first woman to win the French Legion of
Honor. Portrait of the animal painter with bovine ca. 1852.
While studying art, Rosa requested and received the official
police cross-dressing permit—*permission de travestissement*—
needed to allow a woman to wear trousers in the streets of post-
Napoleonic France. Her reason? As she sketched in the
slaughterhouses of Paris, she did not want to bloody her skirts.

mend me in all humility unto her highness!' Charlotte, not comprehending
the irony, dutifully sent the message along.

Jane was too ill to answer. The winters laid her up. But when she
regained strength, she matched Charlotte in hyperbole:

'My Heavens!' Jane wrote. When she had come to see her that first time,
'how very little I *dreamt* of jumping into your arms! and "swearing eternal
Friendship," like any boarding school girl!'

'But it was all right!'

'I feel no misgivings about the somewhat german-looking transaction! rather compliment myself on having so much *Life* left in me after all!'

She looked forward to seeing Charlotte in the summer; she seemed to cling to her strength, as she once nervously clutched at her hand: 'The influence of a strong, brave, loving true woman may be felt at any distance, I firmly believe, without outward visible sign! And then Dear, you are come to me just at the right time!'

She had been '*Playing at Friendship* with the new people I was thrown amongst; and so discouraged in my secret heart that I despaired of both my chances and my ability to ever make myself a *new real* Friend!'

What would she do if she could see Charlotte?

'My Dear! My Dear! I want to put my arms around your neck, and give you—o! such a good kiss! And then,—if you can stand that sort of thing . . . I should like to lay my head on your shoulder and take a good cry! *That* is how nature prompts me to acknowledge your dear letter, and dear new year's tokens—with a good kiss and a good cry.'

Many of Jane's friends copied the Scottish tradition of trying to bring Mrs. Carlyle good luck by being the first foot to pass her threshold on New Year's Day. Charlotte sent her gifts at the beginning of 1862: 'I cannot put into words how touched I was by your new year *bouquet* and the *little* scarfs! I took them not only as Tokens from *you* but as omens of a fortunate year; and—next day I had a relapse and was thrown into bed again for a fortnight!!'

If telling Charlotte of her immediate relapse after receiving her gifts was not enough, Jane squeezed into the borders of this letter: 'One word more and the paper is full. Please love me ever so much but *dont* flatter me or it makes me "*think shame*"!'

It was not that difficult both to love and fear this woman who never minced words. Charlotte's hero worship of Jane turned her diffident, and Jane's desire to lean on a strong woman, to be held, kissed, solaced, was the life she led in her letters, not on Cheyne Row.

That summer Charlotte was in London with her niece. Jane was busy with visiting nieces of her own and the two women did not meet until July. When they did, they simply walked and talked. Charlotte expressed her happiness in being able to *listen* to Jane once more. After visiting her on Saturday, she wrote, 'If I come in an open carriage will you drive with us on Monday afternoon.'

The 'us' were Charlotte and Emma. But the day after their drive, Charlotte wrote to Jane, 'Dear, much like the Temple of Concord that I ask you to let me bring Miss Stebbins to see you!' The Temple of Concord had become their way of referring to the smoothing of Jane's resistance to Charlotte during their first meeting at Islington. Now Miss Stebbins was the jealous party. She was jealous of Charlotte's attention to the visiting Emma Cushman and she was jealous of Jane Carlyle too.

Charlotte did not write to Jane on her return to Rome, and Emma, back in America, wondered why. Was Auntie too busy? It was an *interior* difficulty, Charlotte responded. 'Mrs Carlyle frightens me. She is a chemical test; she criticizes her nearest & dearest. She *uses* up her holiest to ridicule.' How could even a Mrs. Carlyle belittle one's husband, how could she talk of her own mother's foibles in front of others?

But her unease went deeper than that and Charlotte knew it. 'I have never come to be in such relations to her, as to wear off this dreadful awe! I have never been sufficiently with her to forget *her* and *myself* & see only a warm friendship between us! and then somehow I got the idea before I left England that she had tired of my stupidity because unless I can utterly forget myself, I am unutterably stupid! If I am frightened of people—I am powerless—& then it is that I can never take my proper position with very remarkable clever people. Thus it is, that knowing myself—for instance cleverer much than I think Hattie is—I could never take my true position with Mrs Kemble—I was so full of awe & terror that I had no power for myself to show myself. I heard the other day from the Dilberoglues that Mrs Carlyle wondered why she had not heard from me—so I wrote her a little tiny rattling good for nothing note! But darling—if she wanted me, she would write me!'

Charlotte had no idea of Jane's emotional reticence or that what she sharply *said* of her mother and her husband did not reveal her 'homeless' heart. It took a Scottish woman to see that right away—the thirty-year-old author Margaret Oliphant.

If, as Geraldine Jewsbury wrote to her publisher, being a *Miss* anybody did nothing to increase a woman writer's prestige on publication, being *Mrs.* anybody did nothing to contribute to her posthumous fame. By the end of her life, Mrs. Oliphant was on the title page of over a hundred books, novels, travel books, biographies, all written late at night while her sons slept. A streak of alcoholism ran through her family, and after the death of her husband and daughter of tuberculosis, she enabled her sons, an unhappy brother, and a promising nephew to live in comfort, though she would lose most of them through dissipation and all of them to death. A letter from Mrs. Oliphant was always bordered in black.

Margaret, a born writer, was a woman of incredible energy and zest. She first came to Cheyne Row to speak with Carlyle about Edward Irving, for a biography she was writing. Carlyle said he couldn't tell her anything, but his wife could if she wished. Margaret left disappointed.

A day or two later, a woman appeared at Margaret's door: 'I went, wondering, and found in a homely little brougham a lady with bright eyes and very hollow cheeks. . . . She must have been over sixty at this time, but she was one of those women whom one never thinks of calling old: her hair was black without a grey hair in it (mine at half the age was already quite grey), her features and her aspect very keen, perhaps a little alarming.'

In her autobiography Mrs. Oliphant recorded that she understood Jane as few did. What appeared to be detraction and bitterness when Jane spoke of her belongings was a whimsical impulse, a mixture of pride and Scottish shyness, joined to 'the strong Scotch sense of the absurdity of a chorus of praise.' She labeled the chapter 'A Typical Scottish Trait.' 'Though [Jane's] kindness was inexhaustible and her love boundless, yet she could drive her opponent of the moment half frantic with half-a-dozen words, and cut to the quick with a flying phrase. On the other side, there was absolutely nothing that she would not have done or endured for her own; and no appeal to her generosity was ever made in vain.'

Charlotte began to understand this following Jane's terrible accident. Attempting to catch an omnibus after visiting a poor relative, Jane stepped into the street and was sideswiped by a passing cab as she attempted to jump back to safety. Because her left shoulder was immobilized by neuralgia, she had not been able to break her fall to the cobblestoned street and was seriously injured. Carried home in misery and then secluded in her little bedroom, she was surrounded by the four walls she previously wallpapered all in red.

Terribly disabled but used to living like a single woman, she sent for the carpenter within a few days, and had him set up a system of cords and pulleys that allowed her to do as much for herself as she could with her one good hand.

Her husband recorded a significant detail. 'On a little table at her right hand, among books and other useful furniture, she gaily pointed out to me a dainty little bottle of champagne.' She had a kind of leaden straw screwed through the cork so that it only needed a touch for her to tip it and take a drink, without turning what was left in the bottle flat.

'Is not that pretty?' she said to Carlyle. 'Excellent champagne and does me good, I can tell you.'

There were darker, less anecdotal moments.

At first Jane's nerves were so damaged that she could not close her mouth. Carlyle, who had a protruding underbite, was sensitive about an open mouth. It was a sign of foolishness.

'Jane, ye had better shut your mouth,' he told her one morning, leaning against the mantel across from her bed.

She could not, she tried to tell him.

'Jane, ye'll find yourself in a more compact and pious frame of mind, if ye shut your mouth.'

Then, in old-fashioned yet sincere phraseology, he told her she should be thankful the accident had not been worse.

'Thankful! Thankful for what? for having been thrown down in the street when I had gone on an errand of charity? for being disabled, crushed, made to suffer in this way? I am not thankful, and I will not say that I am.'

He left the room, telling her he was sorry to see her so rebellious. He later wrote to his brother John, 'She speaks little to me, and does not accept me as a sick nurse, which, truly, I had never any talent to be.'

Her cousin Maggie, all grown up, was called for. And the ever-loyal Geraldine seemed to live at Cheyne Row during these dreadful days that turned into weeks and then into months. For six months, Jane lay in that red-wallpapered hell.

The pain she was in was incredible. The doctors called it neuralgia. They tried new forms of opiates and narcotics. But nothing worked. 'Any honest pain, mere pain,' she told her husband, 'if it were of cutting my flesh with knives, or sawing my bones, I could hail that as a luxury in comparison!' Her condition led to mental complications as well.

Her demons came to her and she could not escape. Earlier that year, one of her two servants told her a rumor circulating among servants in Scotland that 'you were a she-devil! And . . . *that* tall chair (pointing to a *prie Dieu*) was for strapping you to when you were mad!!!'

The shock sent a stab through Jane's back to her heart. She tried to keep the pain the foolish girl caused her to herself. ('Swallow your vexation.') But was she a she-devil? Was she insane? Better to die than to end in an asylum. She wanted to kill herself, she told her doctor, Richard Quain. Anything rather than madness.

'*Promise me* that you will not put me into a mad-house, however this go,' she pleaded with her husband, who solemnly promised.

'Not if I do quite lose my wits?'

'Never.'

Charlotte heard reports of Jane not only from Sarah and Stavros and other friends when she was in England, but from Dr. Quain himself. Physicians were careless of patient privilege in those days. Before she lay too ill to be seen, Mrs. Carlyle had recommended Dr. Quain to Charlotte for her mother. The man who once treated the first Lady Ashburton was now treating the failing Mary Eliza.

Dr. Quain was a literary man and a raconteur. It was he who told another literary man, Frank Harris, that Carlyle 'jiggled' on his wedding night in his failed attempt to rise to the occasion. And Harris put it in his memoirs, *My Life and Loves,* to be ignored through the twentieth century, the message-bearer in this case long considered a liar. But Quain actually had been curious to learn the exact details of the Carlyles' unconsummated marriage night ever since he assisted Mrs. Carlyle during her menopause. He told Harris:

'I had been a friend of the Carlyles for years: he was a hero to me, one of the wisest and best of men: she [Jane] was singularly witty and worldly-wise and pleased me even more than the sage. One evening I found her in great pain on the sofa: when I asked her where the pain was, she indicated her lower belly and I guessed at once that it must be some trouble connected with the change of life.

'I begged her to go up to her bedroom and I would come in a quarter of an hour and examine her, assuring her the while that I was sure I could give her almost immediate relief. She went upstairs. In about ten minutes I asked her husband, would he come with me. He replied in his broadest Scotch accent, always a sign of emotion with him:

'"I'll have naething to do with it. Ye must arrange it yerselves."

'Thereupon I went upstairs and knocked at Mrs. Carlyle's bedroom door: no reply; I tried to enter: the door was locked, and unable to get an answer, I went downstairs in a huff and flung out of the house.

'I stayed away for a fortnight, but when I went back one evening I was horrified to see how ill Mrs. Carlyle looked, stretched out on the sofa, and as pale as death. "You're worse?" I asked.

'"Much worse and weaker!" she replied.

'"You naughty, obstinate creature!" I cried. "I'm your friend and your doctor and anything but a fool: I'm sure I can cure you in double-quick

time, and you prefer to suffer. It's stupid of you and worse—Come up now
at once and think of me only as your doctor," and I half lifted her, half
helped her to the door: I supported her up the stairs and at the door of her
room she said:

'"Give me ten minutes, Doctor, and I'll be ready. I promise you I won't
lock the door again."

'With that assurance I waited and in ten minutes knocked and went in.

'Mrs. Carlyle was lying on the bed with a woolly-white shawl round
her head and face. I thought it absurd affectation in an old married
woman, so I resolved on drastic measures: I turned the light full on, then
I put my hand under her dress and with one toss threw it right over her head.
I pulled her legs apart, dragged her to the edge of the bed and began insert-
ing the speculum in her vulva: I met an obstacle—I looked—and immediately sprang up. "Why, you're a virgo intacta!" (an untouched virgin), I
exclaimed.

'She pulled the shawl from her head and said: "What did you expect?"'

Jane told Dr. Quain, at his prodding, the specific, embarrassing details
of her unconsummated wedding night years later as she lay in her red
bedroom, besieged by mental and physical agony, and letting all her
demons out. The torment 'burnt up all delicacy in me,' she wrote, 'I "think
shame" to see him; after all the dreadful questions and answers that passed
between us.'

The next summer, Charlotte, unable to see Jane, visited once more with
Stavros and Sarah and commiserated with them concerning Mrs. Carlyle,
who was then at St. Leonards by the sea, so nervously ill and not getting
better. Mr. Carlyle had just gone to her. Charlotte's awful awe of the woman
was being replaced. She felt great sympathy. And with that imitative, empathetic nature of hers, she felt not a little of her friend's vulnerability. Not
only was her own mother wasting away, so was her dear Jane.

Nobody knew what was the matter with Mrs. Carlyle, Geraldine wrote.
'The doctors declare that it is all on the nerves, but both I and her cousin
who is nursing her fear that she injured herself in her *fall* and that there is a
cause for all the pain and terrible restlessness. She suffers dreadfully and her
restlessness is worse than pain.'

The sea air at St. Leonards was a last resort. She would stay there at the
home of yet another former servant, one who married an accomplished
doctor. But how to get her out of her red bedroom after six months?

The way it was done was dreadful. Everyone knew of it. Her neighbor

Mr. Larkin arrived to lift her from her bed and put her into a sick carriage, a wooden box with a little window. Mrs. Carlyle insisted her husband stay away until that part was done. She left Cheyne Row in her coffin. She knew she would never return, but still had the presence of mind to direct the men as they brought her down the slender staircase, out into the waiting carriage. These were her pallbearers, lifting her into a hearse. She traveled to St. Leonards in the baggage car, Carlyle coming to see her every stop along the way. That was how she was deposited at Dr. Blakiston's door.

Carlyle stayed till she was settled. She was passive, quiet, polite. He left her with her trusted servant Mary and her Liverpool cousin Maggie and caught the last train back to London. So out of sorts was he that he lost the cap she had knitted him, leaving it in the cab that returned him to 5 Cheyne Row.

After only a month Dr. Blakiston suggested the Carlyles get a little house of their own. Jane's barbed wit returned for the occasion. Why shouldn't the doctor unload her, as he would not get so much as the honor of a cure for all his pains. She was in a positive torment, day and night, she wrote to her husband. It was some derangement of the womb, some female problem, that affected her vagina as well as her 'lower belly.' To see the lack of control in her handwriting, to see the honest misery in her letters to Carlyle . . . 'Oh my Husband! I am suffering torments.'

Mr. Carlyle was on his way to his wife, Charlotte wrote to Emma, emphasizing that Mrs. Carlyle was suffering enough to kill twenty women.

But Mrs. Carlyle survived and the next summer Charlotte stayed longer in London to see her again. Carlyle had finally bought Jane her own carriage and Lady Loo added a fine horse to the brougham. Mrs. Carlyle would pick Miss Cushman up and bring her out to her ailing and decrepit mother in Brixton. On those carriage rides and visits to Mary Eliza, Charlotte learned firsthand of Jane's kindness, and of how painfully she regretted not being able to tend to her own dying mother. Charlotte remained for Jane the type of strong woman Jane yearned to lean on for comfort. But was there a woman alive with Jane Welsh Carlyle's inner strength, Charlotte wondered. She had literally raised herself from the dead.

One imagines Jane, during their carriage rides, using her narrative gifts to tell Charlotte Cushman the story of what she found on her return home. The servant Mary—the one she so trusted—had given birth to a child there, after leaving Jane at St. Leonards. It was the second child she had secretly carried and birthed on Cheyne Row.

'I shall only say that while she was in labour in the small room at the end of the dining room, Mr Carlyle was taking tea in the dining room with Miss Jewsbury talking to him!!!—Just a thin small door between!'

The baby was not born till two in the morning. Geraldine was long since gone, but Carlyle was still reading in the drawing room, oblivious to this particular noise. He didn't hear the other servant fetching two more women, or the child being taken out to be nursed. 'Need one ask where all my fine napkins went, when it is known that the creature had not prepared a rag of clothing for the child!'

Jane was appalled not so much by the secret pregnancy of the unmarried girl as by 'a great lot of the most disgusting details which struck me like a blow on the breast with a stick, making me *retch* for half an hour after! How she had been keeping the worst company in my kitchen, spending my substance on them . . . and laughing at me as "a simpleton" for my trust in her! *That* was the *worst* of it!

'For two years I have been cheated and made a fool of, and laughed at for my softness, by this half-idiotic-looking woman; and while she was crying up in my bedroom—moaning out, "What would become of her if I died?" . . . she was giving suppers to men and women downstairs; laughing and swearing—oh, it is too disgusting!

A new servant was hired. A respectable widow, past menopause.

Reluctantly, Charlotte left her mother and Mrs. Carlyle, one more frail than the other, and returned to Rome.

When they first met, Charlotte hoped one day to show Jane Rome. 'Do you dream how happy it would make me? No, you cannot!' The invitation had an irony to Jane's ears. For the first Lady Ashburton offered the same invitation years before. Not that Jane was ever up to traveling. From Edinburgh to London was her range, with stops at Manchester, Seaforth, Liverpool, Dumfries, and Haddington. She did not accompany Carlyle to Ireland, France, Germany—and for a while lived in fear that he might locate them closer to the first Lady Ashburton's estate near the Isle of Wight—or transplant them to America!

Art and change were all around Charlotte in the Eternal City, and she would have been proud to show Jane, discreetly, that she was instrumental in a new professional development for women: the first generation of American women sculptors. These women's studios clustered around her at the Spanish Steps. Everyone knew it was she who had brought Harriet Hosmer to Rome, and that she now lived there herself with two sculptors, Hattie Hosmer and Miss Stebbins. Returning from America after the marriage of her lover to her nephew, Charlotte brought yet another young hopeful, Florence Freeman, who wanted to sculpt and was no sooner in Rome than she became Hattie's willing 'fag,' to use Charlotte's designation. Charlotte would mentor other young women sculptors as well, among them Edmonia Lewis, of mixed African-American and Native American blood. She did much to launch her career.

Henry James referred to this circle of women stonecutters around the Spanish Steps, i.e., around Charlotte's home, as 'the white marmoreal flock.' A witty—and inevitably condescending—designation, it came to mask the dead earnestness with which these women made careers and names for themselves in marble (and bronze). These were some of the 'new women' Geraldine Jewsbury envisioned years earlier, telling Jane Carlyle that she and Jane were but imperfect predecessors of those independent working women to come. If it turned out that professional women—such as those clustered by the Spanish Steps—remained more dependent on love than Geraldine had imagined, it simply disproved the more utopian aspects of her vision.

Ironically, since many of these early professional women were lovers of women and remained unmarried, the next century did much to perpetuate the myth of their single-minded, fleshless dedication to Work. This summary exclusion from passion diminished them, turning them as silly and anonymous as Henry James' clever tag. But what excitement and energy existed in those heady Roman days, when independent women were making their own living and bystanders, a bit perplexed yet quite impressed, were applauding.

Jane Carlyle could envision such change in women's lives in private conversations with Geraldine. But at sixty, she was no different than she had been at twenty-six. Jane Baillie Welsh might have once had the chance to, but Mrs. Carlyle would not change. She was attracted to Charlotte Cushman's strength and independence—to her electric magnetism. Attracted enough to draw close to the American's flame, levelheaded or frightened enough to then pull quickly away. In any case, she had a woman she was closer to and more comfortable with in Lady Loo, and a child she could dote on in little Maysie. Jane Welsh Carlyle and Charlotte Cushman would remain half sisters till the end.

The Roman Mosaic

ROME, LONDON

1861–1865

WASHINGTON, D.C., NEWPORT, BOSTON

Summer 1863

R OME. AMERICANS abroad and the British flocked to Rome during the winter season. Political uncertainty did not stop them. 'When one lives in Boston, or St. Louis, or London, you have a sort of social foundation to which you belong. . . . Here you are without a foundation, but your own house and home and its inmates.' Charlotte set the scene for Emma. The ambitious parents who come to marry off their daughters; the callow parson who comes to find a wife with a little money; 'the small, very small heiress, who comes to fish for a husband'; the ignorant rich American jobbers who come to play patron of the arts and buy 'bad copies and still worse originals.' The pretentious wives and daughters of these American businessmen who fall victim to hungry Italians in search of good times—dances, suppers, champagne. 'Such is the Roman Mosaic which is made up winter after winter.'

Still, Roman life had such a 'bright' side. The cold weather lasted such a short time, the skies were so clear, the mode of life so independent, the prudish Miss Grundys so scarce, the artistic society (of the best) so nice, that it would be difficult to find any other place as attractive. Charlotte concluded, 'The worst feature of living in Rome—is the being forced to leave in the summer.'

Adding to her good fortune, Emma would soon be taking her from Babyless Places.

'Do you remember sitting on my knee in my bedroom one day, & whispering in my ear all your discreet plans about Ned & me & perhaps Baby! How strange that it should all have come. And yet how sure it ought to make us that we *can* do what we *will* do.'

Perhaps it was for the best that they could not be together all the time, for the pregnant Emma must now settle down in Boston in the quiet way necessary for the timing of her children. Charlotte planned to be doting 'old Granny Cush,' while still leading an exciting 'Bohemian' life in Rome. 'I had such a wonderful letter from Mrs Carlyle,' she wrote in February. 'She has been ill for nearly four months, poor creature, she is very delicate indeed! I am in despair when I get any such letters for my head at the best of times is not equal to this great woman.'

The cheerfulness that Miss Stebbins exhibited in Islington with Jane Carlyle and at Fontainebleau with Rosa Bonheur faded on her return to Rome. She had a tendency toward depression which menopause did not help, and though Charlotte didn't get such bad flushes lately, she was such an imitative animal that she would have fallen into depression right after Miss Stebbins if it weren't for Hattie. Hattie Hosmer was so cheerful that Charlotte was thankful for the mercury the younger woman brought to Via Gregoriana—even though Hattie was constitutionally ungrateful and spent money like a drunken sailor (a type quite familiar to Charlotte). Hattie had still not delivered the copy of *Puck* she promised Charlotte, and she sold the bust of the *Zenobia* she had also promised her, in order to buy a horse.

She was fickle in love. A shocked Charlotte witnessed Hattie having an affair with Irish feminist Frances Power Cobbe, who was in Rome that season and living with them at Via Gregoriana.

Cobbe remembered the wonderful dinners the two couples shared, replete with American oysters and wild boar, 'including an awful refection menacing sudden death, called *Woffles*,' which Sallie served up with molasses. *Woffles* were so good that the four ladies would often divide up a fifth plate. These were hilarious times, Cobbe wrote.

At the same time Hattie was making love to Miss Cobbe, she received a very beautiful diamond ring from Lady Marian Alford, one of Hattie's most generous patrons. Lady Marian knelt down in front of Hattie and placed it on her finger, Elizabeth Barrett Browning wrote home to her sister. It was the most splendid piece of jewelry one could imagine, a ruby in the form of a heart, both surrounded and crowned with diamonds. Hattie was

Frances Power Cobbe, Irish proponent of women's rights, well known in the intellectual circles of Great Britain and expatriate Italy. This undated picture from Charlotte's album shows her at the time she was living at 38 Via Gregoriana. 'Miss Cobbe is here, & making great love to Hattie,' Charlotte wrote. 'But Hattie is so fickle she makes me heart-sick. Every month or two a new one.'

delighted, and said so with all sorts of fantastic exaggeration. It was Hattie's second diamond ring, Charlotte wrote home to Emma. In America she flaunted a splendid solitaire, not telling Charlotte or the Crows that it was a gift from sister Cornie.

Aglow in diamonds, Hattie, as usual, was out of money. She was reluctant to ask the adoring Lady Marian for yet another advance, but 'just in the nick of time,' her father died, Charlotte reported, tongue in cheek.

Had Dr. Hosmer died of that stroke of paralysis two years ago, before Hattie finally dragged herself back to Watertown, she would not have been so lucky. For in America, she learned her father had made a will in which a male cousin would manage his property. She told her father she'd give everything over to the cousin rather than be put in such a position. The doctor knew she was serious (perhaps he was afraid of his daughter) and he had the will torn up in front of her eyes. Hattie, unfettered, inherited everything. 'I never saw a person who was so universally fortunate in my life & sometimes I think it is a reward for her being so universally cheerful.'

Emma was far from cheerful.

Mr. Crow was shrewd enough to allow his daughter to marry Ned Cushman, knowing nothing but a civil war could prevent it. But he had no intention of handing his daughter over to Charlotte, and before the marriage spoke with Ned in secret, offering to take him into his business in St. Louis. Ned was not one to resist an easy perk, nor would he be sorry to put more distance between Emma and his aunt. Without consent from Emma, he agreed to move to St. Louis after a one-year stay in Boston. Then he had been 'stupid' enough—Charlotte's word—to let Emma know the wool had been pulled over her eyes. The headstrong bride was devastated.

A return to St. Louis next year would be exile for the cosmopolitan Emma.

What was her life coming to, Emma wondered aloud. Did Charlotte still love her?

'Never did a mother love her child so dearly. Never did Auntie think so sweetly so yearningly of her Niece. Never did Ladie love her lover so intensely! Are you satisfied? Must I say more? Shall I say less?'

Was Emma satisfied? She was terribly upset by a cruel, offhanded response like that and her nervous, unsettled letters revealed it.

What a relief when Wayman Crow wrote to Charlotte that his daughter's nervous excitability during pregnancy was a constitutional trouble inherited from her mother. Charlotte's curt responses reflected no lack of love, but fear that she had allowed Emma to be sold into a terrible slavery.

'I could not let you go out of my life—out of my own world to belong to anyone else, hence my worry. If wrong there is, I have my remorse when I see you suffering. . . . Forgive me my own one—do anything but doubt my love or my anxiety for you.' For Emma's peace of mind, 'I would sacrifice my own soul *almost*.' And as for the intensity of her feelings: 'I know no love which admits of such passionate expression. I have never known it— believe this—'

Pregnant Emma was somewhat reassured. A strong woman came nearer one's ideal for a lover than any man could ever come, she told Charlotte.

'You are right, darling,' Charlotte answered. 'Yet do you know I have met very few women in the world whom I could have accepted for a lover or a husband any more than I could have accepted any man.'

A woman's love was 'more acceptable than a man!' just as Emma said. Still, 'we must reflect how exceptional the nature must be that can admit that.' A nature like Emma's. For she now knew by experience that even when a woman *does* find a man as a mate, she would love him better 'if he had all those abilities for loving which exist in a woman.'

Men were 'poor & unworthy' when it came to understanding 'all those little subtle needs.'

But even though men lacked such skill, 'how terribly they use the power they have. How dependent a woman's love makes her upon them.' Charlotte could only wonder at the subjection of women if men 'knew & used all the powers which a woman knows how to use in making love. No darling depend on it God knows better than we do what is wisest & best for us.'

And God was blessing Charlotte and Emma's union. With Emma pregnant, Charlotte for the first time in her life felt her own maternity being developed in a natural way. Her only goal now was helping Emma 'to make a perfect child—as much as one can.' Her advice came rolling in.

Early training was very important.

For example, Hattie had received a boy's education. She was left to run about, to grow up a strong animal with keen perceptions. She had a shrewd, observant, quaint Yankee father on a daily, an hourly, basis. These were the elements which stayed strong in Hattie and which 'go to make her success, much more than an *individual talent for sculpture.*'

The roots of Ned's indolent nature 'is still more apparent for he had no strong example but his grandmother. . . . I was never allowed to have any influence upon Ned—who too often heard me *dis*praised at home, through their jealousy of my friends.' Her mother considered her stupidly weak in regard to the money and time she lavished on these women. Still, she had a hand in the spoiling of Ned Cushman. "I sorrow that I have, that it is done & cannot now be helped.'

English parents were more careful of early influences. A good 'bonne' was important, *not rocking* a child was very important, no matter how it cried. 'Ah dont rock her, & *daze* her little head to sleep.'

And don't be overaffectionate; that was even worse than rocking. Charlotte had seen Emma's effusive affection toward her youngest sister Isabel, had heard Mrs. Crow rebuke Emma for kissing her sister so much. A child's nature was easily tainted by *too much caressing.* 'I could explain this better to you, if I were where I could whisper in your ear—but . . . I don't know if I could speak then.' Perhaps expressing her own needs more than Emma's, she intuited how much Emma wanted 'to have a child—some thing . . . *you own,* one whom no one could have any control over but yourself, a little mind to guide.'

As Emma's confinement grew near, Charlotte imagined their little daughter: 'You will make her call me "big Mamma" & you "little Mamma" until she is old enough to call me "Ladie Mamma."' Emma was sure their baby would be a girl, but Charlotte, as much as she wanted a daughter, had a feeling it would be a boy. 'Remember *my name* can only live through a male child & then after you will find a little Carlotta somewhere.'

Emma *did* give birth to a girl, a girl who eerily resembled the flat-faced, broad-foreheaded Charlotte. It was either stillborn or died immediately after birth, its brain 'too large for health.' The child who so resembled her big Mamma might have carried an extra gene.

The first letter Charlotte sent Emma after receiving the horrid news referred rather cavalierly to her 'Labour Lost,' and offered consolation worthy of Edward Irving: 'The possibility that God saw it was right!' She knew this letter would be read by Ned and Father and Mother Crow, none of whom wanted Emma to be petted too much. So she wrote it for, as she called them, 'foreign eyes,' praying that Emma would see through the disguise. She told Emma that now she would have a year of being a good influence on Ned and his new business when they moved to St. Louis. The baby might have made him a bit jealous.

Of course, Emma would not be nursing; therefore the danger existed that she would become pregnant again too soon. Auntie knew how difficult it would be 'for a woman loving her husband and being accustomed to his caressing' to deny him. Wouldn't it be better if Emma came to her before traveling to St. Louis—that is, if Ned and her parents did not object?

Had Emma's true love instinct seen what this letter covered up, Charlotte asked in a private letter the next day. She spelled it out. The loss of their daughter was 'the very hardest disappointment of my life.'

Once more maternity had been denied her and she reeled under the blow in this second letter. The shock brought back 'the loss of my child-brother (for he *was* my child).' It made her remember the man who had been untrue to her in Albany and another attempt at a relationship with a man. Then, still a girl, she realized she would not marry and have her own children. Instead she had her work, her 'art isolation' and her 'mind children' on the stage.

The loss of their Carlotta brought up another deep defeat as well: her love of Matilda Hays, 'so cruelly tried—so terribly disappointed.'

But there was the immediate compensation of Miss Stebbins and Charlotte's necessary role in encouraging her art. Miss Stebbins led her to her Roman life and Rome once more to Hattie, and Hattie to a letter of introduction to Wayman Crow and Wayman Crow to the great reward of finding Emma, 'my dear daughter, my comfort, my pride, my hope, my help.'

To avoid another pregnancy, Emma did leave Ned and come to England, where she and Charlotte were together once more for a long summer, one in which Charlotte brought her niece to Cheyne Row to meet Mrs. Carlyle. Charlotte was so completely preoccupied with Emma that she had become a very unobservant spouse. When an anxious and dispirited Miss Stebbins finally went off and left Auntie and niece to their pleasure, Charlotte hardly gave it a thought. Sallie, Stebbins' only confidante that lonely summer, looked on in disapproval.

At summer's end Auntie wrote to her little lover: 'Yes darling I do remember the evenings in the country, how short they were, for we had such long twilights as you remember—& how hard we slept—& what jolly little breakfasts we used to have, & what rambles out in the lovely sunshine. It is a very sweet memory to me, & I go back to it often. . . . I feel so happy at having been able to afford you so much enjoyment too. I know you prize the memory of it, as I do! *It will come again!'*

Charlotte just had to figure out *how.*

'I am *a born ruler* you know.'

Miss Stebbins told her that if she could not bend things to her own ideas, the ideas themselves would kill her, so impossible was it for Charlotte to give up the impulse to control circumstances.

Back in Rome Miss Stebbins threw herself into her work. She was no Hattie, busy riding and driving and amusing herself, while she left her workman to set up the third figure for Lady Marian's fountain, paying him '$2 per day!!!'

Nor had Miss Stebbins any of Hattie's blessed cheerfulness. She turned into the most doubtful, doubting, fearing soul Charlotte ever knew, and it caused a great *un*settlement in all ways. 'However I must not complain. She is very sweet & good & gentle & it is better for me than to be alone in the world.'

Ned waited for Emma to return to Boston rather than going to St. Louis by himself, immediately alerting his father-in-law to his tendency to procrastinate rather than work. Nor had Ned written to his aunt of their westward journey. 'Men dont know how to write journal letters like women, at least until they are as old & clever as your father, who writes capital comprehensive letters (for a man!!).'

Emma answered that she arrived in St. Louis with boils under her arms.

Within a month Ned too sounded Job-like. He should be the last to complain, his Auntie replied. He promised Emma that she would never have to live there: 'If Emma does not constantly make you feel it, she is a wiser & better woman than you had any reason to hope for in a wife.'

It did not take Ned long to prove to Mr. Crow and his partners he would leave all the work to them, while he did the hunting, and the billiards, and the dancing. It made Charlotte ready to jump out of her skin, Ned showing such disregard while on his three-year probationary partnership: 'I think he must be crazy or a fool! & you ought to set yourself absolutely against it. A woman has more opportunity of punishing a man than he has of punishing her!'

Emma was obviously not punishing Ned sufficiently. She was pregnant again, and with pregnancy her old doubts about Charlotte's love came back. Charlotte told her she would not go to heaven because she lacked pure faith. If she didn't believe Charlotte loved her, ask Sallie. '*She* knows me entirely & "goes up & down inside my thoughts with a lighted candle" as Mrs Carlyle says.'

A worried Charlotte wrote to Ned asking for a full report of Emma's difficult pregnancy, at the same time warning her nephew not to talk about her pregnancy to other men in the American way. 'I don't think it is any more indelicate to exhibit the picture of your wife naked, than to talk of her ailments with other people.' A wife was sacred, was holy. 'No word should be exchanged with any other man about her.'

On 17 April 1863, poor dear Susan Cushman's birth date, the daughter-in-law Susan would never know miscarried. And again Charlotte's dream of motherhood was thwarted.

Charlotte had already made plans to return to America that summer. And she had an unassailable reason to wave in front of Miss Stebbins and the Crows. Patriotism. The American actress could not stand distance from her country while it engaged in civil war. She would return to the stage to do benefits for the Sanitary Commission (today the Red Cross); she would do her part to help the Union cause. How could anyone object to that?

Miss Stebbins made it clear that she couldn't bear the idea of Charlotte's going to America. She expected her summer to be one of suffering in consequence. She could not come with Charlotte for more than one reason—seasickness, confronting her mother's frailty. . . . The unexpressed reason was that it was obvious to her that her spouse wanted to be with another woman. 'I know she will have a great unhappiness in being separated from me,' but so would she 'if she came to America, & I should want to be with you & had rather she staid behind in England.'

Guilty about the miserable summer Miss Stebbins would have without her, Charlotte called it an act of special providence when Isa Blagden invited Miss Stebbins to join her set at her villa in the hills above Florence.

Charlotte wrote to Emma, 'Miss Blagden is an independent person, she is not intrusive, she minds her own business. She is bright & cheerful, keeps au courant . . . corresponds with all sorts of new people—has a charming villa—and in the nicest situation in Italy I think—& if [Miss Stebbins] should be ill, no human being in the world would be kinder than Miss Blagden.'

By the end of May, Charlotte visited Mrs. Carlyle in London, and then wrote to Emma from her mother's home at Brixton, 'I am this far on my way to you.'

'It was in the spring of 1863, two years after the breaking out of civil war, that Miss Cushman returned to this country,' Emma remembered. 'She could no longer bear the suspense of waiting and watching for news of the success of our army and she came back to be nearer to the events upon which the future of our nation depended.'

Charlotte brought her young lover to a place so respectable that it would be out of the question for the Crows or for Ned to object to their blissful time alone and together. Miss Cushman and her niece went to Washington, where the two stayed for several weeks at Lafayette Square as the houseguests of William Seward, who was now Abraham Lincoln's secretary of state.

'I did not then perhaps realize how impressive were the personalities of these men upon whom rested such responsibilities, nor did I appreciate fully the dignity, the solemnity and grandeur of their carriage. Now, after more than fifty years, the face and figure of the President comes clearly before me as I saw him many times, either walking on the street or coming into the house on Lafayette Square, to speak with Mr. Seward—with, if I had realized it then—the sorrow and the pathos of a savior of his country in his face.'

When she was twenty-four, it did not strike Emma as unusual that when President Lincoln dropped in to consult Seward for a few moments, Seward told Charlotte not to leave the room. So astute was her Auntie politically that Emma often sat with the Seward family for several hours, listening to Seward and Charlotte talking over the events and the eventualities of the war. Those hours probably seemed endless to Emma.

Seward was charmed by the girl, the age of his daughter. She was so joyous, so fresh. Still a newlywed, she was so in love. 'I was able sometimes to make Mr. Seward smile when he came into lunch looking weary and stern after an anxious Cabinet meeting, by saying, "Oh, Mr. Seward, will you not tell me a Cabinet secret? I promise not to tell."'

During the several weeks in Washington, Charlotte gave Sallie a few days of holiday and Sallie reluctantly left her side. She had no confidence of anything going right when she was separated from Charlotte.

One day Seward came back from the State Department and with a smile handed Emma and Charlotte a telegram from Philadelphia addressed simply 'To W. H. Seward, Secretary of State,' which read: 'The rebels are expected here. What shall Sallie do?'

There was great tension at that time, and for a free black, the threat of rebel invasion was even more terrifying. But Sallie's telegram broke the heavy tension and amused Seward, who began imaginary replies to Sallie, giving her whimsical advice about what Sallie should do. Even Lincoln, in those days of deep anxiety, Emma remembered, 'found momentary relief in his sense of humor and I recall his expression when his face lighted up with a humorous smile and then relapsed into the saddest I have ever seen, as if a lamp had been lighted and then suddenly extinguished.'

Charlotte gave a rigorous series of benefit performances in New York, Boston, Philadelphia, Baltimore, and Washington.

During her Boston run that fall, 'Miss Cushman and her niece' passed a few evening hours at a gathering at the home of Annie Fields. 'She lives for effect,' Annie remarked of Charlotte, 'and yet doing always good things and possessed of most admirable qualities. She has warm friends. Mrs. Carlyle is extremely fond of her, gives her presents and says flattering things.' What a triumph it must have been for Charlotte to look out among the assembled guests, many of whom—such as Emerson—arrived at Cheyne Row way before her, and say, on the authority of her own experience: 'Mrs Carlyle is cleverer than her husband.'

Soon after, it was back to Washington with Emma for her performance there. Charlotte had a choice of Ford's Theatre or the new National. She chose the National because of its Shakespeare company and because she heard rumors that Ford's catered to Rebel sympathizers. Everyone came out for Cushman. The theatre was packed. Dignitaries everywhere. Emma sat in a box with Seward, his daughter Fanny, his son Frederick and his wife. Abraham Lincoln sat in the flagged draped presidential box with his wife, son Tad, and private secretary. When Charlotte came onstage, the actress noticed him sitting sober and stiff to her left, the cares of the country still

Miss Charlotte Cushman as Lady Macbeth, around the time of her
benefits for the Union cause in 1863.

on his gaunt visage. But at the end of the performance, he and his family
gave her Lady Macbeth a standing ovation—and Lincoln was smiling.

She played Lady Macbeth next in Baltimore and then with Edwin
Booth in New York. A week later, at the end of October, Charlotte allowed
herself to be persuaded to play one more performance; it was Lady Macbeth
again at the Brooklyn Academy of Music, with Edwin Booth's brother playing Macbeth. As a boy, John Wilkes used to dress up in the tattered rags of
an old withered hag and play 'Charlotte Cushman as Meg Merrilies,' scar-
ing the blacks on his father's farm to death. As an adult, he demanded a
brute realism in his roles, real swordplay and real fights onstage that led to

William H. Seward, 1862, former New York senator and governor, became Lincoln's secretary of state after losing the Republican nomination for president. He was known for his careless appearance and his political savvy. He helped Lincoln with many of his speeches, and through diplomacy prevented England from siding with the South. His great friendship with Charlotte Cushman allowed him to champion her unqualified nephew Ned—this patronage, not the purchase of Alaska, can ultimately be seen as 'Seward's Folly.'

blood gushing and to bruises that he gave and got. He would tell people that the scar he had on his neck was caused by Charlotte Cushman, who opened up a surgical wound when she played against him in Brooklyn in 1863. A madman, Charlotte thought him.

Emma had so many chances to watch Charlotte perform that summer, and her account tallies with those of many of her admirers: 'When she was on the stage her voice was a potent factor in the spell she threw on her audience. She held them with her voice, and moved them to any emotion she intended, there was no trick about it, it was a perfect tone, coming from a perfect heart, through a physically perfectly constructed organ, for her throat was like the Arc de Triomphe and one never missed a whisper however far away he might be.'

Charlotte always said she was an imitative animal. When she interpreted a role, she did so with the force of her passion and her unique understanding of human nature. 'It was not possible for her to accept another person's conception of a character.' When she played Katherine in *Henry VIII,* it was difficult to leave the theatre without thinking that one had actually witnessed the death of the unfortunate queen. In fact, after experiencing the performance one night, Emma ran into her dressing room sobbing, and fell into her lover's arms thankful she was alive.

'Everything in her profession was real to her, her whole duty for the time being—no levity, no taking it lightly. . . . I remember Miss Cushman's once saying to me—"Dear, they talk about my genius—*my* genius is hard *work,*" and truly it was. . . . The only times I was ever afraid of her was when she was at the theatre.'

Yet offstage, she was just like other people, a fact that at first astonished Emma. 'In her own personality away from the theatre she never posed . . . she never acted. She was just her own self.'

A very complicated own self it was.

In the weeks Charlotte conferred with Seward in Washington, about the war, about hedging her investment by switching some abroad, she pressed the secretary of state concerning her nephew. Should a position open in Rome, could Ned be considered for—minister to Italy. She had raised the ante. On her last trip home, she had inquired as to a consulship, but in the interim she had grown more ambitious. For now she had a niece to consider as well as a dissolute nephew—and her own grandchildren yet unborn. What she saw for her beautiful, clever Emma Crow Cushman, child of wealth on her father's and her Auntie's side, was her entrance into the highest society, on the level of an ambassador's wife—a society from which, due to her profession, Charlotte Cushman was excluded.

Whenever she brought up the subject of appointing Ned American minister to Italy, Seward, with alarming pessimism, shook his head sadly and answered, 'If the future of the country shall continue until then.'

Wayman Crow, Jr., by Rose Lamb, the only son of the wealthy, self-made St. Louis merchant.

Was the war going *that* badly, she wondered.

Seward might have been shaking his head thinking of the future of the country after it had been exposed to Ned.

Mr. Crow's exposure to Ned—and Charlotte—was getting the best of him that summer in Newport. This woman bringing his daughter to bed under the secretary of state's roof! Damn those Republicans! Charlotte was finding out that Wayman Crow had a hard and unrelenting side. There was some talk about her returning with the family to St. Louis for a visit. Angrily, Mr. Crow told Emma that Ned was in too great a state of dependency on him and on his aunt.

Wayman Crow was reaching his boiling point. One summer day at Newport, he looked at Charlotte closely and said sharply: 'Miss Cushman, Ned is a sensualist.'

Unlike the uncultured American 'jobbers' Charlotte portrayed in her Roman mosaic, self-made Wayman Crow did not come to Italy to buy bad copies and worse originals, but to support a unique homegrown woman artist, Harriet Hosmer. Mr. Crow, a civic leader and state senator, knew about more than dry goods.

If he hadn't at first, his four strong daughters and one weak son gave him an education. Cornie, his oldest, in a bad marriage with a husband who drank, would soon begin to take her children and go to Europe to be with Hattie as often as she could. When Cornelia Crow Carr later edited Harriet Hosmer's 'Life and Letters,' she changed some of Hattie's salutations, turning letters addressed to her into letters to her father, which made it look as if Hattie might have been sweet on *Wayman*! Charlotte herself was surprised by some of Cornie's letters; they read like those a woman might address to her lover.

The next in age was his tempestuous, outspoken, irreverent, flirty Mary. Charlotte felt Hattie was able to have too great an influence on her when she was young. Mary certainly did like the boys. Charlotte considered she was 'sexually hysterical,' a condition only marriage would change. She flirted outrageously with Ned in St. Louis. 'Don't let him think you love him too much,' Charlotte advised when Emma complained of the way her sister danced with her husband. 'No man living can bear this!' Recently Mary became engaged to Robert Emmons from a very good family, and Mr. Crow had no aversion to settling *this* couple prettily in Boston.

Then came Emma with her stubborn hold on Charlotte which Mr. Crow seemed unable to disengage. If he thought Emma's marriage to Ned would be a curative, especially since he had craftily succeeded in getting the young man to move to St. Louis, he found not only was he wrong, but he had saddled himself with Ned—who ate and drank and hunted and God-knows-what—while Mr. Crow's own partners looked on.

Isabel was still too young to be much trouble.

Mr. Crow's one son, Wayman Junior, was only six years old when Charlotte first met Emma. He just finished school at the primary department at Washington University the summer that Mr. Crow called Ned a sensualist, and was about to be sent to England to a private school in Twickenham, where he would take a prize for correct deportment and punctuality in the discharge of his duties. Eventually, after some world travel, he entered his father's firm.

According to a close friend, Wayman Junior had many of his father's values, was rigorously honest and not careless in money matters (even if he did know Ned in his formative years). But he had a peculiar cast of mind and was a slow learner. This friend witnessed him work diligently at Crow, Hargadine & Company, scrupulously discharging inconvenient and laborious duties, simply because he wanted to please his parents. 'His delicate sense of filial duty led him to comply with their anticipated yet unexpressed wishes.'

Anticipated yet unexpressed wishes.

When Wayman Junior was twenty-five years old he went on a long visit to his sister Mary and her husband, who by then had a home in England. He was recovering from alcoholism and was out of work. With them for a month, he had a relapse and was under doctor's supervision when, a few weeks later, he again appeared to be deranged: 'He was possessed of delusions, which he could not be got to see were delusions,' said brother-in-law Robert, who slept in his room and watched over him. He seemed quite docile the day he excused himself from the family at noon to get ready for lunch, went into his bedroom, took a razor, lay down on his bed, and slit his throat.

Mr. Crow built a Memorial Art Museum in St. Louis in his honor, on the corner of Locust and Nineteenth.

The tragedy was years away, the summer Mr. Crow lost patience with Ned—and with that slippery spinster he could not confront directly.

'Ah what a long time I have been with my darling this summer,' Charlotte wrote to Emma at sea off Ireland. It was a summer that lasted until November, and Charlotte still had to see to her ailing mother before returning to Rome and Miss Stebbins.

In London she found her mother more feeble than ever, and Mrs. Carlyle, having suffered her terrible street accident, too ill to be seen. She was torn about leaving her mother, but had to get back to Rome. What else could she do? It was already December and Miss Stebbins had been back from Florence for three months. Stebbins was moving into a new studio and was surrounded by workmen whose Italian she could not understand; not that Charlotte's was much better, but between the two of them, they got work done.

Of course brother Charles was there near Brixton for her mother, and Charlotte provided all the financial help she would need. She was quite aware that 'I am not much happiness to the poor dear soul, except that I am able to gratify all her physical requirements.' When she went to say goodbye, both mother and daughter thought it would be their last visit. Mary Eliza spent the entire time giving her daughter unsparing, detailed instructions on how to dispose of her remains. Charlotte, looking at her shrunken mother, not only felt guilt and dread, but saw her own future. She went back to Rome, conflicted, sadder.

Emma did not help matters. Perhaps the long summer they spent together in America gave Emma more of a bird's-eye view of what it meant to be too closely attached to a woman who like herself was born to rule.

Charlotte had been quite surprised when Emma wrote that it would be ridiculous for her and Ned to come to Rome until Ned had made more money in his partnership. What was he to *do* in Italy? Suddenly Emma was happier in St. Louis. (And being sensible about money?) Charlotte was willing to give up her personal happiness. If the partners were to continue with Ned after the present term of three years expired, well then, 'God speed you in every way. I will see you as often as I can—& you will see me as often as you can—until you have made your fortunes & are ready to come to me.'

Not that Charlotte was indifferent.

'Never suppose for a moment that I am cold or falling off in my affection—or that I do not love you as "in the olden time when we were young"—or that I am "changed" if I seem willing to let you off from a life with me. I want you to be happy in your own way. I may need you more some years hence—than I *absolutely* do now, while I am able to manage my own affairs—but the day may come when it will be *necessary* for someone belonging to me to be near me—& when that time comes I only hope they will not fail me.'

Charlotte's mother waiting to be buried alongside her favorite daughter, Mrs. Carlyle, lying in her red bedroom, looking like death to the few who were privileged to see her—well, Charlotte Cushman was an imitative animal. . . .

She was also as persistent as a force of nature. Auntie bought Ned a billiard table for his and Emma's new house in St. Louis—hardly an aid to the renewal of his partnership—and waited.

Ned a future ambassador? Ned and Emma living with her in Rome? Miss Stebbins 'has become more irritable than I can have supposed possible—poor dear Soul—I love her so much & am so sorry for her.'

Rome was a center of political unrest. The Victorian pope, Pius IX (Pio Nono), was, with his troops, holding out against Garibaldi's army, Mazzini's words, and Italian unification—which was actually eight years away. Still, for the expatriates, it was a high and spirited season.

Foxhunting had become the rage among the fashionable, taking over from the older, simpler pleasures of drives in the country. Charlotte participated in a two-day foxhunt along with forty to fifty people. Miss Stebbins recalled that the Americans weren't as well dressed as the Roman aristocrats, who added *bella figura,* if not expertise, to the experience. Nor were they the glorious riders that the sturdy English were with their soiled red coats speaking of real work and their unequaled noble horses. But the Americans were alert and ready to profit from their mistakes. They got every bit of energy they could out of their hacks, and would try *anything* (like Charlotte?)—holding on to the death.

There were so many fine balls that season, including the grand Bachelor's Ball. 'Your aunty went in canonicals—that is—the most beautiful white silk dress trimmed with the black lace flowers—which were waiting for me in Paris.' Charlotte arrived looking stunning at ten-thirty and did not come home until one-thirty. 'Young England was out for the night—& I danced until the small hours. The supper was splendid & all went off well. Your aunty was a very merry Bachelor!'

And a very well-dressed spinster, worthy of a wellborn niece. Charlotte threw aside her mannish bodices and Wellington boots and blessed her mother and her grandmother for one element in her nature, her ambition. 'I cannot endure the society of people beneath me in position or character or ability—& hate to have satellites of an inferior caliber.'

Then Seward disappointed her. The newspaperman Rufus King, not Ned, was appointed minister to Italy. Charlotte did what she always did when she couldn't control things. Took what life handed her and turned it to her advantage. She insinuated herself into the new minister's household by professing to like the wife. They were nice people, but would never get along on the seven thousand dollars a year the position paid. If King had just had fifteen hundred dollars of private money to add to that, what a difference it would make!

They couldn't hold out for long. Mrs. King confessed to Charlotte they were running into debt with two children to educate. The daughter was a practical, loving, helpful child. 'She is very fond of your auntie too—though that does not say much in *my* opinion for her judgment.'

Now, if Charlotte's children had the minister's position, with an apartment waiting for them as well as social comforts, carriage, horse, with nothing but suitable clothes to buy and their own receptions to give, why, they would not only live on the salary but save money.

Charlotte was sure that 'Mr Lincoln will be reelected—& Mr Seward kept in his place—with full power!' Emma must try to get some sort of promise that if King should resign, Mrs. Seward (Seward's daughter-in-law) would use her influence to put Ned in his place.

When first in Rome, Charlotte would go to Miss Stebbins' studio in the gardens and sit with her from eleven-thirty to one-thirty while she worked. Now, with Miss Stebbins' studio moved to San Basilico, Charlotte was seeing her less often. When she did visit, she found her not well or happy. 'She must have great sympathy in her work or she cannot work. . . . She is more delicate & poorly than I have ever seen her—& I am so sorry for her—for I cannot seem to drag her out of the dreadful slough into which she is plunged.'

Since childhood Miss Stebbins was a perfectionist. Working on two monumental commissions, to be executed in bronze, the statue of Horace Mann and the Bethesda Fountain for Central Park, her art had become her agony, giving her a wide swath on which to register despair. She modeled a fearsome Satan during these years—on her own, *not* on commission.

To further undercut Miss Stebbins' self-respect, Harriet Hosmer had been attacked in the *London Art Journal,* which reported that the full-length *Zenobia,* in the London International Exhibit, said to be by Miss Hosmer, was really the work of an Italian sculptor. The implication was that the women sculptors in Rome needed men to carry out their ideas, that they could not finish the work themselves. *All* the neoclassical sculptors used skilled Italian artisans to turn their small clay models into full-scale sculptures. Sculptors used such workmen since the time of the ancients, Charlotte pointed out. Miss Stebbins took the attack personally 'as a woman worker.' She was distressed beyond description, while Hattie was furious at this libel and wanted to sue.

When Charlotte was in England tending her sick mother, Hattie wrote to her and put the matter in her hands, as if Charlotte hadn't enough to do. Charlotte consulted an 'Eminent man' who gave the same advice as Charlotte would have. 'Don't let her go to law about it but force an apology from the editor.'

Rabid about the slur on her reputation, Hattie kept the controversy going, writing her own defense and pushing on for a full apology. She soon realized the uproar was turning into a free advertisement for herself. Her defense of the sculptor's method, and of women sculptors, was spreading her name in the art world.

She fanned the flames and did bring a suit for libel. Whatever the outcome, Charlotte shrewdly observed, the publicity from the notoriety would be worth it. All sculptors, male and female, *must* have skilled helpers. 'Hattie has more done for her than any one else—that is she lets the workman advance her figure farther than any of the others—but she is right! I never saw such crucifixion as Miss Stebbins . . . for she cannot accept these helpers & tries to struggle on to do *all* of her own work. I sometimes think she ought not to do it.'

These male sculptors in Rome were 'chiselers,' Charlotte told those who came to her gatherings. Not only did they chisel men out of marble, but they tried to chisel women out of their professional reputations. They were 'a set of vile men.'

William Wetmore Story believed she was trying to wreck all their reputations. He accused her of saying his statues were not his work but the work of his Italian helpers. He, like Hattie, had a studio full of male artisans who worked for next to nothing. '*I have said no such thing!*' she responded. 'I know that all sculptors require assistance from even human tools; all sculptors, I believe, have them, and *if* I say this of *you*, I say it of all!'

A rather legalistic defense that Story, once a lawyer, was sure to recognize. In the meantime Charlotte told Kate Field for one that Story was an 'independent humbug who took other people's ideas for himself.' (Carlyle, by the way, described Story as a consummate dilettante—with a good singing voice.)

The male sculptors were a group of card-playing, whisky-drinking cads, though Charlotte did consider Story, Arthur Drexler, and Charlie Perkins gentlemen. She talked against the whole crass lot of them, and the male sculptors ached for revenge—expatriate style. Cushman often sang at parties—her renditions of Burns and Scottish ballads generally were favorites. Her ruined voice, with its raspy, dramatic range, stirred people's emotions. At one of these Roman gatherings, the sculptor Randolph Rogers stood up and sang Charlotte's songs, imitating her mannish voice and her facial gestures. Instead of the tears that greeted Charlotte's performances, there were gales of laughter. Rogers finished, smiled, and turned to Charlotte—who, good actress that she was, acknowledged his bow and brought her hands together.

The American consul to Rome was a male artist, art editor, and writer himself, William J. Stillman. He thought Charlotte turned against him at that point because he was the male sculptors' friend and played cards with them. Stillman had earlier reported theatre news for the *New York Evening Post* and co-edited *The Crayon,* and Charlotte entertained him when he first came to Rome. But then she found reasons to complain about what she considered his incompetence to Seward. Even Story would be a better consul; of

Horace Mann, clay model, mid-1860s, left, and model of *The Angel of the Waters* for the Bethesda Fountain, ca. 1870, below, both from Emma Stebbins' scrap album. Horace Mann (Nathaniel Hawthorne and Elizabeth Peabody's brother-in-law) was a champion of women's education. The Bethesda Fountain, inaugurated in Central Park in 1873 with both Miss Stebbins and Charlotte Cushman in attendance, stands as one of the great accomplishments of the women sculptors in Rome.

course Ned Cushman would be best, particularly with her advising him. When Stillman realized Charlotte's ambition for her nephew was behind her animosity, he vowed to make Rome 'too hot' for Miss Cushman. He had no idea yet of the danger he faced, of how virtuously ruthless Charlotte Cushman could be when defending—never herself—always her belongings.

Charlotte now had two circumstances to control: her spouse's career and her lover's future. The two came together in her battle against the male sculptors.

As she parried with the sculptors—and Stillman—she wrote Ned a secret letter: 'I look to you—as my one hope & dependence . . . to come to look after me and relieve me from some of my cares and anxieties!' Assuming the partners would not want him after his three-year contract, she told her nephew her home in Rome was large enough for him, Emma, and their future progeny, her means sufficient to keep them all at one third of what it cost him to live in America.

Ned was furious over Auntie's customary disparagement of his worth (and her accurate assessment of his business acumen) and showed the letter to Emma, who became very angry at Charlotte's duplicity.

Charlotte protested that she had only been doing her duty. She wrote to Ned in secret because she did not want to unsettle Emma about St. Louis. She knew what a pride and comfort the girl was to Mr. Crow and she *would not take* that comfort from 'the Pater.'

She herself was ambivalent. She had a terrible yearning for them, but what if they were unhappy in Rome? 'Then what a terrible responsibility I should feel upon my soul.'

Soon she discovered a new ploy among the male chiselers. William Wetmore Story convinced Hattie to move out of her house on Via Gregoriana and take a good apartment that would be available near him and his wife the year after next.

'Mr. Story & I are not on the most intimately friendly terms & therefore the sort of secret underhanded way in which it has been done does not make me think any more of Hattie, for it has come out quite by accident. . . . Of course I am too glad to be rid of her after her being six winters my guest, but the manner of doing it is quite worthy of her. Now after she is gone I shall furnish that apartment & let it so as almost to pay my rent here—and I should have an apartment for my darlings if they wanted one to themselves which would be very reasonable for them & yet they could be under my roof.'

Harriet Hosmer with her monumental bronze of Senator Thomas Hart Benton, ca. 1862. In Rome, her mentor John Gibson wrote, 'The Americans may now boast of possessing what no nation in Europe possesses, a public statue by a woman.'

Harriet Hosmer surrounded by her workers, 1867. Hattie's success is mirrored in the size of her studio; she had as many workers as the male sculptors in Italy. Her former anatomy instructor in St. Louis delighted 'to see a woman dare to scale the mountain height of fame.'

Plotting for Emma's return to Rome and protecting Miss Stebbins from the calumny of the male sculptors, Charlotte became relentless, secretive, and as destructive as possible—a female tiger protecting her cubs, her actions fueled by her most secret, stifled ambitions.

If she had been beautiful, Stillman wrote in his memoirs, Charlotte Cushman would have held all society in the palm of her hand. He considered her the most intelligent woman he ever met. She had impeccable tact, the most refined understanding of the world, and an exquisite ability to put herself in the other person's place—a person of quality, that is. He, like everyone she knew, noted how unlike an actress she was off the stage, how unfull of herself, how concerned about others. But while her friends saw this as her glory, a man such as Stillman, whom she had made her enemy, saw in the very naturalness of her demeanor, the unselfish and generous concern in her eyes, the highest example of her craft.

'My *social* position is very good *privately*,' she wrote to Emma. 'But you can tell Mrs Seward that my former profession bans my being received or presented at any foreign court or Embassy. You would say—in your love for me—I dont want to go to where you cannot go—but this would not satisfy me for you *as your father's daughter*.'

Or as *Charlotte Cushman's niece*. Emma Crow Cushman must have all the honor due her.

How humiliated Charlotte must have been when naïve Mrs. King asked if Charlotte could be present at the French Embassy to greet an old friend married to a count and was told Miss Cushman's *former profession* prevented it.

Her former profession—and her business acumen—however, was what paved the way for her belongings. Charlotte took over the house next door, at 40 Via Gregoriana. She planned to make the main entrance to her house through it. She was going to put a walkway across the garden at 38 Via Gregoriana down to Miss Stebbins' old studio, and make a stable of that part. Next to the old studio was a place she rented for a coach house, over which she made a second studio for Miss Stebbins and an apartment for her coachman Giuseppe.

Had she stayed in America during the Civil War, she told people, she would have made through speculation the greatest fortune a woman in her country ever made. Still, through her patriotism and her business sense, she was becoming wealthier each year, whether or not the court received her.

'When you come again you will hardly know the place,' Charlotte wrote to Emma. 'Sometimes I think I am foolish to do all this for I dont know how long I may live in it, & then comes the thought, "live while you do live" & never mind the cost.'

She was glad that Emma liked the diamond earrings she bought her. If she ever decided to sell them, she'd make a handsome profit. She saw a sapphire and thought of Emma as well. If her Philadelphia deals turned out she'd indulge in a few nice things—including pearls, 'Big ones.'

Emma was pregnant yet again that summer and Charlotte wanted her to come to England for her confinement. Charlotte's frail mother still hung on to life—and opinion. Mary Eliza insisted it was a bad idea: Emma would be anxious and worried and overexcited, as she always was when Charlotte was around. 'Do you see dear what is thought of you by others, never mind—we make our own world & it matters little what anyone thinks—does it?'

Emma made up her own mind. She would *not* return to St. Louis to live and she *would* come to Auntie in London for the birth—and she'd bring Ned with her for a needed respite. The partners did not—or dared not—fire Ned. More insultingly, they were willing to keep him, but no longer as a partner.

Charlotte expected that Mr. Crow believed 'I have seduced you away!'

She encouraged Emma to show her father in a subtle way that he was responsible for Emma's actions. For by bringing Ned to St. Louis, he had made it impossible '*for you & I to be together.*'

Had he just been reasonable when he had the chance and set Ned up in business in Boston, Emma would have been contented and Charlotte could have alternated summers with her there and in England.

Though her father opposed it, the very pregnant Emma sailed to her 'ladie love.'

When Emma and Ned arrived, Auntie was at the waters at Harrogate with her mother and Miss Stebbins, laid up by a terrible blood-red rash that had spread over her hands. This ailment, suffered by the most popular Lady Macbeth of her time, might have given a less focused person a start. But all of Charlotte's energies were directed toward the welfare of Emma and the healthy birth of their daughter. Charlotte rented a house in Manchester for the confinement and Miss Stebbins stayed away. It was Sallie who saw to all the moving, complaining only to an equally drained Miss Stebbins that she was being overtaxed.

So, after the miscarriages and the 'Labour Lost,' Charlotte was with Emma in Manchester when labor began. She sat outside the room, listening to the moans of the woman she loved, praying her travail would soon be over. Ned was sitting by her and she took his hand. They heard a double cry, Emma and Baby at once! Baby shouted out in the most lusty way the moment it was born. When they were called in, Baby, rolled in a blanket, was deposited in Charlotte's arms. All she could do was weep tears of joy. 'I assure you I could scarcely see my way across the room.' She sat down by the fire, not rocking, but holding her own flesh and blood. She was much too thankful to care whether the baby was a boy or girl. In late September 1864, Emma Crow Cushman brought her ungentle mistress away from Babyless Places.

Hattie wrote to Wayman Crow that Charlotte was in a highly emotional state, tense about the welfare of her new charge. 'I philosophically remarked to her that now she sees what it is to have babies.' She couldn't resist writing to Cornie, 'Don't you think Emma will be disappointed it can't be a little Charlotte?'

But a boy was compensated for by the way he linked two families. Baby was named Wayman Crow Cushman—though Charlotte loved to call him Baby.

By the time Emma and Ned and Baby sailed back to the States on the *Canada* at the beginning of December, Sallie Mercer was looking dreadful. 'She has become so pale & emaciated & has a *green* look—which is very bad & which frightens me about her.' The doctors said Sallie's end was near. Though Sallie had made Charlotte indignant at times, 'I cannot bear to contemplate losing her, & I fear I have suffered her to do too much hard work this summer when she really wanted rest.'

Not only did Sallie make arrangements for a very pregnant Emma, see to all the moving about, help with Mary Eliza, and take care of Charlotte's needs, she was witnessing Charlotte's relationship with Emma. Her loyalties in this matter were elsewhere, with Ned and particularly with Miss Stebbins, who *she* had the eyes to see was suffering and whom she listened to and comforted as much as she could.

No wonder Charlotte was indignant at times! Sallie was a one-woman Greek chorus, the discord in the house visible in her emaciated appearance and the green of her face. As soon as the Ned Cushmans sailed back to the States, Sallie foiled the doctors and miraculously recovered.

After President Lincoln was reelected in November 1864, the Sewards wrote to offer Charlotte a consulship for Ned at either Ravenna or Venice. She declined it. 'If Ned has any office, I would prefer it to be one which would give him the right to the *best* society.'

However, back in Rome, she was so lonely for Emma and their Baby that she decided she would consider the Roman consulship. Even if it was not a diplomatic position that automatically led to being accepted at court, the way Ned and Emma could entertain at Via Gregoriana would make it into a more important office.

'Oh it is very terrible to love anything so dearly as to make one's happiness dependent on it,' she wrote to Emma at the start of the New Year.

Listless and depressed, she was not the bohemian 'Granny Cush' she planned to be. The old demons all came back. She *must* have Emma with her: 'I always have loved you ever since I first knew you—better & better each year that I have known you, but I love you now in every way *double,* because I love you for yourself, then as Baby's mamma. Then for Baby and then for myself.' She crossed out 'myself,' changing it to 'Ned's dear self.'

Charlotte was desperate: 'I told Charlie in one of my confidential moments that I could not live in this way any longer & must have you with me.' Her brother responded: 'I think the idea of your having them with you—& letting Ned lead a life of idleness, perfectly absurd!'

This was an example of the help she got from her family—as usual. Show her a business twenty-six-year-old Ned could get involved in and not lose all he had gained, and she would never take him from it. 'I have proved that—by letting him sacrifice my happiness & your comfort by going to St. Louis to live for three years.' Not to mention the seventy-five hundred dollars she had paid for his trial partnership.

He'd be robbed in any future business he attempted alone. There would be nothing in it for him but mortification—as it had been in St. Louis. 'He will have plenty of occupation here—looking after you & baby & me & the stable & keeping himself in health by exercise.'

She wrote to Ned: 'I don't think it would be possible for me to love anything in the world more than I love Emma—but my love for you though differing in kind does not differ in degree.'

Then Charlotte called in all her debts. She alone had helped Ned in life. She stood the only member of her family able or willing to earn any livelihood for him, all through her love, not through any legal obligation. 'Thus you have been like my own child & thus have I loved & cared for you, & through this love & care do I make my claims upon you.'

She prayed Ned would come to her, at least until the war was over. She knew the Sewards were now offering him the consulship in Rome and lived in fear that Ned had already refused it. He must accept. He did not even have to think of the work. There was an old man who acted as vice-consul who would do everything for him. Not only that, the consulship would give him the ability to go in and out of foreign ports without customs or duties. So if he had a yacht at any time, he could go about in it to any port he liked.

Ned accepted.

Auntie told him to order the *New York Times* to come to him in Rome and to bring two big American flags for decoration. He must not forget corn, oysters (fresh, not pickled), and tomatoes from Mr. Murray in Baltimore to bring to the Kings. And by all means Emma *must* accompany him to Washington to thank the Sewards!

Consul Stillman—who needed the meager six hundred dollars attached to the position—said he'd make Rome 'too hot' for Charlotte. 'It seems that in a sort of grim humour, M Seward & Ford have given Mr Stillman a post down south of the Grecian Islands, Candia, where he will find a place—*an island hot enough* for *him.*'

The newspapers, somehow (need one ask how?), picked up the story of Consul Stillman's removal before he got the official word, so he was doubly mortified. Imagine, the man had the gall to excite rich Americans in Rome, telling them he was being persecuted by Charlotte! Did it matter? The word around Rome was 'Miss Cushman has done Stillman up brown.'

Hattie had the last laugh too, writing to Charlotte that in New York, in two days, one thousand and fifty people came to see the exhibit of her notorious *Zenobia,* and a thousand of them paid (single tickets twenty-five cents; packaged tickets one dollar).

Even if the libel case had gone against her, it would have been worth it as an advertisement of her work and her character. The world likes nothing better than to be caught up in and carried away by someone like Hattie, Charlotte opined. 'For she is *selfish & arrogant & bold!* These things which

Isabel Crow, the youngest of the Crow sisters, with her nephew Wayman Crow Cushman, 'Baby,' ca. 1866.

combined with a large amount of self-esteem & love of approbation & secretiveness—go to make up—"Pluck"—an Anglo Saxon virtue.'

And lo and behold, Miss Stebbins was suddenly thriving as well. The overworked sculptor had developed a circle of women who gravitated to her. In fact, to preoccupied Charlotte's delight, she 'has been having many lovers this winter.' These friends had been better than morphine. They seemed to relieve her of her depression.

Then the terrible telegram of 15 April 1865; Mrs. King herself brought it to Charlotte: 'The dreadful intelligence of Mr Lincoln's assassination & death & *Mr Seward's precarious* state from the same dreadful cause.' Seward, recuperating from a carriage accident, had been stabbed in his bed by a man posing as a confidential messenger.

Mrs. King thought Lincoln had been stabbed too, but Charlotte out of nowhere replied, 'No, he has been *shot* by someone going into his box door, shot in the back!'

She could not believe it had been done by one of her own countrymen in these enlightened modern days, and she rejected the idea, telling Mrs. King, 'It is too theatrical a thing to be done by an American!'

A few hours later, a telegram arrived saying the assassin brothers were named *Booth*. She immediately thought, 'The madman John Wilkes Booth!' That perfectly reckless daredevil!

The next telegram: 'The assassin is John Wilkes Booth—Mr Seward is better!'

The name of Booth was disgraced 'forever & forever.' How could Edwin Booth ever act, ever hold his head up in public again? Think of Edwin with his child's name and picture in the papers. Uncanny that Charlotte knew beforehand that Lincoln had been shot, and that the assassination had a theatrical character. 'These instincts of mine are peculiar.'

In personal terms, it should have been her hour of victory. All of her plans were being fulfilled. Her children were coming to her in Rome, Ned to replace a humiliated and defeated Stillman. Mr. Crow was not able to keep them away from her after all. In her love for Emma she had found not only a lover and friend but her own motherhood. In Miss Stebbins she had a woman of genius who needed her support to live and to work. In Jane Carlyle she had the triumph of an important friendship. She had doubled her beautiful home so that all her belongings could live together in comfort—and privacy if they demanded it. Her grand stables and Thoroughbred horses would provide recreation and transportation for all.

Still, at forty-nine, she found herself more excitable, shaky, depressed, and tearful than she had ever been. Part of the reason was physical—a female problem, an excess of bleeding, that would require a simple operation in England that summer.

The greater part was Henry Stebbins arriving in Rome in May with a message from the whole family, four sisters and brother Henry. All— excluding Miss Stebbins' mother—disapproved of Miss Stebbins' relationship with Charlotte Cushman. 'They felt she was morally, socially, spiritually, physically injured by it.'

Previously Miss Stebbins had terrible passages with her sisters and brother about her living with Charlotte. 'They have been always jealous of her love for me.' Now the family had given up seeing Ned and Emma as well. For in New York 'they had spoken entirely too freely of all the family,' and said things they should not have regarding Miss Stebbins' life with Charlotte.

Miss Stebbins, who had been like a stone wall most of the year, finally told Charlotte she thought their relationship was doomed anyway. She was sure Ned and Emma were determined to come to Rome and throw her out. They did not like her, talked about her, mimicked her. 'She has always been a little afraid of you,' Charlotte wrote to Emma, 'afraid of your little satirical speeches, ways & thoughts, afraid of your absorbing too much of my love & devotedness, afraid that you did not love her & would be glad to take me away from her.' Charlotte was kept unaware of all of this the previous summer when Baby was on the way. Miss Stebbins confided only in Sallie, 'for she saw I was anxious & troubled enough.'

Now the doctors told Charlotte straight out that Miss Stebbins was so worn down physically and emotionally that she might die if not kept from anxiety and disturbance. 'I see her pale wasted cheeks, she is like a skeleton, so thin.'

It was only at this juncture that Charlotte realized 'I have not been considerate or thoughtful enough of & for her.' And she admitted: 'I have allowed myself to be untrue to much I promised her. . . . When I first knew her & took the obligation of her life and future upon me [I] did not know of other cares which were to fall upon me—*of other loves & affections which were in store for me.* I was then free to promise. I have not kept my word too well.'

She urged Emma to love Miss Stebbins, who had put an 'Element' into her life that was necessary to it. 'She is high, true, noble & self sacrificing— she has made me happy—& for that my family not being able to live with me themselves ought to be so grateful to her.' Emma must convince the older woman that she did not mean to unseat her in Charlotte's affections.

Things with Miss Stebbins were so awry that Charlotte wished her belongings would not come to Europe to live until the autumn, after her female operation. But in July Emma, pregnant once more, arrived in England with Ned and Baby.

Charlotte had the operation in August and recuperated first at her mother's house, with 'a great friend & favorite of dear Mrs Carlyle,' Mrs. Venturi, staying with her. Miss Stebbins was not there. Neither were Ned and Emma, off traveling with Emma's parents and Hattie. Right before the surgery, Mrs. Carlyle sent her a beautiful shawl. She must have changed it the night she went to see Frances Power Cobbe, and Sallie put it away and she hadn't seen it since. 'I have lost Mrs Carlyle's present.' She would rather have lost anything else.

The wound to the womb was slow to heal and she was in a very weakened condition. She needed to be dressed by Sallie and it was very difficult to walk down stairs.

Henry Stebbins, brother of Miss Stebbins, about the time he went to Rome in 1865. Successful banker, stockbroker, New York City parks commissioner, and member of Congress during the Civil War, Henry was instrumental in securing the commission of the Bethesda Fountain for Central Park and later attempted to separate his sister from Charlotte Cushman.

As she recuperated in North Wales at the end of 'this miserable summer,' she hardly knew how to control herself when she was disturbed by anything that irritated or inflamed her. 'It seems so hard that I should have been given such a bitter cup to drink, just at this time when all seemed so fair for peace, rest & enjoyment. But perhaps my trial has been sent to me in love. I was too proud, too arrogant, too happy, too blest, & I could not and did not bless & love and thank God enough in my happiness.'

For the worst had happened, something Charlotte never deemed possible, never imagined.

Miss Stebbins had not been faithful to her. Among the circle of women who had gravitated to her, her spouse found a lover, in a later century's definition of the word. It could have been Isa Blagden on a long visit to them at the time. Isa wrote a beautiful poem on the death of Miss Stebbins' beloved dog Bushie; Miss Stebbins kept it among her papers. Charlotte made sure to keep up with Isa Blagden, just as she would Emma's future lovers, and she clipped her death notice, which remains among her papers. Small things. Charlotte knew who the woman was, but more importantly, how could she have been so blind! Had any self-absorbed husband ever been blinder? Charlotte could have kicked herself.

'Be patient with me dear darling, if I seem to fail you for the moment,' she wrote to Emma, who was still traveling. 'I am steering a bark through troubled waters but shall come out all right, bringing with me what I have so dearly prized for eight & a half years, that I cannot give it up without struggle & consequent suffering. If I did not feel that I had been greatly myself to blame in letting it go drifting about to be picked up by any one close, I might suffer less, but enough of this subject, which only you know of, except ourselves & those most nearly interested. It will all come right in time. But you know that your Auntie has an adhesive nature, that what she once loves she never wholly gives up. Even though separated by distance time & feeling. There could not come a revolution in her small world—so near the heart—& not bring with it convulsion of suffering.'

On Baby's first birthday, Charlotte was with her mother in Brixton, and again taking rides with Mrs. Carlyle, who seemed suddenly in straits less tragic than her own.

Charlotte wrote to her little lover that she had been very nearly broken to bits over 'my great disappointment in the fidelity of Aunt Emma.' Only the love of her darling daughter and friend kept her from drowning.

But to stay afloat Cushman must not lose either woman. This too would become part of the Roman mosaic.

The Red Bedroom

LONDON, SCOTLAND

1863–1866

S O IT was that Charlotte's belongings came to live with her on Via
Gregoriana. Ned was the American consul to Rome and Charlotte
one of the most sought-after and most lavish hostesses in that city,
making a place in society for her nephew and his wellborn wife. Surrounded by her belongings, the old and curious paradox of her existence
came back to haunt her.

The slow waning of Charlotte's vitality, her vague sadness, would be
attributed to her empathy for Jane Carlyle. To some extent that was true.
'You will be very sorry for the news I have to send you,' Sarah Dilberoglue
wrote to her from London.

There had been nothing left of Mrs. Carlyle really, that summer at St.
Leonards three years before. If she looked like death in London, was as light
as a twelve-year-old child when Mr. Larkin came to her bedroom and put
her in her wooden box, one can only imagine, through her handwriting and
Carlyle's sudden attentiveness—he stayed with her at times in the little
house they leased at St. Leonards—the unspeakable condition she was in.
But somehow, no matter what the doctors said, she knew the pain she was
feeling in her vagina and womb was real, not simply a morbid dwelling.

On the eve of Jane's sixty-third birthday, she made her own decision.
She couldn't sleep, she couldn't eat. First Dr. Blakiston and now Carlyle's
brother Dr. John were doing her no good at St. Leonards. She would make
a run for it. Scotland was where she wanted to go. As she grew older, home
thoughts absorbed her.

It took her eight years after her mother's death to be able to return at all—and only because cousin Babbie married and moved to Edinburgh. 'Oh Babbie! how I wish it had not been your *idea* to pitch your tent in the "valley of the shadow of Marriage."'

By then, the train ran past Haddington: 'I *cannot* fly past Haddington—merely shutting my eyes.' So she stopped there for the first time in *sixteen* years—incognito. She stayed at the old Georges Inn at High Street and looked out its windows up to her old house. 'The same street, the same houses; but so *silent,*—dead,—petrified! it looked, the old place, just as I had seen it at Chelsea in my dreams—only *more* dreamlike!'

She walked through the town, doing the circuit as when 'in my teens.' But where were all the living people one used to meet? What could have come to strike the place so dead?

She threw back her veil finally: 'I was getting confident that I might have ridden like *the Lady Godiva* thro Haddington, with impunity.'

She walked into a cooper's shop. 'Then, in the character of the travelling Englishwoman, suddenly seized with an unaccountable passion for wooden dishes, I questioned the Cooper as to the *Past and Present* of his town.' He told her, 'Doctor Welsh's death was the sorest loss ever came to the Place. His daughter went away into England and—died there!'

Oh, he remembered Miss Welsh famously, and gave her a nice elegy. He used to think her the '*tastiest* young Lady in the whole Place—but she was very—not just to call *proud,*—very *reserved in her company.*'

Jane left the shop feeling more than ever like her own ghost.

The cooper must have had second thoughts about Mrs. Carlyle's death, because the next day when he saw her on the street he demanded to know her name. She told him the truth. He looked pleased and asked how many children she had.

'*None.*'

'None! None at all! then what on Earth have you been *doing* all this time?'

'Amusing myself.'

She woke before dawn that day and soon after six she was '*haunting*' her old house. The garden door was locked, the house needed paint and white-wash. It had a 'bedimmed melancholy look.' Like her, the house had seen better days. 'It was difficult for me to realise to myself that the people inside were only *asleep*—and not *dead—dead since many years.*'

She planned to clear her father's grave before she left town. She saw it yesterday, covered by moss, surrounded by nettles. 'It was strange the feeling

The Jane Welsh Carlyle House, Haddington, Scotland. An interior house, built in 1797, where Jane was born in 1801 and spent her first twenty-five years. Edward Irving tutored her there; Thomas Carlyle met her there. Her parents and Edward Irving were long gone when Jane finally returned on an anonymous visit in 1849.

of almost *glad* recognition that came over me, in finding so many familiar figures out of my childhood and youth all gathered together in one place.'

Naturally she got to the churchyard way before the sexton opened the gates. The surrounding wall was very high; in her letters she called it ten feet high, in her journal seven. For a moment she was Jeannie Welsh again: she made a wild dash, pulled herself up the wall, and dropped safely down the other side.

'A feat I should never have imagined to *try* in my actual phase, not even with a mad bull at my heels, if I had not trained myself to it at a more elastic age.'

Not that jumping the wall at the age of forty-eight made her feel alive again. 'I had none of that feeling—moi.' She knew she was dead. 'Only what one has well learnt one never forgets.'

At eight o'clock the sexton arrived: 'How in the world did you get in?'

'Over the wall.'

'No! surely you couldn't mean *that*?'

'Why not?'

'Lordsake,' he cried in real admiration, 'there is *no end* to you!'

Leaving Haddington, she took a seat in the railway carriage next to an old gentleman whom she immediately recognized. In younger days he made the little obelisk which still hung in her Chelsea bedroom. She felt comfortable enough around this incredibly aged Mr. Lea to lay her hand on his arm, turn away, and say, 'Thank God here is one person I feel no difficulty about.'

'I don't know you. Who are you?' He remained as blunt as he had been.

'Guess!'

'Was it you who got over the church-yard wall this morning? I saw a stranger-lady climb the wall and I said to myself that's Jeannie Welsh!—no other woman would climb the wall instead of going in at the gate—*are* you Jeannie Welsh?'

Yes, she was. They shook hands, they even embraced. After things calmed down, he put his hand on her shoulder and asked, 'Now tell me, my Dear, why *did* you get over the wall instead of just asking for the key?'

In Edinburgh, reunited with her Babbie, she ended the journal of her return to Haddington; 'Much Ado About Nothing' she entitled it. With a 'lily white hand' she gaily 'bid herself adieu,' at the same time making that chilling remark: 'It is only in connection with the Past that I can get up a sentiment for myself—The Present Mrs Carlyle is what shall I say?— '*detestable*—upon *my* honour!'

Five years later, the past came to her again. She was fifty-four years old, and was so ill that cold winter that she only went out one night: to a party given by Anne Procter, her husband the poet Barry Cornwall, and her daughter the poet Adelaide Anne Procter. Would she go upstairs, Mrs. Procter inquired. Her mother, Mrs. Montagu, wished to see her.

She had little enough to do with Mrs. Montagu since she arrived in

London twenty years before. At the end of her stay at the desolate Craigen-puttock Jane confessed to the Noble Lady that she feared she might be going insane. Mrs. Montagu pooh-poohed her, writing that Jane had gotten everything she wished for, and she better be careful lest she wind up with *real* problems to plague her. Jane treated her in a formal manner ever since.

That night Jane walked up to the attic. In a low-ceilinged room, surrounded by artistically arranged pictures that once hung in her grand drawing room, the Noble Lady sat, a proud pagan of an ancient, awaiting her death. There wasn't a fold of her skirts out of place or a tear in her eye. Jane sat down opposite her, on a low chair, and listened to Mrs. Montagu 'speak of Edward Irving and long ago as if it were last year—last month!' In fact, Edward was dead twenty years, dead of the tuberculosis that claimed two of his children, dead the year Jane and Carlyle came to London for good (without telling Mrs. Montagu they were arriving). Dead at forty-two, the same age as her father.

In that ignoble little attic room, with the incongruous chatter of the dinner party coming from below, Mrs. Montagu spoke and the past gathered around Jane too. 'I fairly laid my head on her lap and burst into tears!'

Then, right before her illness, it was Jane herself speaking of Edward Irving to Margaret Oliphant, remembering not the fanatical Edward who came to believe Christ would appear on earth in his lifetime, the Edward who believed God spoke through members of his congregation and who allowed them to interrupt services speaking in tongues. Not the Edward whom the Scottish Church disavowed, the Edward who formed his own church, whose followers were called 'Irvingites.' How Carlyle pleaded to his friend against *that* Edward, how Jane cried! There would not have been any speaking in tongues if she had married Edward!

While the sixty-year-old Jane and thirty-year-old Margaret drove round the park, Jane told her the story of her childhood and of her tutor, the big young Annandale student who set her up on a table and taught her Latin: 'I felt a little as I had felt with my mother's stories, that I myself remembered the little girl seated on the table to be on his level, repeating her Latin verbs to young Edward Irving, and all the wonderful life and hope that were about them,—the childhood and the youth and aspiration never to be measured.'

Scottish Margaret Oliphant was one of the last to come to say goodbye before Jane was carried out of her house in the wooden box to St. Leonards.

Margaret Oliphant. 'Mrs Oliphant, "Authoress of" etc,'
Thomas Carlyle wrote on this undated photo. She wrote:
'I have written because it gave me pleasure, because it
came natural to me, because it was like talking or breathing, besides the big fact that it was necessary for me to
work for my children.'

Right before she was confined to her red bedroom, at Swan & Edgar's in
London, buying some tapes and things, a nice-looking boy served her. He
sounded 'homelike,' though he was doing his best 'to be Anglified.'

'You are Scotch,' Jane said, 'without consideration for the mortified vanity of a youth trying to speak *fine*.'

'Yes, I am,' he answered tartly.

'I should say you come from Dumfriesshire?'

'Yes, I do.' He was 'almost startled.'

'Dumfriesshire is partly *my* country, too; you are from the Nithsdale,—
from near Thornhill, are you not?'

By now the young man was meek. He did indeed come from near Thornhill, from a place called Dabton, if she knew it.

'Oh don't I?' Then she asked him if he knew Holm Hill.

He answered in the most 'unadulterated Scotch': 'Oh, fine! . . . I know it fine!'

That was where Dr. Russell lived! Now, finding St. Leonards was doing her no good, Jane craved one more visit to Holm Hill, to see her cherished friend Mary Dobbie Russell, who, along with her doctor husband James, had nursed Jane's mother in her last illness. She resolved to return to the kind people, the unsooty white lambs, the pure milk, the green meadows of her Scotland. Mrs. Carlyle was dead, but in Scotland Jeannie Welsh once lived.

Carlyle was with her at the house on 117 Marina at the time. Displaying the duality that existed at the very core of his being, he would remember the place: 'Dreary and tragic was our actual situation there, but we strove to be of hope, and were all fixedly intent to do our best. The house was new, clean, light enough, and well aired; otherwise paltry in the extreme—small, misbuilt every inch of it; a despicable, cockney, scamped edifice; a rickety bandbox rather than a house.'

London was home, not Holm Hill, he told her. Well then, she'd return to London. But not to that red bedroom, not to Cheyne Row, never, never. She'd stay with the Forsters if they would have her. They had come to visit her in St. Leonards, but she had been too ill to see them and sent down a pathetic scrawl of a note instead. Carlyle called this sudden desire to leave a fixed resolution of her own and she executed it. With Carlyle's doctor brother John escorting her, on the eve of her sixty-third birthday, she got on the express train—and 'shot away.'

At the Forsters' that night, even through the sounds of traffic, she got some disturbed rest, her first sleep in twelve nights. On her birthday morning, she came downstairs and 'found there much kindness, and much state, and a fine expectation that I was merely passing through!'

Then another decision. She *ordered* Dr. John to get ready for the night train to Scotland. Since she'd find no rest in London, she'd leave that very night. And off they sped. On board she drank four glasses of champagne. At the Carlisle border where they had to detrain, she ate a good breakfast. 'John was dreadfully ill-tempered: we quarreled incessantly, but he had the grace to be ashamed of himself after, and apologise. On the whole, it was a birthday of good omen. My horrible ailment kept off as by enchantment.'

John brought her to his and Carlyle's relatives in Dumfries, but she was as sick there as before. Added to that, she and the relatives were in a carriage accident the first week she arrived.

A week after her birthday she wrote to Carlyle, still at St. Leonards: 'Oh what a fool dream that by putting myself on a railway I could get whirled away from my misery! or that there was any place quiet enough for me to sleep in than the grave. . . . I have put hundreds of miles between us—and am as ill and *need* you as much as ever. . . . Oh my Dear my Dear I am so lonely and miserable.'

By now, Carlyle's letters too were ripe with tenderness and panic.

Brother John was a different story. She'd never gotten along that well with him. Carlyle had helped his brother through medical school; his career consisted of becoming the personal physician of an aristocratic lady and being in attendance for her as she traveled. He became a translator of Dante as well and was often to stay at Cheyne Row, like a younger brother still, whenever and for as long as he wished, without attempting to pay back hospitality. Jane thought the man was as subtle as shoe leather. And now that he had taken over her case from Dr. Blakiston (and from his absent eldest brother), his ego was involved. Just like Dr. Blakiston, Jane wrote, 'he is bent on making me out 'much better' because he had had charge of me.'

This doctor's daughter was the worst kind of patient—one who did not get well no matter how good her doctor's opinion of himself. She told her in-laws she was going on to Holm Hill to stay with the Russells, who had tended her mother, to put herself under Dr. Russell's care. They were good people, and Jane loved them. They brought back the only thing that soothed her: the golden days of the past.

Dr. John was obviously offended. She even refused to let him accompany her to Holm Hill. 'I have not had so much pleasure in him as to prolong an intercourse a moment beyond that I could help,' she wrote to Carlyle. 'He has been very hard and cruel—and MEAN inconceivably! but THAT is *his own* affair.'

It actually was inconceivable: 'Fancy him telling me in my agony yesterday that "if I had ever done anything in my life this would not have been; that no poor woman with work to mind had ever had such an ailment as this of mine since the world began"!!!'

'She never could forget again,' Carlyle wrote on this letter. Or forgive. Carlyle's own brother, a doctor to boot, had blamed *her* for her childlessness. She who had been cast in Babyless Places before she had a realistic understanding of what Carlyle meant when he told her he could not love. She accepted the barren existence, the lack of the wine of life, the lack of giving mother love. But according to Geraldine, she could never forgive Carlyle for her childlessness. That was what made her bitter. The racking pain in her womb, the irritation in her genitals were illnesses that fit her situation, surely. But illnesses of the flesh they were, of her very real and throbbing nerves, not of her imagination; on that, frail as she was, she insisted.

The Russells met Jane at the railway station that summer and brought her to their home, Holm Hill.

There, Mary Russell, less than two years younger than Jane, became 'a nurse like my own mother—I have had no such nursing.'

And Dr. Russell, Thomas Carlyle's age, was a healer of Jane's father's ilk, albeit one who had studied in the United States. He was a doctor, a contemporary remembered, who put on his short trousers, thick-soled boots, and his distinctive drab overcoat and walked briskly to tend to patients scattered all over the district. He often covered thirty miles a day, no matter what kind of weather. And he was the kind of doctor who listened to what a patient had to say. He was the trusted depository of many family secrets.

James Russell was close to seventy and retired from practice—though he was still the bank agent for the district—when Jane came to him in dire need. The Russells, like the Carlyles, were childless.

They were charitable, well-loved people. Mary's father was a minister of what was called the Relief Church. After their deaths, the Russells were commemorated in a long stained-glass window over the altar of their Church of Morton, Thornhill. Mary's good works glint there today as Tabitha distributing food and clothing to the poor. And the doctor is celebrated as the Good Samaritan, his skill as an oculist remembered by Jesus restoring sight to the blind. All fitting images for the couple's effect on poor Jane.

From the drawing-room windows of their beautiful home at Holm Hill, Jane looked out at the rolling Tynron Hills and down toward the sprawling white house where her mother was born and spent her last years, and where she herself was married. She wrote a good thumbnail sketch of mortality: 'It is terrible to look over to Templand and think how *all* who were there are dead and gone! and the place itself green and bright looking as if nothing had happened!'

Dr. Russell, from the day she arrived, believed her. He said, as had Carlyle (a master of complaints of the lower region), 'that my illness is only to be acted thro' the stomach but does not make light of my *nervousness*—does not say slightingly that "nervous pain does not kill, that people can live without sleep."'

Two days after she arrived, 'he made me bathe my feet in hot water, and I slept—very brokenly but still I slept.'

He collaborated with her. When Jane couldn't sleep, he suggested she take tincture of hops. 'Hardly to be called a Narcotic,' he said.

'But I decided to try again—with only bathing my feet—and taking a glass of wine during the night.' All right with him. In fact, he told her two glasses of wine wouldn't hurt her if she 'needed it so much.'

'By the by,' Jane wrote to Carlyle, 'or by the direct—will you make them send me a dozen or two of that sherry from Leith—I am in the fourth bottle of what I brought from St Leonards!!' The wine had no bad effects 'and is certainly good for the fluttering at my heart.'

Everything was comforting to her at Holm Hill: the quiet airy bedroom, the new milk, the beautiful drives. But it also made her realize that she could not blame her state on a noisy bedroom or badly cooked food. 'Now I can only lay it to my diseased nerves, and at my age such illness does not right itself.'

But seeing a situation more clearly was restorative. She was better than she had been and she gained five pounds, even though she was still not sleeping.

Brother John came by and managed to wolf down more of the Russells' strawberries and cream than was good for him. He was disgusted that Jane stopped taking quinine because she believed, rather than helping her sleep, it excited her further. 'I being *in* the thing could not *see my way*,' John explained.

Dr. Russell thought 'it best to discontinue the quinine *that* being my idea—and last night I had what, for me, may be called a good night with no aids but utter exhaustion and God's mercy.'

She was enough her old self by the middle of August to be furious with two servants at Cheyne Row who had not brought Carlyle his castor oil on time. 'Oh if I were *well*! wouldn't I make these lazy stupid creatures alter their figure.'

She was well enough to ask Carlyle to put these miserable letters of hers out of the way and not to show anything she wrote to John.

'John Carlyle appeared last evening to tea. He plays the part of consulting Physician here which I find a farce—when I needed his help . . . he only aggravated me with brutal impertinence. As I was more even than usual *ill* with my pain last evening, he kept assuring me I "looked well—fuller in the face." '

That night she took her wine and had her 'waking sleep' till six in the morning. 'It is the strangest thing this sleep in all my sick experience. I believe I sleep it with my eyes open; for when I wake wide up, there is no difference in what I am seeing.'

But the next night she had a dream: 'I dreamt about Blakiston and my Mother was in it! All thro' this weary illness I have hardly dreamt at all and *never* about my Mother before. I could not help regarding her return to me this morning as a good sign. Yet I was doing something to vex her—going away with Dr Blakiston when she expected me *home*.'

And a week later, she had a bad dream about poor Lord Ashburton, who had recently died. He had left Carlyle two thousand pounds outside of the will so his friend would not be taxed. Lady Loo wrote to Jane, underlining that she always *knew* that Lord Ashburton loved Carlyle, phrasing it in that ambiguous way. What has been wished for comes too late, Jane wrote of the money. In her dream Lord Ashburton's face had become as pure and transparent as waxwork. When she remarked on it, he told her hers would be as transparent when her illness was over.

'Poor Ld Ashburton and his transfigured face,' Carlyle answered. 'I had him one night too, in my dreams.'

During her stay with the Russells, from late July until October, Jane's health went up and down. But she was also learning something about her body.

'I wish that when my education was going on there had been wise women appointed to give a course of lectures to young Ladies on *The Bowels*!' It was Dr. Russell who recommended she pay particular attention to hers. 'I am so much in the dark as to the whole matter, that I don't know when to take physic and when to let it alone. When I came here first, I was nearly having an attack of jaundice, from the mistaken idea that these same perplexing bowels had returned to a state of primeval innocence!'

She was taught better at Holm Hill. There was nothing moral about virginal bowels. She would later tell Mary Russell that she now looked on her bowels 'as a sort of sacred charge laid on me by you and the Dr!'

What she had to say of the physical components of her illness was most often edited out of her published letters. The terrible irritation that she was '*shamed* to complain about,' which seemed to affect her vagina and her

Holm Hill (above); 'Mrs Russell, Holm Hill' (left). Mary Dobbie Russell, two years younger than Jane, was one of Jane's closest Scottish friends. 'I am still hanging between life and death,' Jane wrote from St. Leonards. 'I have thought of you and loved you always thro these dismal months of silence. How often looked at the picture of Holm Hill on my bedroom wall, and mourned to think I should never be *there* again, never, never—.'

anus; the exact nature of the pain she knew was 'specifically *female*' and was located in her womb. The 'rubbing in' of opium that alleviated the torture for periods. The fact that she had to get out of bed fourteen or fifteen times a night, until Dr. Russell prescribed something for that. The color of her 'water,' as she called it, clear until she returned to London, when it had red sediment in it. The fact that the irritation of her genital area was so bad that she had to take a laxative to calm it before she attempted to sit on a train. She might have had what we now call irritable bowel syndrome or cystitis, or both. Though she was past menopause, her symptoms resemble those of endometriosis or enlarged fibroids as well. She knew she did not have cancer. She knew she did have neuralgia. And then there was the pain when she was anxious which seemed to stab her in the back. Some sort of heart condition that she believed her mother died of and that she would die of too.

One day Dr. Russell handed her a medical book on neuralgia, 'that I might read, for my practical information, a list of "counter-irritants." I read a sentence or two more than was meant, ending with "this lady was bent on self-destruction." You may think it a strange comfort, but it was a sort of comfort to me to find that my dreadful wretchedness was a not uncommon feature of my disease, and not merely an expression of individual cowardice.

'I think Dr Russell much the best Dr that I have had. *He* does not treat my sufferings as "hysterical mania," as something *in the air*—that has no *positive* existence. *Nerves* are *real things* for him, to be seen and acted upon like muscles or any other part of the human body. If I had had *him* or such a one beside me in the beginning of my illness, I fancy it might have been prevented from attaining such a fearful height and such a grim hold.

'But it is no good thinking of what *might have been*! There are plenty of aids to insanity without indulging in reflections like *that*!'

Carlyle believed Dr. James Russell saved his wife's life. Jane knew him to be an even better doctor. She was fully conscious that Dr. Russell helped her to save her own life.

It looked as if she might be coming home, but never to the hell she had experienced in her little bedroom. The bed she was born in seemed in her imagination 'a sort of instrument of red-hot torture.' All that red wallpaper had to be torn away first. In the middle of September she had a relapse, but was not too ill to instruct Carlyle to have the paperhangers *leave* all the odd pieces of the new wallpaper, for repairing in case of accident.

The sofa must stay out of the room. 'I dont want the sofa in my bedroom again—Oh mercy! That sofa!' And the bed had to be placed so that it would not be seen too plainly. With the door open, pictures and books should be seen first.

One of her servants was to sleep in her bed now and then to keep the bed up—not the one who perspired so heavily. It should be Mary, who had returned to Cheyne Row. 'When the rooms are done, pray charge the maids not to rub the clean paper with their abominably large *crinolines,* and not to push back the chairs against it, as their habit is.'

Imagine, Carlyle seeing to alterations. But he did. Even at that, she was afraid of returning to Cheyne Row, dreading it to be 'a sort of suicide.' She did not want to travel with Dr. John. If he simply brought her to Carlisle and put her on the train there beside some other woman, she would be just as well cared for. As long as she could stand and talk, why did she need an escort? However, John insisted. At least on the night train there would be less need to talk with him.

She dreaded the moment 'of re-entering a house which I had left in a sort of hearse, with a firm conviction of returning no more.' But fate had a kindness in store for her. Dr. John had stupidly given Carlyle reason to expect Jane an hour and a half earlier, and as Carlyle waited he kept expecting a telegram at any moment telling him Jane had died on the road.

When he heard her carriage stop, in violent agitation, Carlyle rushed into the street in his dressing gown, and as Jane was descending from the carriage he grabbed her and kissed her and wept all over her—'much to the edification of the neighbors at their windows, I have no doubt,' she reported to Mary Russell with underplayed Scottish pride.

Carlyle, without a cigar in his face, bounding out in his dressing gown, kissing her, crying over her, making such a fuss.

And the two maids appeared behind him with flushed faces and tears in their eyes.

Everyone was astonished at the improvement in her appearance. 'Mr. C. has said again and again that he would not have believed anyone who had sworn to him that I should return so changed for the better.'

'It is not an unhappy life,' she wrote. 'I am no longer obliged to overexert myself, as I used to be. Mr C. has had such a fright, that it has developed in him a quite new faculty of *Consideration.*'

For years Carlyle had talked about getting her her own brougham, and now he actually took the time to go out and shop for one. Lady Loo bought her the horse to draw it. Jane drove every afternoon from one to three. The air did her good. While in London, Charlotte saw how much she had

Dr. John Carlyle was the same age as his sister-in-law Jane, and a confidant of his brother Thomas. 'Jack,' as he was often called, disregarded the physical roots of Jane's illness, considering her nervous and hysterical for no reason, a view perpetuated by Carlyle's family in later years.

Dr. James Russell, a year younger than Carlyle, was respectful of Jane's perspective on her mental and physical derangement, and helped to save her life.

improved. Jane would pick her up and bring her out to Brixton to see Mary Eliza, happy to do a kindness for a friend. Grace Welsh was much on Jane's mind, and seeing Charlotte's concern for her mother would only intensify her memories.

The pain of anxiety that at times stabbed her in the stomach and then in her back, Dr. Russell called a spasm of the diaphragm. He advised she have her limbs massaged, but she could not stand physical contact with any stranger. Again, it would be Geraldine who rubbed her feet, her legs, her aching arms and shoulders, literally hour after hour. Geraldine was her Consuelo, Jane said, her comforter.

Her neuralgia was so bad that she once more consulted Dr. Quain. She hid from him the first two times he tried to see her. She was so embarrassed about what she told him while confined to her red bedroom that just hearing he was calling sent the pain from her back to her heart. 'Not that I did not feel grateful for his kindness last winter—but I remember how wildly I used to talk to him, imploring him to give me poison, etc, etc, and all the horrid questions he had to ask; and I could not look him in the face.' When she finally consulted him about her pain, he scolded her for not sending for him at once. 'How could I when he would never accept a fee from me!' Now Dr. Quain agreed with Dr. Russell. She might lose all movement. But she fought against this prognosis, would not have it.

When her right arm was useless and Carlyle was away, she dictated her letters to him. Carlyle responded, complimenting Jane on her 'hand perfectly firm.' Of course it was Geraldine's distinctive long, looped handwriting. 'And *you* not to know that!'

He would read all her letters over more carefully in due time.

He would look back on those next eighteen months, which Jane called not unhappy, 'as . . . a second youth (almost a second childhood with the wisdom and graces of old age), which by Heaven's great mercy were conceded her and me.'

Then, at the age of seventy-one, Thomas Carlyle received an honor from his own country. The former enfant terrible was elected rector of the University of Edinburgh—a vindication and recognition that did not require residency, just a speech. A speech! Carlyle was extremely miserable for getting himself tangled in a coil of vanity, and was, as on every day of his vigorous, horseback-riding life, in sadly ill health. Jane, now sixty-five, encouraged him to speak extemporaneously. For it was in the free flow of his ideas and fancies that he excelled.

Left to right in foreground: Thomas Carlyle, Louisa Ashburton, and Jane Carlyle in 1865.

He agreed to do as she said, which precluded her going with him. For she was afraid that if he made a slip as he spoke, she might get one of those stabs in the back that came to her in moments of anxiety and that seemed to stop her heart. What if she fainted in the crowded room?

They parted, both looking pale and ill. Nothing like an honor to play havoc with their nervous constitutions. Jane handed her husband a small flask of fine brandy to mix into the water as he gave his address. They actually kissed before he left Cheyne Row.

The day of his speech was the most gloomy, chaotic one Carlyle could imagine. Jane knew it would be torture.

'Now they will be telling him it is time! now they will be pinioning his arms and saying last words! Oh mercy!'

In her imagination she saw him get up in front of an awful crowd of people, and then, in the fuss and bad air and confusion, drop dead.

Carlyle began his speech in a mood of defiant despair, goaded on by nightmares. But he was an old man speaking to youth, and in the extemporaneous flow of his ideas, he told the young audience something of his own personal struggles with writing, and urged them on to hope, to the future, to work, and to truth. It was a howling success. He was applauded and cheered and the young students followed him through the streets as he wended his way to George Street. It was only then, at his brother's door, that he turned and faced them, and, in a sudden heartfelt gesture, lifted his hat. Poor young men, he thought, to be so affected by their poor old brother—or grandfather, he added. But before Jane could receive this Carlylean version of a grand and popular success, she received a telegram from their friend the physicist John Tyndall, who accompanied him:

'A perfect triumph.'

Jane was among friends, dressing for a party at John Forster's, when she received the word. She read it to herself first and then to her friends, who gasped and clapped their hands and danced around—until Jane fainted.

'Get her some brandy!'

'Do, ma'am swallow this spoonful of brandy; just a spoonful.'

She recuperated from her hysterical fit in time to bring the good news to the Forsters and share it with them and with Charles Dickens and Wilkie Collins. 'We drank your health with great glee.'

Carlyle decided to stay in Scotland for a little while longer. While visiting relatives, he sprained his ankle and that added to his absence. He missed her letter one day, which gave him time to dream of her in bitterly bad circumstances. On Saturday, the twenty-first of April, she wrote that it was a waste of time to send all her news since he would be home on Monday. She was quite busy, giving a tea party that night for Geraldine Jewsbury and Margaret Oliphant and Froude and his wife among others. Eleven guests and only ten teacups! 'To-morrow, after the tea-party, I may have more to say, provided I survive it!'

Her preparations did not stop her from taking her daily ride in her own brougham.

The day before, she had gone out to Richmond with Sarah Dilberoglue, bringing the little dog that had been left in Jane's care after the death of its owner. She let it out for a while to run by the carriage. Sarah suggested Mrs. Carlyle should sometimes drive in the park and let it run, and Saturday, after lunch at the Forsters', Jane did just that. She told Mr. Silvester, the old coachman, to drive through the Queen's Gate, close by Kensington Gardens. At the uppermost gate, she got out and walked very slowly for about two hundred paces with the little dog running. Then she and the dog got back into the carriage and Mr. Silvester drove on to a quiet place near Victoria Gate where Jane put the dog out to run along by itself.

Toward Marble Arch another brougham came along and seemed to swipe the dog. When it passed, the poor thing lay on its back screaming. Shades of Nero having his neck run over by the butcher cart. Shades of Jane plashed down by a cab. She called for Mr. Sylvester to pull up, and jumped out of the cab like Jeannie Welsh of old.

The little dog had struggled up and wandered to the side of the road. The lady in the brougham that swiped him got out and spoke to Jane, as did several ladies who had been walking. Jane went to her charge, picked him up, put him into the carriage, and got in herself.

Was he hurt? Mr. Sylvester asked, but as other carriages were passing, she seemed not to hear. The dog squeaked, as if Jane had been feeling it for injuries—only a toe was actually hurt—and the coachman continued on.

He got no further directions from Mrs. Carlyle and for close to three quarters of an hour drove on. He looked back. Her hands were on her lap, right hand palm up, left hand palm down. She did not sign to him. So he continued, but began to feel a bit uneasy. He looked back again and her hands had not moved. Becoming alarmed, he made for the street entrance and asked a lady to look in. It was a quarter past four. Jane was leaning back in one corner of the carriage, rugs spread over her knees. Jane's eyes were closed, and her mouth just slightly open. The woman said, 'I dare not open the door for I am afraid the lady is dead.'

Carlyle was sitting at his sister Jean's in Dumfries that Saturday night, favoring his ankle, thinking of his voyage home. A telegram arrived, to brother John. But since John was not at home, it was forwarded to his sister. Jean did not have her glasses on and so she passed the telegram to Carlyle to read for her. It was from, of all people, John Forster. He opened it. . . . Mrs. Carlyle was dead.

'Yr saddest of messages came to me last night at 10. The stroke that has fallen on me is immense; my heart as if broken.'

Carlyle would not let his friends convince him to spare himself, and insisted on returning to Cheyne Row to escort his wife's body back to Scotland. He told Forster he must. 'I have just now a letter from her hand, written in the most perfect spirits, date "Saturday" 21st!' The day she died.

Carlyle's stunned pain is spelled out to Forster in his small, unendingly even hand, every semicolon in place as always, 'broth-er' neatly hyphenated when the word did not fit the line.

Through the considerable efforts of John Forster and Dr. Quain, who wrote the obituary for *The Times,* there was no autopsy performed on Mrs. Carlyle at St. George's Hospital. Dr. Quain called the cause of death paralysis, but they all believed it was apoplexy, Sarah informed Charlotte. The important thing was that her body was not violated; that would have upset Carlyle tremendously, his friends agreed. One cannot help wondering if an autopsy would have caused Carlyle a particular personal embarrassment, for it would be discovered that Mrs. Carlyle was a virgo intacta—to quote Dr. Quain.

His friends told Carlyle that Jane looked peaceful, in perfect repose in death. But to some who saw her at St. George's Hospital, it was quite evident that death, as she predicted, had stabbed her in the back.

Geraldine was at Cheyne Row preparing to receive Jane's remains. Mrs. Warren, Jane's older housekeeper, came quietly up to her.

Mrs. Carlyle's mother once bought a beautiful pair of candles for a party her daughter was giving, but Mrs. Carlyle was young and headstrong and would not have her guests see such an extravagance. She put them away. The last time she was ill, Mrs. Carlyle told her housekeeper where those candles were: in the closet in the spare room, wrapped in paper. When her end came, she wanted them to be lit at her bier.

Geraldine went upstairs. Her heavy heart and inflamed eyes aside, she easily found them.

Jane was brought back to Cheyne Row and carried for the last time to her bedroom, the room she once thought she was leaving dead. The room she would not return to till it was altered and stripped of all its red. They laid her out on the bed she was born on. The hardly injured little dog stayed by her feet. Grace Baillie Welsh's elegant candles were placed by her head. They burned for two nights.

Carlyle brought her back to Haddington. The apse of the church had been restored in the years since Mrs. Carlyle jumped over the churchyard wall. The long rectangular stone which marked Dr. Welsh's final resting place was now embedded in the church floor. Jane was lowered into her father's grave, her wish when she was eighteen, her wish when she was sixty-four.

All was ended, Carlyle wrote. If only he could have five minutes more with her, only five minutes more to tell his wife of forty years that he loved her.

Jane Welsh Carlyle with her dog Nero, July 1854. 'It *is* really a comfort
to have something alive and cheery and fond of me, always there.'

From the moment of her death, she was everything to him. Sarah Dilberoglue's prediction to Charlotte Cushman turned out to be accurate. 'He
will feel as if life were indeed ended—his work done, its acknowledgment
received, and his wife gone from him.'

All of Carlyle's writings and editing from then on revolved around her
memory, as if he were writing her one long letter. He began this new, one-
sided correspondence on the tombstone she shared with her father in the
apse of the restored church, where one can read it today:

Here likewise now rests
JANE WELSH CARLYLE
Spouse of Thomas Carlyle, Chelsea London

She was born at Haddington, 14th July 1801, only daughter
Of the above John Welsh and of Grace Welsh, Caplegill,
Dumfriesshire, his wife. In her bright existence she
Had more sorrows than are common; but also a soft
Invincibility, a clearness of discernment, and a noble
Loyalty of heart, which are rare. For forty years she
Was the true and ever-loving helpmate of her husband,
And by act and word unweariedly forwarded him, as none
Else could, in all of worthy, that he did or attempted.
She died at London, 21st April, 1866; suddenly snatched
Away from him, and the light of his life, as if gone out.

In death Jane became what for forty years she steadfastly aimed to be: the Necessary Wife.

Changing Times

LONDON

1866

ROME, NEW YORK, NEWPORT,
ST. LOUIS, EDINBURGH

1866–1870

C HARLOTTE WAS soon back in London herself. The shock of
Mrs. Carlyle's death relayed by Sarah Dilberoglue was followed in
less than two weeks by a garbled telegram. Was it possible that her
mother had died seven years to the day of sister Susan's death? She traveled
all night in a diligence to get to a train. But then the train was stopped in
Pisa the next day. The Italian government needed it for the transport
of military. She was running at a crawl, and arrived in Liverpool too late to
see her mother once more, to kiss her forehead before she was laid to rest
next to her favorite daughter. 'They had *closed* the leaden house—& my
mother—the best & Truest & dearest & most self sacrificing of mothers &
friends—had passed to heaven without a word of blessing or comfort to my
wretched heart.'

Back in London, Charlotte was left with the saddest of duties—ordering
her mother's affairs, disposing of her effects, closing her overfurnished, cluttered little house in Brixton, bucking up Charlie. She herself felt so old and
used up that she thought she should be setting her own affairs in order.

She attributed her condition to other people's ills. Sallie, middle-aged now, was ill with rheumatism. Dear Fanny, Seward's wife, had tuberculosis and Charlotte intuited the worst, though it had not yet been told her.

Thomas Carlyle was at Cheyne Row ordering and rereading all of his wife's letters, from the first one-sentence note to 'Mr Carlisle' to her last, which he received sixteen hours after her death. He had come upon her private journals as well. Her whole life was welling up in front of him, one long letter which he now read carefully.

His sin had been lack of confidence in himself, he believed.

Forty years before, in his abandoned novel fragment 'Wotton Renfred,' he wrote of the character based on him: 'Wotton had never known love: brought up in seclusion from the sex, immersed in solitary speculation, he had seen the loveliest half of our species only from afar . . . with impossible abysses intervening; and doubting and disbelieving all things, the poor youth had never learned to believe in himself.' That 'any fair soul should ever languish in fond longing, seemed a thing impossible. Other men were loved; but he was not as other men; did not a curse hang over him? had not his life been a cup of bitterness from the beginning? Thus in timid pride he withdrew. . . .'

Besides loss, Carlyle felt guilt—the way only a son of darkness, an old Teufelsdröckh, an old Devil's Shit such as he, could feel remorse. Just like the husband in Geraldine's novel eighteen years earlier, he blamed himself for Jane's suffering and never got over the death of his wife. Once so long ago in Haddington Jane had been his sun. Now he saw her sparkling once more; images of Jane he drenched in light. There was another history for the author of the recently completed eight-volume *Frederick the Great* to write: hers.

He began his 'Reminiscence of Jane Welsh Carlyle' by accident. Geraldine sent him the small, leather-bound notebook in which she had written down many stories of Jane's youth—of the Haddington days that an older, sadder Jane loved to remember. She asked Carlyle's permission to send the notebook to Constance, Marchioness of Lothian, who requested Geraldine to jot down her memories. Carlyle read of Jane's fight with the turkey cock, her crawl over the Nungate bridge, her socking a boy student in the nose, her wanting to learn Latin like a boy. He stopped at Jane's fascination with her dandy of a cousin. He exclaimed, he annotated. At the end of Geraldine's scrawl, right there in Geraldine's notebook, he began his own reminiscence of his wife. He wrote with a haunting lyrical spontaneity. His pen loosened into an artist's brush. He walked through the valley of the shadow of remorse scattering stardust over gloom.

During these sad months, Miss Stebbins came to visit Charlotte in England. Miss Stebbins had had an awful summer too. 'Her brother has behaved badly to her & she is very low, depressed & ill.' Charlotte pitied Miss Stebbins and she pitied herself: 'My heart bleeds over *her* mistake & my own.'

The Bolton Row house was costing Charlotte a fortune. Angrily, she wished she could get rid of it, drop a match on it, furniture and all. 'Ah, why did I ever leave it to make a Roman home? *That* was the mistake of my life—leaving it to attempt to make another for any body! and now it is like a millstone about my neck!'

Often she stayed with Stavros and Sarah. There she heard more and more of the details of Mrs. Carlyle's sudden death and had the chance to compare her increasingly nervous symptoms with those of her poor friend.

'Darling daughter of my heart,' Charlotte wrote to Emma that sad autumn. Emma was presently in England saying goodbye to her parents, who were returning home after a year abroad. The Crows snubbed Charlotte, insulted her deeply, by not staying with her at Via Gregoriana in Rome that winter season. She had even delayed the construction of a billiard room to have ample room for them. Instead, they allowed Hattie, brilliantly settled in her own sunny apartment at Via delle Quattro Fontane, to arrange 'more comfortable' rooms for them at the Hotel Europa.

The Crows could not do enough for Hattie, who traveled with them, while Charlotte suffered under the public, humiliating neglect.

Charlotte wanted Emma to stay in England with Baby after the Crows left. They could meet up in Brighton, where Emma could choose a lodging and they'd have a quiet week together, though *not* at the Grand Hotel. Surely Emma could find more economical accommodations.

Instead of being glad to have a quiet week by the seaside with her own dear 'Mum,' Emma did not wait for Charlotte at Brighton. She began her trip back to Rome; she was afraid of a quarantine—she said. 'If your father had asked you to stay for any reason, you would have done so—only he would have been wiser than I—he would not have asked you to be refused.'

Emma was very annoyed by Charlotte's letter. There she was, interfering in her life again.

Charlotte insisted she did not want to rob Emma of her resolute independence. But as usual, her apology turned into a lecture. 'One of the joys of a mother's life to think that her children had rather do what would please her, than what they might.' And Mum had nothing left in all the world but

Emma, who must take care of herself—especially now that she was pregnant with their second child. 'Our own little daughter is coming.'

Charlotte needed a daughter, the type she had been: 'I want some one to take me up bodily & lift me along. I no longer seem to have energy or spring left in me, & I want some one to do for me & think for me & feel for me.'

Back in Rome, the unhappy actress entertained; at times she had close to two hundred people at her Saturdays, from artists to businessmen to cardinals of the Church. Never was she a woman to be alone, especially when the invited elite might be of help in advancing her belongings. When Miss Stebbins returned to Rome and took up residence at Via Gregoriana again, Charlotte once more attempted to advance her career. Though both Miss Stebbins and Emma lived in her house, they were not truly *with* her. 'I shall learn in time to be indifferent to your movements—perhaps,' she told Emma.

Not a daughter but their second son was born in Rome. 'Ned was so excited & knocked up by Emma's confinement that we sent him up to Florence for a few days, he is now away,' Granny Cush wrote to Grandpa Crow, being sure to note that his new grandson looked just like him—even though Allerton Seward Cushman was named after his godfather, the secretary of state.

The summer after Emma's confinement, Charlotte and Miss Stebbins attempted a reconciliation, vacationing together in the English countryside. Preoccupied with saving her marriage, Charlotte did not understand the implications of Consul Ned's latest foray.

The American Civil War was over, but not the war in Italy. The Italian city-states were struggling toward unification. With the death of Elizabeth Barrett Browning in 1861, the international community had lost the voice of the 'Poet of the Italian Risorgimento.' Most of the expatriates in Rome were not interested in popular uprisings. Mazzini's 'God and the People' meant proletarian rights, which would dilute local color. It was freedom at aesthetic (and perhaps financial) expense. The *stranieri* did not come to the Eternal City for change.

In Paris at the end of October 1867 Charlotte heard that Ned, her 'soldier boy,' had gone out to see what a small military engagement was like, riding with the papal mercenaries who were fighting Garibaldi. She considered Garibaldi's advance on Rome to subdue the Pope a form of suicide and was glad Ned was able to prove and testify to the bravery and worth of the Pope's men, but 'I don't like you going into such places & running such risks.'

Consul Cushman rode off with the Pope's troops as if he had simply joined in a fashionable foxhunt. For an American official to enter a battle in a *foreign country*, to have ridden on the side of *one* faction, to have been seen *armed* on one side was an error of such fabulous stupidity that perhaps only Ned could have pulled it off. He had allied his country to the cause of those who wished to suppress Italians in their drive toward 'a Nationality,' as one furious English artist wrote Seward. Seward upbraided Ned. That slap on the wrist might have humiliated Charlotte, but it was not enough for Mazzini himself: 'My American friends and I want him dismissed.'

Ned had absolutely no understanding of the position Auntie had gotten for him—and to some extent, neither had Auntie. It was only when she had to deal with the ramifications that Charlotte labeled her nephew's actions 'Ned's folly.'

But when she first heard of his actions, she had been so terribly distracted. Not only was she attempting to placate her alienated spouse, she knew her niece was entertaining Fran Noble and the Kelloggs while she was away. These people were her enemies. They had talked against her and Miss Stebbins to Miss Stebbins' family; they had whispered about Charlotte and Emma's relationship too. How could Emma allow them into Charlotte's house?

Wasn't it bad enough that while Charlotte was in mourning for her mother, she made the mistake of allowing Ann 'Nannie' Lemmon, a young acquaintance from Baltimore, into her home? Nannie certainly would not have been invited if Charlotte knew of her depravity! 'It seriously injured the character of my home—it had a most demoralizing effect upon Ned—& was of great harm to you physically & morally—*I think!* for you have never been the same since. Ned has never been the same since & my home has never been the same to me since! The form of entertainment & moral disease has poisoned it for me.'

Emma Cushman—and perhaps Ned as well—had taken a new lover.

If Charlotte thought open disapproval of Emma's relationship with Nannie Lemmon would curb Emma, she was more than mistaken. Charlotte could travel the moral high road by herself.

When Charlotte returned to Rome for the winter season, Emma and Ned went to as many parties and balls as they wished. If Emma's friends weren't welcome, perhaps it was time for Emma, Ned, and the children to establish their own residence in Rome. Charlotte, as always, played the cards she was dealt. After Emma's threat of leaving, Charlotte stayed as friendly as she could with Emma's lover.

'Emma Cushman longs for you,' Charlotte wrote to Nannie back in Baltimore. 'At times stretches out her arms in a longing moan for the sight of you. She had a very miserable summer, but since she got back to Rome is all right & is as jolly as a "schoolboy," though far from being as strong as I wish she was.'

As Miss Stebbins continued to work on the Horace Mann statue (a plague of problems), Mann's sister-in-law, Charlotte's dear friend Elizabeth Peabody, visited, and it was Miss Peabody, not Miss Stebbins, who helped Charlotte ward off her bouts of depression.

'Rome is *fuller* than ever,' Charlotte wrote to Nannie. 'We have quantities of new people, a few of the English ones are very clever & very bright & very badly dressed as usual—but after all—worth having, for they *mean* what they say.'

Charlotte was floundering. Her whole emotional world was crumbling. Her relationship with Miss Stebbins was unsteady. The New York Stebbinses disapproved of her. The St. Louis Crows snubbed her. Emma was not only insisting on her own life but threatening to move out. And Ned's position was even more precarious, now that he rode out to battle with the Pope's men. Her life was completely out of control. She had to do something to regain her self-respect.

'My affairs in America require my coming,' she wrote to Emma's new lover, telling Nannie, 'I shall see you—& we will talk. "God how we will talk."'

Charlotte's mood can be seen in her description of New York. 'The streets are even worse than ever, the holes, the dirt, the smells.' And the prices!

'For a small bedroom for myself & a dark one for Sallie next door, they charged me $9.00 per day, with board, & the food really without taste—my heart sank within me—& I thought I must have lost the taste of my childhood.' It did not help her appetite that she and Sallie were living in a hotel, not on Gramercy Park with Miss Stebbins, who had also returned.

The first order of business was to travel to Washington to see Seward, now a widower, about Ned's Folly. Seward was forced to appear to take the *high hand* with Ned. But no matter the harshness of the letters that Seward wrote to the father of his godson, 'Ned shall not lose his post.' At least not while Seward was still in office.

Ned and Emma, against Charlotte's wishes, insisted on taking the children and traveling with the fast set to Germany for the summer months. Since officially Ned was required to be in Rome, Seward's son, the assistant secretary of state, could only give Charlotte good advice, not official sanction. Ned should leave behind an efficient vice-consul, and when anyone asked where the American consul was, the answer should always be, 'Mr Cushman is only absent for a few days.' With those words from Washington to guide him, Ned took an extraordinarily long lunch.

Seward brought Charlotte to meet the man who was finishing Lincoln's term and she found the President, who had avoided impeachment by one vote, gentlemanly, dignified, and amiable. He had made his mistakes—'Who hasn't?'

'I have never been more completely satisfied than I was & have been right about him from the beginning. . . . Andrew Johnson is a true man.' Imagine that treacherous woman sculptor Vinnie Ream helping the effort to impeach him. It confirmed Charlotte's belief that women should not get the vote.

Charlotte read that Elizabeth Cady Stanton was offering the vote of women to whatever party was the more influential in obtaining suffrage for them. 'I would not raise my voice one note for woman suffrage. In this country where women can do much what they like and what they choose with men . . . I don't think votes are worth struggling for.'

Returning from Washington, Charlotte stopped in Baltimore. When Nannie Lemmon answered her door, she made a lively moment of it. She told the actress, with melodramatic flair, that there was nothing to do but throw herself out the window and actually bounded toward one. Charlotte stopped her on the sill, and with their arms around one another, Nannie begged her to stay for a visit.

Charlotte was absolutely relentless. Emma might no longer be her lover, but she would always be the daughter of her heart and her legal heir. She did her duty. 'I made everything right in Washington for Ned,' she wrote to Emma. Now it was time to make everything right with her spouse and the Stebbins family.

Back in New York, in time for her fifty-second birthday on July 23, Charlotte was no longer at a hotel. She and Sallie were living with Miss Stebbins on East Seventeenth Street. From that vantage point, the city appeared less dirty. It was the place to *make* money and the society was very good. 'Not among *fast* people either.'

Nannie Lemmon, in an undated photograph from Charlotte's
album, became Emma Crow Cushman's lover during the
Roman years and undoubtedly added to Charlotte's general
malaise. Excusing herself to Nannie for not writing sooner:
'There is not fire in me any more dear. I am a broken winded
hunter & have no longer any spring.'

But her nerves often got the better of her and she suffered a pain around
her heart when she hurried too much. Was she suffering from an ailment
similar to Mrs. Carlyle's?

'It makes me very sad to think how completely a woman may lose herself,' Charlotte wrote to Emma.

While on her way to Germany Nannie wrote to Charlotte saying she hoped Ned would come over to Frankfurt to meet her and conduct her to Emma.

Would Emma want to see her? Nannie asked, and Charlotte answered honestly: 'Yes.'

'But for all that I am sorry that you are going to be bothered with her, not that I think she can harm you.' Charlotte had a bilious attack of colic after she got Nannie's letter. All night long she felt as if she were being cut across her navel.

No pain was severe enough to stop Charlotte from mending her fences. Resolutely, she joined Miss Stebbins at sister Mary Garland's estate at Hyde Park. There she sat with the well-bred Stebbins ladies on the spacious lawn under a mosquito net large enough to accommodate a half-dozen chairs and a little table. She read to the women as they did their needlework. Or they talked. At times Miss Stebbins darted off with a butterfly net in search of the large beautiful-colored butterflies that haunted the place.

By the end of the summer, Emma, pregnant with her third child, was heading to St. Moritz. Charlotte was very relieved. The Stebbins family had told her enough about the fast set of Americans in Germany to make her approve the move, though last winter she was against Emma going to St. Moritz as well. 'But you have forgiven me long since for all those fears & jealousies, have you not?'

Emma appeared indifferent. 'You are very good & very sweet to tell me not to mind about writing every week,' Charlotte responded, '—but I wish to write by every steamer when I can do so. It is *my* pleasure.'

She would not return to Europe until the end of November, after the election. Andrew Johnson was a gentleman (albeit a Democrat); he was not like Ulysses S. Grant, whom the Republicans had chosen to run. If Grant won the presidential election in the fall, the country would fall to the philistines. 'I shall see who is going to be President—& will do what I can to have Ned continued.'

Meanwhile, it might be wise for Ned to return to Rome. Those miserable creatures trying to see the consul all summer were exasperated and might report him.

Nannie was welcome to stay with them at Via Gregoriana—at least till Charlotte and her entourage returned, and then Nannie would have to find other accommodations, simply because there would no longer be room.

No matter how Auntie extended herself, Emma was still thinking of moving. She mustn't! She just must stay at Via Gregoriana: 'No matter about any body else. It is all over & done & your being away from me or with me wouldn't make the slightest difference *now*.' For both their sakes, she begged Emma to put the idea of leaving out of her head.

'I loved you & love you & you are more necessary to my happiness now than when you first came—for I have nothing in the world now *but* you & your babies. . . . My trouble last winter arose from the thought that you were not as desirous to make me happy as you used to be & that made me so utterly lonely in my house—that I dare say I exaggerated all things. However, it is past I believe. You love me earnestly & tenderly I believe no one loves me so well, & why should you think of leaving me. I suppose you are having great fun you & Nannie. I hope you will be careful of yourself.'

Ned and Emma Cushman were obviously part of what Charlotte referred to as the set of loose-living American 'demireps' in Europe. Her belongings were making their own sexual accommodations. Whether Emma looked the other way at Ned's affairs, or whether she found women for him, or whether she and her husband were both involved with Nannie is unclear. But husband and wife were now intent on living as they liked under their own roof.

'But darling—don't worry or fret about any thing. You have not cast your lives very wisely I fear in this world—for your well-being or for a love of high morals—but you know you have always your father & me at your back & you must find comfort in our love for you.'

And so Charlotte completed her sea change from ungentle mistress to unconditional mother.

A mother who would gladly loosen, rather than lose, control. She wouldn't be home until the end of December: 'So—you can do with the house as you will until that time.'

The entire Stebbins family disapproved of her? Charlotte grabbed her butterfly net and headed to Hyde Park. She was snubbed by Emma's family during their year in Europe? In Newport, Mr. Crow slipped and gave her an opening. Hattie and Cornie would be coming to St. Louis and Mr. Crow seemed to have extended a polite invitation for Charlotte to refuse. 'I said yes to please him.'

Please him? She knew full well 'there is a restraint in the atmosphere with all your family & me. Your mother is sweet & good, but she is naturally reserved & restrained. Your father is queer with me. *I* think on Hattie's account & the jealousy he feels with regard to your love for me which he thinks swallows up everything else. And then sister [Cornie] is very constrained with me—on Hattie's account & altogether I am less happy or comfortable with them, than any where else in the whole world.'

Mr. Crow was hardly comfortable himself. Realizing Charlotte actually was coming west with the family, he bowed out of the plans and sent her ahead with his wife.

'I thought to go with a man & be taken care of—& now I have to go & take care of myself.'

Charlotte left Miss Stebbins with her family, and as in happier days, she and Sallie traveled to St. Louis. 'Here I am, my precious darling, in your old home, which looks exactly the same as the first day I came into it so long ago.' She was pleased to be sitting in Emma's own bedroom, 'where I slept when I first staid with you here.'

When Wayman Crow arrived, he showed Charlotte a warmer hospitality in his own home and at his own table than he had in the East. Part of it, she believed, was that he was away from the influence of Hattie, who would be coming later.

'Your mother & I have had much better opportunities of knowing each other & she thinks *something* of me now.' The actress entertained the children. They were transfixed by her apt imitations of farm animals and fairies. Little Wayman was growing into a fine boy.

At dinner one night, Mrs. Crow told her husband that the principal of the institute Wayman Junior was attending told her he had taken a 'sudden jump' and was now the most studious and attentive in the school. Mr. Crow was so pleased he had tears in his eyes.

Wayman Junior looked up from his plate and blushed: 'I dont know what Dr. Stone knows about it. He dont hear me my lessons.'

Charlotte was attempting to persuade Mr. Crow to be less exacting with Wayman and Isabel. He wanted them only to associate with the children of his friends and with people he entirely approved of. 'This standard is too high for children!' Still, little Isabel was harder to win over than Wayman. 'She dont take to me as much as her sister Emma did but then she is so much younger!'

What a city St. Louis had become. Charlotte saw it all with new eyes, thrilling at 'its suburbs, its people, its enterprize.' Its streets were paved now. New houses of all kinds were going up all over 'with French roofs & every improvement. I have never been more surprised with the growth of a city in my life.'

She visited the public schools and looked into the 'splendid' mode of

education. Why, here there were ten-year-olds 'working out sums in frac-
tions which would crack my head open.'

What a healthy place to raise children! Far away from the 'brothels' of
Europe.

Such fine people, such good society!

'Your mother took real comfort out of me . . . & your father was like a
hen with one chicken. I could not have imagined such a difference in their
behavior in the west.' And at the end of her visit there was the crowning
glory. A wedding party where everybody who was anybody clamored to be
introduced to Miss Cushman. 'Your father's letters have been much nicer
ever since!'

And of course everyone in St. Louis knew that Charlotte and Sallie
would travel from Chicago to New York by themselves in the presidential
carriage of the train. They had their delicious meals cooked in a dear little
kitchen and served by 'a man who combined cook & waiter.'

Back east Charlotte called on the man who attempted to separate her
from his sister, and thanked Henry Stebbins himself for his great hospitality. Miss Stebbins came into the room while Charlotte was writing to
Emma and asked her to send along her love.

'I think she is in a better state of mind than she was, I am sure *I am*,'
Charlotte commented. 'I dont mind now what she does. . . . I think she
wont bother me any more—at all events she is well with *me*!'

The important thing was that Charlotte had recovered her 'self respect.'

She appreciated herself once more, had become more self-reliant. 'I have
found a true appreciation of me by others—one & all—& all things are
much better with me than they were. I dont care now! and this makes all
things easy, & makes other people more anxious to please me. And I am
now satisfied that much of my trouble was in my own nervous distorted
vision. . . . I had lost possession of myself . . . even my darling came in for
her share of my jealous doubts of my power to hold her love & so all things
went ill.'

She prayed God she would not fall into so unworthy a slough as she had
been in for the last three years, since Miss Stebbins was unfaithful and
Emma came to Rome—and was unfaithful too. It was no vague sadness
concerning Mrs. Carlyle that embraced her during those years.

Auntie and Miss Stebbins returned to Rome just in time for the birth of
Emma's third child, but again no Carlotta. Emma Cushman had so hoped
for a girl as Nannie played the pianoforte for her and amused her during her
pregnancy.

'Try to think how much better & happier for it to be a boy,' Charlotte told the disappointed mother. 'Boys have so much better time in the world & so much less physical pain to bear and there is already so many more women in the world than men that the balance is on the wrong scale if it's a girl.'

Edwin Charles was named after his father, but his nickname reflected Charlotte as well. 'Carlino'—a child never easy to handle—quickly became her favorite.

The self-respect Charlotte reestablished in America was ravaged in Rome. She was humiliated to find how completely she had lost the place she once held in Emma's thoughts and heart.

'These last two winters others have held an influence on you which has shut out mine entirely. I have tried to hide my mortification—though I have succeeded badly.' Her moral sense made her do her duty and object to Emma's behavior.

'If you loved me at all—you could never have behaved to me—under any provocation as you did at the end of last season & this season.'

The European Republican Committee brought influence to bear against Ned's reappointment, at the same time that Emma was threatening to move out of Auntie's home.

'The whole four years that Ned has been abroad your father has considered—& not far from rightly—that Ned was indulging his pleasure.' To remain in Rome now, without any ghost of an excuse, would rightfully disgust Mr. Crow. 'Ned has few friends—few who care for him—but as they can use him—he should strive to keep your father's regard.' It was time to go home—and not to Boston, where Elizabeth Peabody, the pioneer of the American kindergarten movement, promised Ned and Emma the loveliest school for the children. St. Louis was the place to raise a family.

She wrote this from the baths at Malvern. Miss Stebbins was with her and would go for her own holiday as soon as brother Charlie came to prevent his sister's loneliness.

She really did need her belongings by her in these dark days. Fate had just dealt Charlotte its most terrible blow.

BEFORE SHE left Rome, two months before her fifty-third birthday, on 9 May 1869, Charlotte felt a small lump in her left breast, rushed to her mirror, moved her arm up and down, up and down, and was horrified.

Her maternal grandmother, whom she so resembled, had died of breast cancer. As a child of seven, Charlotte heard Grandmother Babbitt's awful, agonizing cries and had never forgotten them. Her grandmother suffered so for four years.

At first Charlotte tried to disguise her panic and calm her own fears. It was thought that only hereditary cancer spread and was fatal, whereas non-hereditary malignancies stayed in one place. Charlotte had no pain, she did not see any other lumps or marks. Perhaps it was nothing.

As much as she attempted to control her anxiety, she could not sleep and could not stop bursting into tears. In Rome Miss Stebbins attributed her outbreaks to Emma's selfish disregard of Charlotte's feelings, coming and going as she pleased—and with whom she pleased. Finally, Charlotte raised her bodice and directed Miss Stebbins' hand to the lump. And from then on, the only silver lining to the horror was Stebbins' steadfast devotion. They reconciled completely and the consultations with the doctors began.

A trip to the waters in Bavaria was suggested, but instead the women sought opinions in Paris. The doctor there said it was too early to tell what the trouble was and Charlotte should wait. He prescribed a quiet summer at Malvern with fresh air and exercise and careful diet.

'My heart sinks within me—with dread and fear,' she wrote to Elizabeth Peabody from Malvern, even though her doctor ordered her to amuse herself and try to *forget* her trouble.

To Emma she wrote that she was taking the water treatment and feeling better, but wouldn't Emma join her? 'I do so want to see you—all—& want so much to see the children—my eyes & arms & heart call out for them.'

Emma, still smarting, accused Charlotte of compromising her reputation, of talking against the way she lived. Unless Miss Stebbins moved out, she herself would leave.

'If you knew how deeply you have hurt me,' Charlotte responded. She had said nothing of the goings-on at Via Gregoriana, often escaping to her bedroom rather than be pressured for opinions by Nannie.

'My mistake was made through my great love! I never distrusted your actions I never thought you could do anything unprincipled or that should make me or yourself blush. I thought you were making a mistake & leading others to think injuriously of you—& in my older knowledge of human nature—I wished to influence you in that matter. *I did not try to mortify you into doing as I wished!*'

Emma was mistaken thinking Miss Stebbins was an influence at work against her. Perhaps she said something once or twice, but wasn't it only natural that there should have been some jealousy on the part of 'the influence' toward Emma?

Charlotte herself knew what that passion was, how 'easily it may be excited when one loves much & is very disappointed.' She had been jealous over Emma, over Miss Stebbins, and never meant to wrong either of them. But to write about this subject made her 'ill with sad memories & painful regrets.'

And then Emma accused Charlotte—and not for the first time—of leading her into a wasted life.

'You did what you did with your eyes open—as open as any girl's eyes ever are—you loved me—you wanted to help me—& *you have helped me.*'

It was his marriage to Emma that lifted Ned from his low connections and saved Charlotte from the consequences of his want of judgment. If Emma loved Charlotte at all, she must dismiss this idea that she had wasted her life by marrying Ned. Whatever pain Charlotte was suffering, 'you have saved me from very very much more—that might have broken my heart long ago! Darling I love you . . . I am very grateful to you & if I have ever hurt you—I grieve.'

Emma must not leave.

'Darling, I will not go back to Rome—& have you anywhere but in my house.'

People would say that even her children couldn't live with her. 'I cannot give this triumph even to your father, who I confess gives me as little love as he owes me. Therefore if you make up your mind that you cannot go back to my house—with "the influence" there, I will make up my mind not to go back there. I am too physically weak—& even too nervous about this trouble—which I am fearful is growing upon me . . . to have any heart trouble weighing upon me as this mortification would.'

In London, Queen Victoria's personal surgeon, Sir James Paget, diagnosed breast cancer and advised Charlotte to have the tumor cut out.

Instead, she consulted another doctor, who gave her a lotion to try for six weeks, until the symptoms became more definite. Isa Blagden, 'one of my oldest & truest friends,' suggested she eat well and avoid surgery. Elizabeth Peabody was zealously against surgery as well.

She waited, the tumor grew, but, as Charlotte herself said, it was still considered very small, only the size of three quarters of an egg.

Because of her own imagination—thinking of an eventual operation meant she died a little every day—she decided on surgery before the tumor

Sir James Simpson, Charlotte's friend and doctor, the singular and eminent Scottish surgeon who originated the use of ether as an anesthetic in childbirth in January 1847. Experimenting on himself later that year, he discovered the required properties in chloroform, which he administered to Queen Victoria on the birth of Prince Leopold in 1853. This undated photograph is from the actress's album.

enlarged. It would be performed in Edinburgh by Charlotte's personal friend the renowned Sir James Simpson, who was working wonders with 'blessed chloroform,' as Queen Victoria called it after Sir James administered it to her during childbirth.

Miss Stebbins settled her at the Clarendon Hotel on Princes Street in the middle of August, and Sir James came to Charlotte very punctually for him (and her), an hour late. After a half-hour examination, he told her that the tumor was malignant and that she had been wise to elect surgery, even against the advice of family and friends. According to him, the tumor *had* grown rapidly in three months and she could not afford to wait. If she were younger, Sir James '*might possibly* advise waiting, but that now every moment increases my danger.'

Some great blow to her breast might have caused the lump. More probably, Charlotte believed, the cancer was the result of her corset rubbing against her breast as she sat at her desk writing her journal letters through the years.

'I am so truly thankful to my God that it is where it can be so easily dealt with.'

Still, these might be her last words to Emma. 'My years & my experience are worth much & you grieve me by your utter & entire disregard of both.' It was so different in the beginning: 'I love you as truly & deeply as you love me & am ever faithfully fondly your own loving Auntie.'

But Sir James did not operate the next day. He found her breast less hard after a night's rest and 'asked me to let him bring the Professors of surgery from the College!' Apparently everyone was going to get a look at the actress's chest.

Waiting for her operation, Charlotte sent Ned some good business advice, along with the type of advice that drove him to distraction. He would be traveling to the States by himself that summer in search of future employment: 'By the way dear, one thing to know to be particular about is to make sure that your postage is rightly paid so that your correspondent is not called upon for double postage, & your own stamp thrown away. This is to burn the candle at three ends. You are always much too careless in these things & dont try to remember that "the penny saved is the penny earned." I had to pay 2 d for your letter. You wrote on heavy paper.'

After a week, all the Edinburgh doctors conferred. 'Sir James says I have taken it in such good time, that it may not come again after the *gland is removed—which it is to be, entirely.*' The egg-sized lump was cut out of her left breast.

Her first thought after surgery was Ned's job hunt. In pencil, her handwriting drenched in pain, she managed from her bed: 'My dear Boy, My first written word will be to bid you goodbye & God speed. . . . Love to Mr Crow, dear kind Miss Peabody, Mrs Crow and all who care for me. I shall pull through this dark valley, as I have done through many others. God bless you. Your loving Auntie.'

Emma came to Edinburgh for a short visit during the six weeks Charlotte was kept in bed, not the ten to twelve days Sir James predicted. For her wound became abscessed and her phlebitis was treated by keeping the leg in one position for two weeks. No wonder, as Sir James phrased it, she developed 'no slight touch of pneumonia.' She could not draw a breath free of pain.

At the end of September she sat up for the first time; it took two to hold her. Her legs had no sustaining power. 'Oh darling I am so thankful to be out of bed.'

The good news Sir James brought her was that under a microscope her tumor was found not to have advanced to a malignant state. The chances were a thousand to one that it would ever return. Charlotte was so relieved. Miss Stebbins, on the other hand, lived on valerian and sulfuric ether, her overstrained nerves completely giving way. She hadn't been out of the house since Emma's visit.

Charlotte did everything she could to gain strength—'I take quantities of milk, white of egg & brandy'—but still her legs would not hold her. Her breast was slowly healing, she wrote to her niece.

'Sir James came this morning. . . . I begged to know when I might leave & he said "this week." '

'I shall go Thursday,' Charlotte called to him.

'I will see tomorrow,' he answered, rushing out the door.

So there she was.

When finally allowed to leave, at the end of October, Charlotte, with her entourage, rushed to Malvern, where Emma and the children were waiting for her at the station.

But that joy was short-lived. Emma told her she would soon be off to the Paris dressmakers, for repairs and refittings, as if Charlotte wouldn't know she was rushing off to a lover. It was the same excuse Charlotte provided the visiting Emma years before, so Emma could leave Brussels and the two could consummate their love.

Charlotte wrote to Mr. Crow that Emma would come home next summer with a much more satisfied feeling if Ned were in a first-rate business. 'Therefore if anything is done, the sooner the better.'

Auntie wanted her nephew in an ironworks business in the West, and was very disappointed when she found out that he was not (at first) taking her advice. 'It always seems to me so strange that all my family, my mother, brother & now Ned (& perhaps you),' she wrote to Emma, 'may entertain the same idea—that I am always falling into the hands of strangers, always trusting knaves, always being cheated & made use of—& yet—more than half what means I have, have been made by other than the labour of my profession, by just these strangers and knaves.'

Constant pain did not stop her from making inquiries about slaughterhouses and manufacturing albumen in the States. The superiority of pigs' blood was on her mind, as were artificial manure and calico printers. There were such commercial opportunities for Ned in her native land. But Ned was not impressed by the profit in animal waste and returned to Europe.

Rome the winter of 1870, six months after Charlotte's surgery. She built her home there for Miss Stebbins and her sculpture, and expanded it to include her belongings, her fine stables, her carriages, and her wonderful Thoroughbreds.

People always did say she had the nicest houses, filled with the best taste of her time. It was a house full of things, from her early Renaissance furniture to her weapons collection. From Hattie's *Puck* (she finally got her copy) to William Page's fine portrait of her. All her prompt books were displayed behind glass. Thanks to the portrait bust Miss Stebbins modeled a decade ago, she was immortalized in the whitest Carrara marble as well. Over her bed, she had a portrait of Jane Welsh Carlyle. She must have looked at it often in those days of her own pain. Once, returning in triumph from Emma's wedding, she hoped Mrs. Carlyle would visit her in Rome. Now she was breaking up Via Gregoriana.

Everything had to be inventoried, separated, packed, shipped, or stored. She was shaken 'to the center of my being, as I was packing up many things—which I shall never see again—& to which I bade adieu as though they each had a soul. The peculiarity of my physical trouble made me feel that I must "set my house in order," in all the ways I could.'

But it was not illness that sent her from Rome. As usual in her life, her love of a woman dictated her movements. She was tearing her house down before it fell around her, before the daughter of her heart humiliated her by taking her family and leaving.

Emma protested, telling her Auntie that she loved her, a love that 'could only go out of me with my last drop of blood.'

'I do not doubt that I am necessary to you,' she responded, 'when I say that I think you care more for the society of others of your friends—that you are more in harmony with others than me. This is perhaps natural, but this is one of the excuses for any falling off in demonstration on my part (& *consequently* on yours perhaps) which you may have perceived.'

Charlotte still loved her 'with all the earnestness of our earlier days together, subdued to tender earnest anxiety for your well being and doing.' It sounded like another Sonnet from the Portuguese. That love had endured a great deal in the five years they lived together: 'Impatience, doubt, fear, anxiety & pride (& perhaps some other passion less worthy in itself but no less natural) has had each their separate & united sway.'

Charlotte would not be swayed, and she broke up housekeeping trying to keep the shame of it all to herself. People believed she was leaving Rome because she had cancer.

She did not give up Via Gregoriana. Instead she leased it through her agent, Mr. Shea. What a boon for Hattie, on the lookout for something not so easy to find. A superb furnished let good enough for a fine lady and her teenage daughter.

THE WINTER after Jane Welsh Carlyle's death, Jane's dear friend Louisa Lady Ashburton traveled to Rome with a note of introduction to Harriet Hosmer.

Lady Loo, with her usual careless aplomb, did not stand on formalities. The door to Hattie's large and airy studio was open; she simply walked in. She stood there among Hattie's marbles and classical casts, her beautiful lush plants and exotic foliage. Hattie turned from her work and stared in disbelief, 'stonily gazing at the lady . . . gazing with no thought of advancing to greet her.'

Had a flawless marble come alive? 'It seemed to my bewildered senses that the Ludovisi Goddess in person, weary, perhaps, of the long imprisonment of Art, had assumed the stature and the state of mortals and stood before me. There were the same square-cut and grandiose features, whose classic beauty was humanized by a pair of keen, dark eyes.'

Lady Loo gazed back with an expression of amused surprise; then came a lovely smile, followed by a rich, musical voice of inquiry that awakened Hattie to the situation.

Just before New Year's, 1868, Hattie received seven hundred pounds in advance from Lady Loo for

Marble of Puck
Will o' the Wisp
2 Putti upon Dolphins
Yellow alabaster pedestals for statues

Hattie added a P.S. to her receipt. 'You are too full of humility—when you say I am doing these things for you for the sake of the Queen [of Naples]. . . . I am doing them for you yourself.'

She was pleased to have 'her babies so beautifully housed' at Lady Loo's

Melchet was purchased for Lady Loo by her husband to replace the estate she
would lose at his death. The Carlyles and Harriet Hosmer spent time there.
This undated photograph is from Harriet Hosmer's papers.

splendid estate at Melchet. Lord Ashburton bought the place for Loo during his last years, in the knowledge that she would lose some of his extensive
holdings after his death, when his title would pass to his brother. It would
have been different if Maysie were a boy. Still, Loo was left extremely
wealthy, a patron of the arts, free to entertain as lavishly and carelessly as
she willed.

Hattie addressed her letters to Loo—often on lively colored paper—to
'My Beloved,' the extravagant thickness of the paper such a contrast to the
tissue-thin paper of international correspondence of the time. She outdid
Ned Cushman in terms of epistolary expense. She was as lavish in paper as
in life when writing to the woman who became her 'little sposa.'

But even Hattie was never as lavish as Lady Loo. Of the studio in
England Lady Loo wished to give her: 'I am profoundly touched by your
magnificence—I know my little sposa would do almost everything for her
little unworthy hubby but that would be a little too much.' (In the long run
it wasn't.)

Speaking of a royal marriage, Hattie wrote, 'They will be as happy in
their married life as we are in ours.'

Harriet Hosmer, Louisa Lady Ashburton, and the Queen of Naples. All three are from Harriet Hosmer's papers. Hattie is pictured ready for the foxhunt; Lady Loo has a cloak thrown over her shoulders, possibly a witty reference to the Queen of Naples' famous gesture at the siege of Gaeta; and the Queen of Naples herself, with her sister the Empress of Austria's 'Staghound,' which Hattie sculpted.

Speaking of the color of her stationery: 'My Beloved, This Green does not mean jealousy.'

Speaking seriously: "Now I wonder what my Beloved is doing & where she is—& how she is. I thought the last letter sounded as if she wanted her Hubby to bully her a little. How I wish we could be together for a little coze just now & talk instead of writing. I see but one thing in store for us—To pass our mature years & our old age together. . . . Everybody says they never saw me looking so well . . . sign that that delicious Highland air did me a world of good—and a little of this soft Roman air would do you a world of good.'

As time passed, one Friday night in Rome Hattie did have a jealous dream she believed based on fact. 'For you never take any notice of me now any more than if I weren't your wedded wife. Well, last night, I thought I reached England & you—but you didn't smile so profusely upon me as of yore,' and instead it was 'an unknown female who basked in the entire sunshine of your favor.' Hattie knew that Lady Loo now had 'Lady Marian [Alford] back again,' and teased, 'I really don't see but what I must get somebody too.' Lady Loo should tell Lady Marian 'for her comfort & yours that we are devoted to each other.'

In another letter, this one quite fittingly on green paper: 'Oh you little flirt! I wonder flirting doesn't keep you warm—& then the audacity of sending my rival's effusions, poking them under my very pug. Oh I'll pay you off. I'll go to Garatshausen [to the Queen of Naples] & see those beautiful eyes. Wont I. . . . Well I never was jealous in my life so I begin at my age—besides I have got a lady here who consoles me for a great deal. Now it will be your turn to grow green & I dare say you would unless I be as kind & tell you that she is a statue.'

The Queen of Naples, by the way, was the young Bavarian princess Maria Sophia, who married the Crown Prince of the Two Sicilies by proxy when she was eighteen and joined him in time for him to become king and be quickly deposed by Garibaldi. The royals retreated to Gaeta, between Naples and Rome, with those in the army who remained loyal. At the standoff in Gaeta, the handsome, militaristic queen, dressed like a soldier, wearing her Calabrian hat, and wrapped in her ample cloak, reviewed the troops and encouraged the soldiers.

When Gaeta was reduced to rubble, the stones of its enclosing wall tumbled into the sea, King and Queen accepted the hospitality of the Pope in Rome, took up residence in the Palazzo Farnese, passed the season in

Rome, and summered in Austria or Germany. They moved to Paris in 1870, the year the Pope claimed infallibility and lost Rome, retreating behind the walls of what was left of his terrestrial realm, Vatican City. 'Rome belongs no more to the dear old gentle man with the Tiarra!!!' Hattie wrote to Wayman Crow in disbelief.

While living in Rome, the Queen came to the studio to pose for Hattie, in the clothes she actually wore during the siege of Gaeta, the riding habit nearly concealed by a large cloak. It was the sculptor's 'happy' idea, as Cornie called it, of placing on the base of the deposed despot's statue the simple inscription 'Gaetae Maria Regina.' Charlotte couldn't get her foot into the court, while Hattie slept with royalty.

'The romance of my life was centered in Garatshausen and the Queen of Naples. My intimate friendship with this lovely woman was an episode to be remembered,' Hattie told Cornie. She was fascinated by the grace and beauty of the 'violet eyed' queen.

The *passion* of Hattie's life, however, was not the militaristic queen but the woman who descended from Highland chieftains and became Jane Welsh Carlyle's great friend, the second Lady Ashburton.

Hattie's letters are full of fun, flirting, high spirits, and the jealousy of a woman who sounded relieved not to have to posture a pious monogamy. She and Lady Loo were well matched when it came to erotic adventures and they loved each other in their free fashion all their lives. Lady Loo's daughter Maysie, who once brought Mrs. Carlyle from 'Babyless Places,' was nicknamed 'Twinniekins' by Hattie. The joke was that they looked alike and that Hattie was Maysie's 'fat little sister.' Lady Loo became 'the mother' or 'the dear mother.' Hattie too had become a daughter of the heart.

It would be Hattie who sent notes to Mr. Carlyle through Lady Loo, Hattie who would travel to Addiscombe and Melchet, as had Jane and as Carlyle continued to do.

When she was staying in London with the King and Queen of Naples one season, she saw Carlyle and 'his watchful friend Froude' often. Hattie recalled:

'One day being at his house in Cheyne Row, the conversation turned upon art, and Carlyle, always more philosopher than artist, delivered himself of the following original remark:—

'"Yesterday I visited an exhibition of Japanese Art, and there beheld figures thoroughly bestial in form—Art is not dead yet."

'"Is that your idea of art, Mr Carlyle?"

'Little Mary Baring again,' Carlyle labeled this photograph of Lady Loo's daughter, ca. 1865. Maysie grew up to marry Lady Marian Alford's nephew, Lord William Compton, later the Marquess of Northampton.

' "Well, they looked natural."

' "Now that is the equivalent," I returned, "of saying that what looks natural is artistic. I thought that art meant the study of beauty as well as of nature." '

Carlyle did not take Hattie's opinions very seriously. But then, Hattie once heard Carlyle growling that the well-known physicist and author of *On the Connexion of the Physical Sciences,* her elderly friend Mary Somerville, had never done or said anything original. Hattie remarked, 'To the Carlyle mind, wherein women never played any conspicuous part, perhaps not.'

Hosmer kept up her connection with another widower as well, Robert
Browning, who had not returned to Italy since the death of his wife. He
along with the Storys and Lady Marian Alford sent Hattie a round-robin
while vacationing in Scotland at Lady Loo's hunting lodge, Loch Luichart.
They wanted her to join them:

> *Dear Hosmer, or still dearer Hatty—*
> *Mixture of* miele *and* latte,
> *So good and sweet and—somewhat fatty—*
>
> *Why linger still in Rome's old glory*
> *When Scotland lies in cool before ye?*
> *Make haste and come!—quoth Mr Story.*
>
> . . . .
>
> *Nay, though past clay, you chip the Parian,*
> *Throw chisel down! quoth Lady Marian.*
>
> . . . .
>
> *Don't send an old acquaintance frowning,*
> *But come and quickly! quoth R. Browning.*
>
> . . . .
>
> *Lady Ashburton . . .*
> *Thus ends this letter—ease my sick heart,*
> *And come to my divine Loch Luichart!*

Hattie answered in part:

> *They think perchance, those loving friends*
> *Who made that lucky hit,*
> *That though stuck fast in Roman clay*
> *I do not care a bit. . . .*
>
> *Believe me if I had my weigh*
> *Though Fortune is a chary 'un*
> *The scales I'd turn, to take in turn,*
> *A turn with Lady Marian.*

She ended addressing Lady Loo:

And tho' fair hostess, though it seem
I'm seeming to be ill,
Yet sight of thee and of thy Loch
Would make me Chubbier still.

It may not be—may not—alas
Is the refrain I sing,
Yet comforts me this fling at thee,
This little Highland fling.

She signed it 'Your very lovingest, H.G.H.'

They were all such good friends. Until Browning did not marry Lady Loo. Then Hattie dropped her long and intimate friendship with Robert Browning and his son without a second thought.

If Lady Loo wanted to marry a famous poet, Browning should be delighted. How dare he insult her! telling her his heart was buried in Florence, saying he might consider marrying her for his son's sake. Hattie would spread rumors all through Rome concerning the terrible behavior of 'the great Elizabeth's widower.' Not only did she champion the union, she thought she could influence it through her long friendship and was humiliated when it did not work out. She wanted Browning for her Lady. After all, it wasn't as if Loo were marrying another woman.

Charlotte, who still yearned for the aristocratic connections denied her because she was an actress, could not get over Loo's relationship with Hattie. She called Loo's leasing of Via Gregoriana Lady Ashburton's folly.

In America, when Wayman Crow would not accompany her to St. Louis, what was his excuse but that he had to go to Philadelphia with Cornie and Hattie, to help Hattie do some business for Lady Ashburton. A few years later 'the Pater,' as Hattie called him, would search Lebanon, Pennsylvania, for half a dozen 'SHAKER HATS!!!!' for the Queen of Naples and her even more beautiful sister, the Empress of Austria. With those sisters purchasing them, the hats would become all the rage in Europe, Hattie predicted.

'What would I give to see you & have you in my arms if only a moment,' Hattie wrote to her spouse Lady Loo; they would soon be on Via Gregoriana together. Hattie would be reunited with her thirteen-year-old 'Twinniekins,' her 'sister' Maysie. 'The dear mother' would be once more with her *two* daughters. 'This will enable us all to do Laocoön once more.'

The three of them would wrap themselves around each other like the classical nude of Laocoön and his two sons, in deadly embrace, as they were surrounded and devoured by the serpent. Careless as ever about the deeper implications of her metaphors, Hattie was ready for fun.

CHARLOTTE WASN'T as lucky. The terribly hot European weather wreaked havoc, exacerbating Charlotte's pain as she traveled to the cures of Vienna and Munich and then on to Paris.

Finally back in London she had so many papers to destroy, as well as some to seal up for her darling Emma alone.

Sir James had died in Edinburgh, so when two new lumps appeared she consulted once more with Paget. They would burn the lumps out with sulfuric acid, rather than attempt another surgery. For a time she endured this treatment every two hours.

Homeopathically, ten drops of extract of arsenic was to be taken three times a day after meals. When she became toxic, nitric acid was substituted.

Her friends were angels of patience, watching her as if she were the treasure of the house—*la stella di casa*. Still, as she told Emma, at fifty-four, she was finding out that constant pain made one very selfish and very hopeless.

Emma bewailed her separation from her Auntie and regretted she had not been able to wait upon her the way Miss Stebbins had. The rivalry with Miss Stebbins continued.

Charlotte thanked God that Emma *was* away and could not see the hourly agony. Sallie was her only necessity—for Sallie comforted her through the nights.

'I wake every half hour or hour as the case may be to sit up & holding up my two breasts with the palms of my two hands . . . let Sallie rub my back & otherwise soothe me from the stiffness which comes from lying on my side.' Once when Charlotte was in severe pain, she asked Sallie to come into bed with her to 'rub my stomach round & round until I fell asleep for half an hour.'

Emma brought the children to their 'big Mamma' at the baths of Malvern by the end of the summer, and soon left by herself.

Well, not exactly by herself. Nannie Lemmon was at Malvern as well.

The morning Emma left, Nannie dropped by on her way to the spa to tell Charlotte she was leaving the next day. And she asked Charlotte one of her questions.

'Do you think I came to Malvern purposely on account of Emma being here, and do you think Emma made arrangements beforehand for such a meeting?'

'I told her frankly, *I did not.*'

Emma would not consciously make an arrangement so discomforting to Charlotte, would she? Plan to meet her lover at her Auntie's sickbed, then leave the children with Auntie and discreetly make off with Nannie? 'We had much talk, but to little purpose.'

Charlotte would be very glad when Ned and Emma and the children were at St. Louis. 'I hope you will not entertain the idea of Emma's fixing herself in the East anywhere,' she wrote to Mr. Crow in a secret letter. 'I am anxious the little boys should be brought up there.'

On 9 October 1870 Charlotte wrote Emma her last letter from abroad: 'One little word—precious daughter & friend & niece & lover (the greatest comprehends the least & visa versa).'

Emma must not think their '*real home*' was broken up. 'I have henceforth & forever no home—such as a house & furniture makes,' Charlotte declared.

'Darling . . . To a woman, there where her dear ones are is the home of her heart. . . . Home has heretofore meant *house* to me. Now my home is anywhere in the world . . . with you & Ned & the children. Wherever your home may be—will be mine & I shall be in it, as much as I can.'

Lady Ashburton took over the house on 38–40 Via Gregoriana, and Charlotte sailed home.

The Door of Exit

E VEN AS Charlotte tore her house in Rome apart, writing that she would henceforth have no earthly home, she was already planning to build a new life for her belongings. Emma, Ned, and the children would live far from sin in St. Louis, Missouri, in the winter and join her in Newport, Rhode Island, for the summer (a season which in those days extended from 1 June through the middle of October).

Within months of her return, Edwin Booth, who survived his brother's disgrace, wrote to Charlotte, begging her to act with him next fall in New York. 'He says I need only act Queen Katherine—which will not fatigue me very much.' She was also contacted by Mrs. Kemble's agent to give readings at three hundred dollars a night—except in Boston, where she was offered her own terms. 'Does it not seem hard that I should not be able to pick up these crumbs.' In one month she could make enough to buy a house.

Emma lamented 'dirty' St. Louis to Charlotte. 'It makes me heartsick to think of your being shut up in what your own dislike has made a prison to you,' Charlotte responded. 'I cannot but be frightened sometimes that your rebelliousness should bring some calamity to you which would show you how much better it would have been for you to be satisfied with the comforts which you had in your power.'

As far as the dirt went: The coal smoke in St. Louis will be good for her children, give them a robust tone and add color to their blood which the effete, exhausted air of the continent of Europe never would do. 'Dirt is healthy for children.'

Emma had become *demoralized* ('and I use this word in a respectful sense') by her expatriate life. Every day Charlotte found more cause to repent of having ministered to Emma's six years of pleasure in Rome.

'Darling, when I tell you that I sincerely think that Rome & its association & above all, Nannie, have served to undermine the high sense of duty & religious respect which you had when I first knew you, you will see how troubled & unhappy I am, about and for you. You have developed, but in a way which is, I fear, unhealthy for yourself & all belonging to you.'

It was useless for Emma to say she wanted to be with Charlotte: 'I dont believe you would be happy *with me* any more.'

Her 'breast trouble' (she put it in quotation marks for Emma) came back while she was in Newport thinking of a summer home. She felt a little soreness in the hollow of her arm, but hoped it was the effect of the cold. It *was* cold in Newport in the winter, she found out. What concerned her more was the hard lump she felt in the scar on her left breast. 'The earth is from under my feet again.'

She wanted to try electrolysis. But when she went to the electrician in New York he told her she had put it off too long. He advised her to have the mass removed immediately and he would use electricity after her surgery.

Only one of her doctors told her he did not want her to have further surgery. He dreaded it, believing it would hasten the end. She was going to take a week to decide what to do. But she took longer.

She heard of a woman physician who treated *the blood* by herbs, so she went to Hartford, Connecticut, to consult her. She was hardly comforted when the herbalist told her that the trouble was all through her system. 'I had a day yesterday of the very worst fatigue I ever had in my life.' She almost fainted by the time she arrived back at Stamford.

She began taking the medicine the woman in Hartford gave her and was in more pain than before. 'The gland in my arm is very sore, for the first time, & all down my arm inside it is very sore—but I strive to keep up a cheerful outside & not let people know all I feel.'

A gentleman who had close to a miracle worked upon him by a Philadelphian was coming the next day. The clipping about this new cure remains in her papers. A Professor Scott treated cancer by applying chloride of chromium on the surface of the sore. It was said that in a few hours it converted the tumor into carbon and the lump crumbled away.

'You would not imagine how thin I have become with this last three weeks of agony & anxiety. I am trying to go without meat & without brandy—for my hands are in an unutterable state.' A condition of the blood and a form of psoriasis were tearing at her finger ends and palms.

Nothing helped. She had Mr. Crow draw up a new will, as she decided to have a second operation. But then she changed her mind, writing to Mr. Crow: 'I have had reason to see that I should get only another slight reprieve by an operation, & after mature deliberation, consulting what I believe to be the best wishes of all who love me most, I have come to the conclusion to submit myself to God's will without doing any further violence to myself.'

She would do for herself all she could do within reason, and for the rest, God knew best. Leaving herself in the hands of God, she separated herself from her illness. Returning to Newport, she concentrated on something she very much enjoyed: scouting prime real estate.

She rented a place for Emma and the children that summer, and by July bought a corner lot in the most fashionable section of town. She hired Richard Morris Hunt to design the house at the intersection of Rhode Island Avenue and Catherine Street to be ready for her and her belongings by next summer. She herself would not have time to supervise construction. She would be too busy paying for it.

'I *may act*,' she wrote to Booth, 'and if I find it too much for me, I must give up! But you know I have indomitable energy and I shall try to take care and not overdo myself.'

So once more she came out of permanent retirement. And what an entrance it was. Everyone knew she was suffering from cancer. Her Edinburgh operation had been reported in the *New York Evening Post* under the headline SUFFERING PATIENTLY BORNE. In the item, Sir James was quoted as replying to a dinner guest who innocently remarked Miss Cushman was complaining of a slight illness and would be unavailable for a few days:

'Slight illness! Do you know that I operated on her for cancer this morning?'

Her reappearance at Booth's Theatre in New York on 25 September 1871 as Henry VIII's doomed Queen Katherine could not have been more dramatic. Her audience were saying goodbye to a legend as they watched Queen Katherine die. Her every word, every look was applauded. 'I am not ignorant of the value of my return to the stage as a *finality*.'

A month later she was playing Lady Macbeth once more. 'I am called out everywhere on the slightest excuse.'

'My breast is somewhat better than it was two weeks ago, when it gave me severe alarm again. I believe it will pass,' she wrote in November. 'Ah God is very merciful to me! The houses the last week have been wonderful. On Saturday yesterday matinee & evening the receipts were $4,935!'

In Boston, she took to the reading desk. They paid her $750 a night and in the smaller houses $500. If her voice held out till Christmas, 'I can easily make $50,000 this season.'

When she played the doomed Queen Katherine there, 'the people, the masses, dont applaud but they cry & that satisfies me better.'

Just before Christmas, she was cauterized for the second time. Not a word to anyone, she cautioned Emma. She was glad to get away from the excitement of Boston, 'but I have had too *triumphant* a time in every way not to be sorry it is over.' After church on Sunday—Episcopal church, she converted in Rome—so many people waited to see her that 'the consequence was a regular reception—more people than I can tell you.'

There was joy when she counted her receipts before joining Miss Stebbins at Hyde Park: 'Only to think that I have earned & recd $39,000 in 13 Weeks! I feel like a child going away from school for holidays to think that after tomorrow's journey . . . I shall have 10 days freedom from night work.'

It was as cold as Siberia that winter, but Miss Cushman missed none of her scheduled readings in New England. Why should snow stop her when cancer didn't? Her readings were a huge success. The reviews were superlative. Miss Stebbins, in a state of 'wonder & *praise*,' said, 'I declare you walked upon that platform as if you had not done anything else in all your life.'

And Sallie said, 'I expected nothing but to see you die at the end. It was perfect.'

The next night she was reading in a small village of only fifty-two hundred inhabitants. Yet they 'had an *auction* for sale of the choice of seats!!'

She was a living legend, applauded for her own well-advertised brand of Pluck.

She toured the West. One week in February it was Cincinnati, Dayton, back to Cincinnati, Columbus, Cleveland, Detroit.

Detroit particularly thrilled her. Everyone knew she was staying with one of the first families there, and that, as it often did, brought out all the people.

After the disastrous Chicago fire of 1871 which destroyed that strong city, she still performed—benefits.

In her Western tour that winter Charlotte went back and forth to Emma in St. Louis, but she was first in the service of her audience. 'Oh darling I was so thankful I was coming back to you & am only sorry I came away, though I thought I was right to earn the money if I could.' But it was so much more than money.

Even Charlotte, with her no-nonsense approach to her work, knew she was first and foremost in the service of her one faithful lover. How many times in her life had it saved her, her blessed Work.

Nor was she deluded. She knew she was not the actress she once was. Early in her run she wrote to a friend in England: 'If you have seen any of the New York papers from about the 26th September and the 17th October to 29th of the same, you would have seen that my country-people give me credit for growth in grace, and *believe* now firmly that they have a Siddons of their own! Of course it is not displeasing to me to be so considered, but *I know better!* I dare say I have grown intellectually, and my suffering has been sent to me in vain if I have not improved in spirit during all the time I have been away from my profession; but as a mere actress, I was as good, if not better, eleven years ago than I am now. But what is printed lives for us, and what is conceived and acted lives only in the *memory* of the beholder; thus I am glad that such things should be *printed* of me.'

Charlotte found in her life what no novel of her time could posit for a woman: the only happy ending was the persistence of her work.

Emma, carrying her fourth child, was in the blush of yet another friendship, one with the sensational Swedish opera and stage star, the young Christine Nilsson. Nilsson had risen from the humblest beginnings in Sweden to world fame. To make a living for her peasant family, the thirteen-year-old sang at traveling fairs and was discovered at one of them. Nilsson had no claim of Mayflower roots to sustain her as she climbed, but she did have *beauty* as well as talent.

'She is now twenty-seven years old,' Annie Fields, who hosted her in Boston, noted. 'Her light hair, deep blue eyes, full glorious eyes, are of the Northern type, but her broad intellectual brow, her beautiful teeth, and strong character belong only to the type of genius and beauty. She is not only brave, but almost imperious.' Henry James, who met her at the Fieldses', concurred.

Charlotte wrote to Emma, 'I do so wish Ned would not be so wilful & domineering in the matter of Baby's name.' Charlotte thought the new child—when he came—should be named Christian Nilsson Cushman. She had long since given up the hope of a little Carlotta.

'I think it would be sweet to have the two names of the times, "*Nilsson*" & "*Cushman*"—one in its prime, the other in its passing away, associated together.' Why should Ned mind? 'If I am not jealous of your friendship for her—I am sure no one else need be!'

By the end of April 1872, Charlotte made certain she caught up with Nilsson in Philadelphia. Nilsson was delighted to hear Charlotte call Emma's child-to-be by her own nickname, Nils. 'She always professes the extremest affection and admiration for me, but—dear—she has no more head than heart! She has had a splendid success here—has conquered all the critics, has the world at her feet.'

Nilsson and Charlotte talked about Nilsson's forthcoming marriage '& she told me a good deal in an epigrammatical way. . . . "He is every man & no man," as Shakespeare says. She will always be master of the situation, *because* she does not *care* as much as to be miserable about him in his doings. We bade each other goodbye! swearing eternal friendship! I think she cares for you, as much as she *can* care, but her head—her heart: she says if she had a trouble she would come to you with it sooner than any woman she knows—& this is, after all, a good test of feeling.'

Hunt completed Villa Cushman, that gingerbread fantasy, by the summer. But without supervision, there were many disappointments. Hunt had actually constructed the master bedroom without a fireplace. Architects! Still, Charlotte spent the following summers in Newport with all her belongings, the winters at work.

'Celebrities Near Newport.

'. . . At Miss Durfee's Tea House, near the Glen, Miss Cushman the distinguished tragedienne, and her friend Miss Emma Stebbins, of New York (who bids fair to take rank with the greatest sculptors the world has ever produced), have taken refuge from the heat and crowd of the cities and hotels.

'. . . The number of women distinguished for artistic and literary attainments, who have been in town this season, has been commented on universally by correspondents. For the one which we have added to the list (that of Miss Stebbins), we predict a brilliant future. Some of her works—a bust of Miss Cushman among them—will soon be placed on exhibition in New York, where they have arrived from her studio in Rome.'

Two years after the house in Newport was built, Lady Loo did not renew her lease on Via Gregoriana. Only then did Charlotte send Ned back to Rome to see that Auntie's possessions and Miss Stebbins' art were shipped to what would become a jam-packed Newport home.

But her Roman affairs were not the sole or most important reason for sending Ned abroad. As ill as she was, her concerns were with her belong-

Above: Charlotte Cushman reading. One in the last series of pictures taken of Charlotte Cushman, who resumed her acting career in America after being operated on for breast cancer. The ample bodices of her well-made dresses skillfully concealed bandaging, just as she herself valiantly concealed her pain. Right: Christine Nilsson, Swedish singer and actress, singing Ophelia in America and receiving the accolades which once greeted Charlotte when she too was in her late twenties, making her London debut.

Villa Cushman. When she left Rome, Charlotte dramatically vowed to make her home nowhere but in the hearts of her belongings. When she reached America, she bought property in Newport, Rhode Island, and hired Richard Morris Hunt to build Villa Cushman, for her and her belongings.

ings. 'I sent him abroad,' she wrote to Susan's daughter, her niece Rosalie, 'first to settle this matter of yours, then wind up my Roman affairs—but if he does nothing else but only the settlement of your affairs—I shall feel satisfied that the money is well spent.'

For Rosalie Muspratt was being prevented from marrying the perfectly decent man she loved, till Ned arrived in Liverpool and did better for his half sister than Charlotte thought he would. 'I am so thankful, darling,' she wrote to Rosalie, 'that it is settled—and that you are able to marry the man of your choice—so few girls do that. Circumstances are often such that it is impossible, & when a woman marries from interest & not from the highest & truest affection, I do not see how she can expect any true happiness— marriage at the best is but a lottery. The coming together into one life & one house—two people who have been brought up very differently with different opinions & associations is very very difficult at the best. . . . When people love each other much this is easier.'

From what Rosalie told her of Mr. Roberts, Charlotte believed her niece chose wisely for her own happiness. 'Herein you are happier far than your poor mother was—who was not able to marry the man she most cared for, hence she led anything but a happy life.'

In the same year as this letter to Rosalie, a friend read out loud to her a poem by a struggling, unknown poet that appeared in *Lippincott's Magazine*, a long poem about the energy of America itself, entitled 'Corn.'

Charlotte wrote the young Sidney Lanier a letter of appreciation that began an epistolary friendship interspersed with occasional visits. To him Charlotte became 'Art's artist, Love's dear woman, Fame's good queen!'

However, by the time Charlotte settled Rosalie's affairs and Sidney Lanier entered her life, Charlotte was ready to cut back her activities, if not her friendships. Her health was deteriorating and so was the box office, though not as badly as the general economy. There was a financial panic in 1874 that affected even Mr. Crow. Charlotte was surprised by his evident concern, and did not miss a beat in telling him his firm could borrow money she had for her *four* grandsons. (Baby 'Nils' was named Victor.) The interest she wanted for the children was 10 percent and it did not matter to her who paid it. This was actually quite a tactful way of showing Mr. Crow her complete confidence in him and in his business. Ned's ironworks—he *had* listened to Auntie in the long run—were lying idle and he and Emma had moved into a smaller house in St. Louis.

Between cancer and economic crises, Cushman decided it was once more time to bid farewell to the stage—and reap the box office receipts of an emotional goodbye. The event was advertised in New York that November. After eight performances at Booth's Theatre, Miss Charlotte Cushman would perform for the last time, in the role that first brought her to the dramatic stage, Lady Macbeth. The theatre planned to have a carriage with white horses waiting for her and an escort by torchlight back to her hotel after her final performance. She forbade it, saying if they did that she would not leave the theatre.

Charlotte was extremely nervous. She wrote her own farewell speech but dreaded giving it, always afraid she would forget what she had written. But the reason went deeper. After the performance the stage was crowded with so many of those in art, literature, and the drama. And Charlotte reappeared, not as Lady Macbeth but as herself, devoid of ornamentation, in an ample, tastefully simple, steel-gray dress. She took her place on stage left as a long ode was recited to her: *Salve, Regina.*

After that William Cullen Bryant, head of the presentation committee, delivered the address. In the speech she prepared in response, she said, 'If the few words I am about to say, savour of egotism or vain glory—you will, I am sure, pardon me, inasmuch as I am here only to speak of myself!'

And it was that which affected her nerves: appearing on the stage not in a role but as herself. 'You would seem to compliment me, upon an honorable life,' the unmarried actress told her audience. As she looked back, 'it seems to me that it would have been absolutely impossible for me to have led any other. In this I have, perhaps, been mercifully helped more than are many of my more beautiful sisters in art.'

She was thrown at an early age into a profession for which she had received no special education or training, 'by the press of circumstance.' She found, paraphrasing her friend Longfellow, 'Life sadly real and intensely earnest,' and resolved to take from this her text and watchword. 'To be thoroughly *in earnest*, intensely in earnest. . . . I do not believe that any great success in any art can be achieved without it!'

Her great success that night was unprecedented. 'They say such a demonstration has *never been made to any human being in this country*. Not even political demonstrations coming anywhere near it. The number of people must have been 25,000 . . . & it looked exactly like the Piazza del Popolo—at the fireworks.'

Before the performance, the big square in front of Fifth Avenue and Twenty-third Street was crammed with human beings, all the way across Madison. The streets were so jammed that the '*horse* cars' were stopped fifteen minutes at a time for the roadway to be cleared.

'The sight in the Theatre was magnificent & crammed to the door with $2. admissions, & the speculation waxing fat rather increased prices they made people pay. Then the ceremony at the end, which was what had made me ill all the week.'

Afterwards, the management stuck to their word, in the sense that she was taken from the private carpenters' entrance at Twenty-third Street, but there she was put in an elaborate carriage which went up the street, 'all the way surrounded by a howling mass of human beings—with torches & fireworks.'

Rockets shot up all along her drive, and she was taken not to the back but to the front entrance of the Fifth Avenue Hotel, where a room had been reserved to which she invited a 'few' private friends.

Once she was in the hotel, the corridors were so jammed with admirers that she could hardly move along.

When she finally got to her room, 'I had to go upon the balcony, & then

'Address & Presentation at Booth's Theatre,' above, and 'The Torch Light Procession,' below, from *Frank Leslie's Illustrated Newspaper,* portray the ceremonies held for Charlotte Cushman's farewell from the stage on Saturday evening, 7 November 1874, and give some idea of the adulation the actress received in her lifetime.

the shouting was something awful to hear. I stayed until I thought I should die with fatigue—& then waved my handkerchief at them & went in. I did not get to my bed until 2 o'clock.'

New York had outdone itself for Cushman.

After that, the actress proceeded on to her *next* farewell performance—in Philadelphia. 'I never had stage fright *so badly* in my life—as I have had in these two speeches I had to make in New York & here. The same way, when as a girl I came out in opera, I stood with my hands clenched tight together in terror—so did I stand in New York—& here last night—& on both occasions it has made me heartsick. I had a good cry last night after it was over. . . . I cant make speeches, at least written ones. The few words I speak to my audience at the reading desk—I get along with very well, but speeches are not my forte.'

She found herself weaker after the two evenings.

She realized her cancer was progressing when she arrived in Cincinnati. 'A new phase has set in—in this inflammation—swelling & hardening of my left arm—& it has frightened me.' She was more depressed than she ever remembered being, and had a feeling she ought to get back east. By the time she arrived in Chicago, she did not think she'd be able to make it to Emma or fulfill her engagements in St. Louis.

She blamed the progression of her illness on the aftermath of the farewell to New York, which made her so angry that it inflamed her physically. What did those New Yorkers think a farewell performance meant—goodbye? What was all this uproar about? All through the country the papers had picked up New York's lead and criticized her for performing after New York gave her a hero's send-off. She was at the center of a growing controversy.

Didn't she have a disclaimer in her farewell speeches? 'I have reserved to myself the right of meeting you again where you have made me believe that I give you the pleasure which I receive myself at the same time,—at the reading-desk.'

Readings she gave. And through the West performances. Previous commitments, she explained, as she continued to pick up new commitments along the way. She still entertained the hope of getting to California to act, to see the whole sweep of her beloved America before she died. She was pressuring Jay Gould to lend her a railway carriage for the trip. She was sure if he granted her a personal interview, he could be persuaded. She would travel to the West with Ned escorting her. It was her California dream.

She returned to unforgiving New York before Christmas. The pain in her breast was almost continuous. Unable to be with her grandsons for the holidays, she directed Emma to buy for each the gift he most wanted in the world, and not to spare expense. She was so weak she could only write one letter a day. You should see my poor breast, she told Emma.

Incredibly, by February of the New Year, despite her physical condition, Charlotte was back in Chicago performing.

It was another brutal winter. Like the North Pole in Albany, twenty-two below, and in Chicago 'I have blankets up at all the windows & only the light coming in from the upper pane. . . . I can but do my best & not work any harder than absolutely necessary to get through the play.' Miss Stebbins was with her, as was Sallie.

She got to St. Louis through an awful snowstorm just in time to dress and play Lady Macbeth. The next day, Saturday, the thirteenth of March, she collapsed, and it took her three and a half weeks at Mr. Crow's house to come to herself. Emma's post-panic house was too small to accommodate her. During her illness the weather became very warm. 'The grass around the house becoming very green & the little bushes budding,' she wrote to brother Charlie. But the wind from the south felt just like the sirocco of a Roman spring, enervating her at a time when it was hardly sweet to do nothing.

Back in Philadelphia in April to do readings, she actually forgot Emma's thirty-sixth birthday. 'It is not that my love is any less—only I seem to be less thoughtful of others—you must forgive me & believe in my love just the same as of the old old time when we knew each other first.'

Then on to yet another farewell performance; in her hometown she played Lady Macbeth. For the last time? The audience's credulity grew thin.

'In leaving the stage finally it has always been my intention to make my last appearance in Boston,' Cushman said in this farewell speech. 'It has been *implied,* if not declared and repeated in the newspapers about the country, that I should not have appeared upon the stage after the great ovation which was paid to me in New York.' She told the Boston audience, through them she told America, she was only fulfilling her prior commitments, only doing her duty.

Miss Stebbins backed her up in her *Memories:*

'After the farewell in Boston on May 15, 1875, Miss Cushman went on a short reading-tour to Rochester, Buffalo, Syracuse, Auburn, and Ithaca.

'On June 2d she read at Easton, Pennsylvania, and from there she went for a few days to Lenox, Massachusetts, where she was much interested in altering and furnishing a small cottage, to which she hoped to retreat in the late days of summer, when the damp heat of Newport became oppressive and baleful to her.'

It was Miss Stebbins who fell in love with the small cottage; Miss Stebbins who bought it. A house just big enough for her and Charlotte and Sallie.

Charlotte felt better in Lenox in the little house that September. She joked that Lenox had become fashionable enough to have its own burglary. The post office was broken into and about fifteen dollars taken. Then the same people went to the store nearby and blew open a safe and got another fifteen.

She wrote to Emma every day, sending her penciled bulletins about her health. She was now consulting a young English doctor she met in Boston, one Dr. Thornton.

Charlotte had reached a stage in her illness where she could hardly walk. The 'jar of walking' caused her great pain in *both* her breasts, and her swollen left arm pulled her to one side.

She loved it in Lenox with Miss Stebbins. It was so beautiful by the end of September that she hated to leave. 'My inclination & *pleasure* want to keep me here while the weather will permit me, for the good I am getting to my general health which shows itself every day.'

But it was her duty to go to Boston, where Dr. Thornton would start a series of treatments. The doctor was so sanguine that she submitted to the treatment for the sake of the result. 'It seems strange that this should always be with me a *necessary* sort of struggle between my duty & my pleasure & inclination!'

Dr. Thornton constantly showed her changes in her condition that neither she nor Miss Stebbins could see. He treated her with external and internal medicine, gave her sedatives that allowed her to sleep.

She could no longer hold up her arm. 'Ah, it is so sad to suffer, apparently unnecessarily.' The doctor spent a lot of time sitting by her and watching her arm, claiming *he* could see the swelling decrease.

Charlotte's daily bulletins are filled with accounts of her asking the doctor if she was getting better. She was, he told her, and pointed out invisible improvements. Constantly she reported the doctor was sanguine, the doctor was elated, the doctor was sure she was progressing.

In the long run, Charlotte treated her illness so differently from the way Jane Welsh Carlyle treated hers. Once more they were half sisters, half contrasts. Mrs. Carlyle knew it was she who, in collaboration with Dr. Russell, must save her own life. At the end of her life, a desperate Charlotte gave over to the doctors.

'Dr T . . . chuckles with delight over this case—& says he will stake his life in the result. [Dr.] Jones says he wont cure me. We shall see.'

In one sense it was good that pain, not duty, ultimately encouraged her to leave Lenox, where she had her last taste of wild blueberries, changing leaves, and the exquisite beauty of a New England fall. For Thornton could do no more for her than be, as Sidney Lanier called him, her inspired quack. Perhaps deep down she knew it: 'The Dr continues sanguine. I am sorry to say I am not so.'

Of course his treatments internally and externally caused her more pain. How was she to get well if she did not suffer more cures? A new acid he applied externally increased her suffering twenty times, 'but he is satisfied that he is doing rightly.' That from the Parker House on 21 October 1875. To Thornton's temporary credit, he did concoct a 'calmant' that lulled her as other sedatives including morphine, ether, and opium could not. But then that drug no longer worked and terribly upset her stomach.

The Parker House was where she spent her last five months. She wrote to Emma that she and Ned should leave the children in Newport, do the business they had to wind up in St. Louis, and then come back to the house in Newport to be in easy call for her, at least until February.

February 1876. That must have been a case of her instincts again. She wrote to her 'sweet little boy Carlino,' her favorite, in late October, 'I have a great deal of pain, but the Doctor thinks I am going on all right . . . & if I ever do get well—wont we all be very happy? We will have a jollification & a bonfire & all sorts of fun.'

At the Parker House, friends came and went. The one doctor's order Charlotte could not obey was refusing her visitors. She *must* not be separated from her friends. As late as the third of February she spoke to Miss Stebbins about the possibility of reinstating the California tour.

At the same time, just as she once meticulously laid out stationery for her mother and informed her—and later Ned—about appropriate postage, as she once adroitly kept abreast of the shipping news to send her letters by the swiftest route and to plan itineraries for herself and others, she now meticulously made the arrangements for her funeral service and burial. King's Chapel for the service. Mount Auburn for her final rest. When she visited her plot in the tranquil, wooded cemetery, she was so pleased with its hilly setting and its view of dear Boston. She talked about the site and its beauty with a cheerful brightness peculiarly her own, Miss Stebbins recorded.

By Christmastime she slept, but not Mrs. Carlyle's waking sleep. 'The deathliness of sensation on waking was more dreadful than anything I ever felt in my life.'

'Still the Dr is satisfied,' she wrote on Christmas Eve. 'During the last week, my state had put him through a tremendous struggle with himself & his methods & he had had to go away from me to have his fights alone.' He was better pleased this morning, she told Emma, and she quoted lines from James Russell Lowell's 'Columbus':

> *One faith against a whole earth's unbelief,*
> *One soul against the flesh of all mankind.*

Obviously Thornton was Charlotte's last hope and she clung to it like an American on a Roman foxhunt, getting the last bit of energy from her hack. The way she saw her own bodily illness through the doctor's eyes and empathically appreciated his struggles over it was of course the attitude of a woman in the last stages of incurable disease, grasping at any straw. But was it as well the way she had lived her life, insisting that she gave of herself, that everything she did was out of duty for her 'belongings'; that her own well-being was sacrificed for them, was in them, in others?

Was this strong woman as privately dependent on others for her well-being as she was openly dependent on Dr. Thornton? She had to be at the center of a circle of love—and somehow, by hook or crook, no matter how disappointed she became in her life, by Matilda Hays, by Emma Stebbins, by Emma Crow Cushman—by Jane Welsh Carlyle's refusal to know her—she picked herself up and with time, energy, and relentlessness reinvented the circle. The great empathetic range of her acting had something to do with the centrality of other people to her own well-being. She seemed to find her own reality through others: 'I am sympathetic & so, more a lover of my kind than *most* people—hence I *must* see people, & it is useless to attempt to pen me up. I cannot be saved in *this* respect & it is folly to try!'

One day she shocked her visiting friends by a violent fit of retching—the next day it was reported in the papers (and the day after that denied). She demanded her private life, she had to have it, but to the world she was a very public person. Beyond the corridors of the Parker House, the world waited.

She wrote to Emma, at the end of Dr. Thornton's twelve-week treatment: 'He says my sufferings would have been worse if I had *had* no treatment—& I dare say it is true—but oh—the chances seem tempting to me to have left it alone.'

However, she listened to the doctor, not herself, and allowed Thornton to extend her treatment, till the end of January. 'The doctor nearly stood on his head when he came into the room, he was so delighted—to find the arm exactly ¼ of an inch less all the way down, after I had been up & about for 2 hours—so *that* looks like progress.'

By February Charlotte Cushman was living day by day. On Tuesday, 6 February 1876, 'I have been sitting at the side of The Looking Glass slab,' she wrote Emma, '& destroying any quantities of letters which have accumulated since I came here.'

It snowed two days later: 'For me as I sit here, a cripple, unable to get about, & the area of my rooms being so small . . . I dont suppose I feel the change as much, though the sudden cold I feel, very palpably!'

Her mood changes were violent. She had fits of hysteria. She woke at two and rang for Sallie, who came in and got her up and shook her pillows and then rubbed her feet until she went off to sleep once more. She woke at five-thirty and then napped off and on till seven-thirty, when 'Sallie opened my shutters to the gorgeous sunshine & I lay and watched my pigeons getting their breakfast.'

Miss Stebbins remembered it too, how they watched pigeons and sparrows negotiate the snow-filled sill. Always the birds were fed before the two women had their breakfast together on Charlotte's bed: 'They are so tame now, that when the expected meal is delayed they crowd the window-sill, and as the morning sun pours into those windows they are pleasant objects, with their burnished necks and bright glancing eyes.'

Charlotte's handwriting was terrible on 9 February, full of pain, but always she wrote to Emma herself when she could. She knew how seeing Miss Stebbins' or Sallie's handwriting caused a fright. She had had an awful night and an awful chill. The doctor insisted she take her medicine, though it was not agreeing with her:

'He is sorry to say that in taking this medicine I must get thinner. What shall I look like if I get thinner?'

On the tenth she could not sleep. She had Sallie read to her, hoping the monotony and her indifference to what was being read would send her off. But 'No!' And so, extinguishing the light, devoted Sallie rubbed Charlotte's feet for an entire hour. Nothing sufficed.

On the twelfth, in her last letter to Emma written in her own hand, she told her she had walked up and down the hallway of the Parker House, 'not quite all the way to the first skylight. Do you know that I have been 46 days confined to my two rooms? as long as Edinburgh, after all the ailments

Columbus, mid-1860s, model from Emma Stebbins' scrap album. Lowell's poem 'Columbus' was always a favorite of Charlotte's, and that she asked to hear it on her deathbed was much reported. One newspaper published a poem comparing her to Columbus: 'For wast not thou, too, going forth alone / To seek new land across an untried Sea?'

which followed the operation. Ah, I am so very weak & good for nothing—but still yours & Ned's & the dear little boys most fond & loving Big mamma.'

She caught a chill in the hotel corridor, which, though painless, weakened her. She did not realize that she had reached the end.

On the night of the seventeenth she asked Miss Stebbins to read 'Columbus' aloud. It was Charlotte's favorite poem; it had already inspired Miss Stebbins to a statue.

A popular jingle kept popping into Charlotte's mind as well. Mark Twain mischievously quoted it in print, saying that to get it off *his* mind he had to pass it on to the reader:

> *Conductor, when you receive a fare,*
> *Punch in the presence of the passenjare!* . . .

It had a chorus:

> *Punch, brothers! Punch with care!*
> *Punch in the presence of the passenjare!*

Miss Stebbins read 'Columbus.' When she stumbled over the lines, blaming the dim light, Charlotte supplied them in a thickened voice. It must have been very difficult for both women to come to the end:

> *Our poor day—*
> *Remember whose and not how short it is.*
> *It is God's day, it is Columbus's,*
> *A lavish day. . . .*

Perhaps that's where Miss Stebbins stumbled, leaving the conclusion to what remained of Charlotte's voice and determination:

> *One day, with life and heart,*
> *Is more than time enough to find a world.*

Before dawn on 18 February 1876 Ned and Emma were notified and they rushed up from Newport. They were all with her. Miss Stebbins and Emma, Sallie and Ned. Her belongings. Just as she always wished. Ned bent down and brought a cup to her lips. 'Come, Auntie, here is your milk punch.'

She smiled. 'Punch, brothers,' she said. 'Punch with care.' They were her last words. She died peacefully at ten minutes past nine that morning. She had outpunched her final enemy for close to seven years and almost achieved the age of sixty.

Life and Letters

S H E   W A S   a Samson and Ruth in one,' the Reverend Murray intoned at Charlotte Cushman's funeral service. 'In her the strength of the masculine and the tenderness of the feminine nature were blended. She seemed to stand complete, with the finest qualities of either sex.'

As her coffin passed from the church to Mount Auburn Cemetery, people lined the way and applauded. Reverend Murray's address was printed on the funeral cards sent out to her adoring fans, with no attempt to blunt the masculine and feminine mixture of her nature.

The newspapers in her native land devoted entire middle spreads to her obituary. Then feature article after feature article was written: 'In the English-speaking world there was hardly a place where her name was not a household word. She had lived and died "a Virgin Queen of the dramatic stage."'

In the last years of Charlotte's life, Nannie, in her usual mischievously prodding way, had suggested Emma write her Auntie's biography. Both Charlotte and Emma were alarmed at the thought of one being written. A columnist suggested it was a pity for a woman who had seen everything and known everybody for over forty years not to leave a record. 'Even if modesty had let her consider it, there was no time to make an attempt,' her twentieth-century biographer Joseph Leach wrote.

There were reasons far beyond modesty. Charlotte's private life must remain private. For posterity—which Cushman knew for an actress meant what was said *in print*—better she remain the Virgin Queen of the stage. She also realized before her death that her immense popularity cried out for a written memorial and in the last year of her life began to dictate early memories to Miss Stebbins. Should she survive, she told her spouse, 'We were to make a business out of it.'

When Charlotte talked with Emma and Ned and Sallie about *not* surviving, Miss Stebbins left the room, unable to deal with the subject. 'All she ever said to me, was in reference to the Memoir and that was only in answer to my suggestions—she wanted *me* to do it—the darling always believed I could do anything I willed to do—but I was never anything but through her—she bore me up in her strong will & made me whatever I was.'

From England brother Charlie explained to journalists that his sister remained single due to the miscarriage of an early love affair in Albany, and newspapers carried accounts of an earlier engagement as well. Posthumously, the Samson of Charlotte's nature was being quickly absorbed by Ruth, a Ruth who followed intense duty to family and to Work.

Soon after her death, the family came together in the way Charlotte wished it could have in her lifetime. Ned was solicitous of Auntie Stebbins' welfare—in fact, he became her trustee as well as one of Charlotte's—and Miss Stebbins found herself in daily communication with the Cushmans. The women's rivalry had been such that one of Charlotte's doctors once was amused by Emma's accusing him of caring more for Miss Stebbins' liver than her own. Now the women consoled each other, and they shared more than their grief. There was the serious business of protecting Cushman's memory.

'I must consult with you about that memoir,' Miss Stebbins wrote to the poet Sidney Lanier. Within two weeks of Charlotte's death, friends already were pushing to write it themselves. It 'must be written by those that loved her, lest unworthy and careless hands undertake it.'

The family wondered, what *material* was there for a memoir? Miss Stebbins never kept journals or diaries, having been too overworked during her Roman years. However, she once had a large correspondence from Charlotte—the many journal letters she received while Charlotte was away with Emma. Not being able to carry the weight home was the excuse she gave for destroying the lot.

Emma kept a storehouse of letters, but was too distraught to look through them yet. Those long, weekly journal letters were written in such a small hand that each would take an hour or more to go over. It would be quite some time before she could give them to Miss Stebbins, who believed she would eventually read them *all*. Stebbins' expectation points to the possibility that she never fully discovered—or fully admitted to herself—the passionate side of Emma and Charlotte's love affair. Emma, in her grief, was certainly not about to cause more pain, and had quite a task in front of her

Miss Stebbins in 1870 (left); Charlotte Cushman (right) from a photograph by Sarony prominently featured in many newspapers after her death in 1876. The marriage of these two women artists went through many unexpected changes and trials over eighteen years. It weathered disappointments, separations, and betrayals.

when she was up to it: picking out letters that Miss Stebbins *could* read and which could become part of a memorial.

The family continued to lament that there was so little material. None of them knew anything much about the very important English years, when Charlotte became a great international star. They wrote to old friends in England such as Geraldine Jewsbury, as well as to brother Charlie, but such firsthand recollections—to be written by elderly people—took time and very little information came through at first. Sallie Mercer, with her long association with Charlotte and her razor-sharp memory, was relied on for exact information about these early years; she was close at hand, living with Ned and Emma and spending time with a very lonely Miss Stebbins.

Emma found some material she could share with Miss Stebbins and brought her Charlotte's daybook for 1844, the one recording her arrival in England; the daybook on which Charlotte's first initial was intertwined with Rosalie Sully's. The notations were so faint and cramped that Miss

Stebbins said she could hardly make them out and could only hope to deci-
pher them with a magnifying glass.

'Why did I ever leave home?' the young Charlotte wrote aboard the
Garrick. 'I almost wish I could sleep away 6 mos.'

'If only I had Rosalie here.' She dreamed about her and Rosalie on *their*
sofa, Rosalie's 'arm about my neck, her cheek resting against mine & my
lips pressed upon her hand.' If Rosalie were only with her, her dear voice,
her endearing smiles. 'While I write I am blinded & will take a few steps
upon deck.'

At night, lonely and homesick, she took to talking out loud to the
absent Rosalie, begging her to answer. She did not hear her voice, but suddenly she visualized Rosalie's lips moving to kiss her. She almost sprang
from her berth at the mere thought of her usual reply to Rosalie's kisses.
Then she sank back: 'Imagining I had her head upon my shoulder, I
dropped asleep.'

Miss Stebbins decided this was not the stuff of memoirs and began to
speak of her responsibility as 'this labour of love,' which would take much
more time and would have to await the arrival of letters Emma was still
'totally unfit' to go over. She appointed Sidney Lanier the writer, the one to
put the material together when it came, while she would take her customary place with her loved one—behind the scenes, not even her name on the
title page. Lanier was overjoyed at the assignment; tubercular and poor, he
looked forward to at least eight months of paid work, and time enough to
devote to his poetry as well. If only writing a sonnet could alleviate *her* grief,
Miss Stebbins regretted.

When Ned returned from St. Louis and consultations with his father-
in-law, Wayman Crow, he brought the news that Charlotte's estate could
not pay for the publication. Like all the best excuses, it was also true. Charlotte left more than six hundred thousand dollars, yet there were heavy
expenses in the settling of the estate and in the paying of the generous
annuities she bequeathed each of her belongings.

Though Ned was attempting to exclude Sidney Lanier from the family
business in a polite manner, Miss Stebbins took the excuse at face value. If
the estate could not pay, she'd query publishers herself with a proposal for
the book. Within some months Osgood and Company of Boston accepted,
offering to pay all charges, including Lanier's advance and a payment to
Miss Stebbins of 10 percent of the retail price for copyright. Still, the Cushmans had to approve; Stebbins would speak with Emma, in New York at

the time, as she was certain Ned would do whatever his wife wished. Lanier took this as a formality, since he and Miss Stebbins had already signed with Osgood, who was confident the book would sell very well.

How could the book sell thousands, when there was such a lack of material for it? Ned wrote to Lanier. Should Miss Stebbins fail to bring the book to completion, wouldn't Osgood go after Miss Cushman's estate to settle accounts? 'Pray excuse my suggestions, they come from Emma Crow Cushman, Trustee, a heartless being, who has to account to other trustees . . . for all expenditures of whatever nature.'

A week later, Stebbins told the poet, 'It seems to me I am justified in asking you to annul—or if possible to *postpone* our agreement with Mr. Osgood—until I can see what time brings in the way of health and additional material—& before we are finally committed to what might prove a failure.'

Lanier responded indignantly. They were already committed to Osgood, and hadn't Stebbins herself said that Ned should be kept out of the arrangements? He sent on her own earlier letter on the subject.

'I am not a business woman and cannot weigh the value of my words,' she answered. She was in no position to ignore Ned, even though she feared his inexperience. 'He is my Trustee—as well as the Trustee of the Cushman estate, and has been extremely kind to me ever since his Aunt's death, so your letter to him frightened me. . . . It is needful for me to make you understand my position entirely. I am unwilling to rest under the imputations of having acted weakly or capriciously.'

The unpleasantness almost caused Stebbins a nervous crisis and made her 'feel more & more deeply the loss of my helper & comforter who always stood between me & care of all kinds.'

Sadly, she realized that Emma, through Ned, did not want Lanier, an outsider, involved in the project. Emma's voluminous correspondence was 'so purely personal & private—that she cannot find anything suitable for the public,' Stebbins wrote, and could not think of putting it in anyone else's hands. *Facts* are what the public wants, 'and facts we have not got.'

By the first anniversary of Charlotte's death, Stebbins was writing the memoir herself, just as Charlotte had wished, and she sent the ill Lanier that news along with a 'loan.' It was slow going, she told the poet, 'but I *do* work a little and I think that little keeps me alive. Sallie's wonderful memory helps me—and her absolute confidence that I shall get well and be strong to do this—is better than medicine or doctors.'

Emma was encouraging as well and approved of the chapters which Stebbins read to her in Newport, where the family gathered to work together and where Emma kept careful control of her letters.

Though Stebbins could use the money the project would bring, especially since Charlotte's 'handsome estate' was shrinking in value and might not be able to pay out its annuities, she would not allow financial considerations to tempt her to hurry the book. She worked painstakingly and slowly, as usual, until there was the threat in April 1878 of another memorial appearing before hers. Suddenly there was a rush for her to publish by the middle of May. 'Now that I am fairly committed to the public—I feel the full force of that ancient utterance of the Psalmist (was it the psalmist—or Job?)—"Oh that mine enemy had written a book"!'

Afterword

Whenit came to the critics, Miss Stebbins compared herself to a soft-shell crab: 'Very vulnerable—but I have been that all my life—forced by circumstances into hard shelled positions.'

Miss Stebbins eulogizes her heroine ad nauseam, fails to arrange her materials in anything like an effective manner, and does not succeed in drawing a very striking portrait.

By sanctifying its subject, Stebbins' memoir trivialized its author as well. One reads nothing of Stebbins' creative power or real life. The only sculpture of her own that she mentions in the book is her bust of Charlotte. Stebbins' output was small though distinguished and her consistent need to hide herself from any professional praise so self-obliterating that not only was Charlotte's memory obscured by Stebbins' genteel and idealized prose, but so was the memory of the sculptor.

Both women attended the gala, well-publicized unveiling of Stebbins' *Bethesda Fountain* in Central Park in 1873, but the occasion is ignored. To this day *The Angel of the Waters* is known throughout the world; its creator all but forgotten. The reviews of *Charlotte Cushman: Her Letters and Memories of Her Life* helped to demoralize whatever spirit Stebbins had left, though she lingered on another four years, crushed by the belief she failed Charlotte.

Emma Crow Cushman held on to the idea of a better book in the future and entered the twentieth century with Charlotte's letters intact.

In 1913 Emma's sister Cornelia Crow Carr published *Harriet Hosmer: Letters and Memories.* Cornie deleted much that was too blatantly 'Samson-Ruth' in Hattie's nature, but she left more than one clue as to Hattie's lived

life. It was a much more substantial effort than Stebbins', though it shared
the form of the old-fashioned Victorian 'Life and Letters' where the subject's life is extolled around selected correspondence.

Hosmer had lived a long life. Neoclassical sculpture went out of favor,
but she was one of its most talented and successful practitioners, and, perhaps more importantly, through her determination, talent—and pluck—
she opened a new profession to women. By the end of the nineteenth
century, successful and extravagant as always, she spent more and more
time among the aristocrats in England, where she remained devoted to
Lady Ashburton. When Lady Loo developed breast cancer—'a very fashionable trouble,' Loo called it—Hattie stayed by her side, the way Miss
Stebbins and Sallie had stayed at Charlotte's. Soon after Lady Loo's death in
February 1903, Hattie returned to America. She had more or less given up
sculpture by then and gotten very interested in inventions. She produced an
imitation marble that was malleable and could be cast in plaster and, not
unlike the French artist Nadar, spent a lot of time and money attempting to
make a 'perpetual-motion' machine.

Hattie died in Watertown in 1908 and was buried at Mount Auburn, on
'Narcissus Path,' not too far from Charlotte's obelisk on 'Palm Avenue.'

Five years later, after Cornie's biography appeared, Emma thought more
seriously of the fate of her own letters.

As an older woman Emma turned again to the spiritual values Charlotte once insisted won her heart, and she was known as well for the
breadth of her cosmopolitan interests and her ability as a conversationalist. 'It is impossible to analyze this subtle, exquisite power of personality
that she possessed,' a friend wrote, noting that in her later years she was
blessed by 'the constant presence and congenial companionship' of one
Miss Ludwig, a younger woman, with whom she shared intellectual and
spiritual interests, making 'the relation between them one of singular
beauty.'

Emma C. Cushman published a volume of lyric Christian poetry in
1917 and *Insight: A Record of Psychic Experiences* the next year. *Insight* was
the name given to the channeled spirit that visited her and her family.

'*Insight,* are you present in this room . . . ? How do you happen to come
to us?'

'I am one of the links in the chain that connects heaven and earth. . . . I
am a part of a channel through which the Divine flows.'

Around the time she channeled *Insight,* at the age of seventy-seven,
Emma wrote 'Charlotte Cushman. A Memory.' It began, 'I once heard Miss

Cushman say, "While painters, sculptors or poets leave some visible proof of their work behind them, an actor leaves nothing but a memory, and even that is not left when those who knew him personally have gone."'

Most of the family—Sallie Mercer, Ned Cushman, and even Charlotte's favorite grandson Carlino—were lying beside Charlotte on 'Palm Avenue' by then; the deceased Miss Stebbins—laid to rest in Brooklyn—was the only one not buried beneath Charlotte's unadorned obelisk at Mount Auburn. Emma was free to entertain the idea of publishing a truer memorial than Miss Stebbins' of the woman who set the course of her life.

'The letters which Miss Cushman wrote to her friends were almost too intimate to publish, even in these days when nothing is too private or too sacred to be withheld from the public, but if I were able to print them as I hope may be done later, I should try to choose portions of them which would show what a wide range of subjects she dealt with and how far-reaching were her interests. Her letters were like miniatures in the minute detail she entered into.'

The eighteen-page typed manuscript recorded Emma's excitement the first time she saw Charlotte—onstage performing Romeo in St. Louis—and it described the transforming effect the actress had on her audience. Emma wrote of the days of the Civil War when the actress returned to support the Union cause. She remembered the weeks with President Lincoln and Secretary of State Seward and told the anecdote of how Sallie Mercer's telegram—'The rebels are expected here. What should Sallie do?'—made the sober Lincoln and the Secretary of State smile.

The short memoir, well written and fact based, was never accepted for publication. Once people clamored for Charlotte Cushman; now one couldn't even get a 'little article' about her in print. Emma understood the reason: 'Only things bearing on the great and absorbing topic of the World's War are interesting to the public at large.'

Miss Stebbins' completely misleading contemporary account would stand alone.

'How delicate, decent, is English biography, bless its mealy mouth!' Thomas Carlyle wrote. The historian/biographer must *not* succumb to society's expectation that 'Your true hero must have no features, but be a white, stainless, impersonal ghost hero.'

Carlyle, the historian, saved, put in chronological order, and edited the letters of his wife's life. He threw away nothing. And he wrote the only bio-

Thomas Carlyle with Ralph Waldo Emerson's grandson, in a
photograph requested by Emerson. On Emerson's last visit to
London in 1872, he came to see his old friend Carlyle. The
much younger Emerson, who once found his way to remote
Craigenputtock on his own, was so ill that he had trouble
finding his way to Carlyle's oft-visited house and needed a
map. Carlyle seems to be staring wistfully through Emerson's
grandchild (living in London at the time) to the past, and perhaps to memories once shared with Jane.

graphical account he ever would of a woman. Publication of the 'Reminiscence of Jane Welsh Carlyle,' Jane's letters, his letters, was another matter.
He would rather nothing was written about him after he died. He explained
to his biographer James Anthony Froude that no one would understand his
history because he had a secret in his life that was unknown even to his closest friends.

Still, like Cushman, Carlyle realized people would write about him. In

The Bethesda Fountain, 1873, by Emma Stebbins.

his case he insisted that the primary material speak for itself—his last flagellation would be with the truth. He gave all of his and Jane's letters and journals to Froude and would let him, along with two other of his executors, decide what to do with them. Dyspeptic Carlyle, complaining of his health daily, continued to gallop on his horse and lived to be an octogenarian.

Froude was the only one of Carlyle's three younger executors who outlived him, and he did what he told Carlyle he planned to do. After the Sage of Chelsea's death in February 1881, he published many of Jane's letters (three volumes) and the *Reminiscences* and used the remaining material in his four-volume biography of Carlyle.

The barrenness of Jane's life, the discord of her marriage, was exactly the material ripe for exclusion from the *Lives* of the period. Carlyle did not even destroy the sad penciled outcries from Jane's year of mental and physical pain at St. Leonards, or the journals from the years in which he abandoned her for the first Lady Ashburton. After the publication of Froude's biography of Carlyle, the chimneys of literary London gave out an abundance of smoke.

One can only imagine the letters Jane must have written to Geraldine Jewsbury through the years. In her late sixties, suffering from cancer, alone in a clinic, Geraldine was true to a promise she made to Jane and destroyed all of Jane's letters, ripping up as many as she could each day, until the task was accomplished. She died late in 1880, predeceasing the eighty-six-year-old Carlyle by four months.

So it came to be that Carlyle insured Jane's immortality by preserving her literary legacy; she is today considered one of the finest letter writers of the period. All of Jane's letters are in the process of being printed in the Duke-Edinburgh collected edition. In terms of posthumous recognition—no less fame—none of the professional women fared as well as Jane Welsh Carlyle.

It was particularly important that an independent woman be turned into a white, stainless, impersonal ghost. A woman who found meaningful work outside the home had given up her primary role as wife and mother to serve a different master. What made her respectable was that she was too devoted to her craft to have an emotional life. She might work, but she was no less 'pure' a woman, English-speaking reformers argued. Miss Somebody was as white as Carrara marble. She was a virgin for art's sake—or duty's sake, or both.

Cornie quoted Harriet Hosmer on the subject: 'You see, everybody is being married but myself. I am the only faithful worshiper of Celibacy, and her service becomes more fascinating the longer I remain in it.' Later generations took Hattie's punning words seriously without recognizing—or perhaps wanting to recognize—the hidden scroll. They misinterpreted these unmarried women's devotion to 'Celibacy.' Hattie would never marry—a man:

'An artist has no business to marry. For a man it may be well enough, but for a woman, on whom matrimonial duties and cares weigh more heavily, it is a moral wrong, I think, for she must either neglect her profession or her family, becoming neither a good wife and mother nor a good artist. My ambition is to become a good artist, so I wage eternal feud with the consolidating knot.'

LATER GENERATIONS perceived many of these independent women as prim and passionless 'old maids' detached from reality. (Such women routinely burned the personal letters that proved otherwise.)

Jane Welsh Carlyle's letters tell of an unhappy married woman, once a brilliant girl who, refusing to acknowledge her own light, would only marry genius, devoting herself to her husband's work and future fame; of a middle-aged woman who learned to take comfort in a circle of friends which came to include the American artist Charlotte Cushman. The married woman was attracted to the independent woman's strength, just as the actress was attracted to the wife's brilliance. The friends remain half sisters.

Charlotte Cushman's letters tell a different story. More than seven volumes of them are to Emma, more than two thousand sheets of just the *dated* correspondence, and they remain unpublished. With a skill equaling Jane Welsh Carlyle's, these journal letters portray the times and are Charlotte's legacy, her afterlife. The correspondence Emma refused to burn captures the inner nature of a self-made woman and points to a fuller understanding of a culture. The letters show that in the process of creating a professional life, neither Charlotte Cushman nor her circle of friends forgot to live.

NOTES

BIBLIOGRAPHY

INDEX

Notes

Abbreviations of works appear in the bibliography on pages 315–316.
The following abbreviations are also used in the notes:

Babbie	Jeannie Welsh
CC	Charlotte Cushman
ECC	Emma Crow Cushman
ES	Emma Stebbins
GEJ	Geraldine Endsor Jewsbury
HH	Harriet Hosmer
JBW	Jane Baillie Welsh (Miss Welsh)
JWC	Jane Welsh Carlyle (Mrs. Carlyle)
Lady Loo	Louisa Lady Ashburton
MR	Mary Russell
TC	Thomas Carlyle

A Home in Rome

PAGE

3 old at the time: Charlotte Cushman was born on 23 July 1816.

4 six people in tow: The fourth of the independent women living on the Corso was the rather flamboyant redheaded American journalist who wrote under the name Grace Greenwood. Then there were British Miss Smith and American Miss Vaugh.

   signed 'Charlotte': CCP, vol. 8.

   from Boston days: Dr. Hiram Hosmer delivered Story's first son, Joseph, in Boston. Joseph would die in Rome the following autumn, at the same time that Story's friends Robert and Elizabeth Barrett Browning arrived in Rome for their first winter season. For a fuller account, see Markus, *Dared and Done*, pp. 88–91.

5 'in so short a time': HH to Cornelia Crow, Jan. 1852, Carr, *Hosmer*, p. 17.

6 attain her end: Brewster, 'Miss Cushman,' p. 10. Cushman's Lady Macbeth 'had a strange reality which I had never noticed before. The bleak far-off time became our

291

own present moment. It was a being that might be one of ourselves—an ambitious, energetic young woman possessed with one mad selfish desire, and ready to peril all that was high and holy to attain her end.'

7 *si fort, si fier:* See Carr, *Hosmer,* pp. 3–7.

that 'Elizabeth' nonsense!: W. W. Story to James Russell Lowell, 11 Feb. 1853, Hudson, *Browning,* p. 271.

9 gray-blue eyes: For a fuller account of William Page, see Markus, *Dared and Done,* pp. 197–206.

termed a 'female marriage': New information about Matilda Hays' life and about her stormy relationship with CC can be found in Lisa Merrill's recently published *When Romeo Was a Woman* (Ann Arbor: University of Michigan Press, 1999), a valuable study of CC which debuted just as I put this book to bed.

11 dissatisfied wife: Leach, *Bright Particular Star,* p. 241.

12 'my own terms': Knowledge of Cushman's early days in London, what she ate, what she said to Maddox, Maddox coming to see her, was the result of Sallie Mercer's sharp recollections of that time. See Stebbins, *Cushman,* pp. 45–46, and Leach, *Bright Particular Star,* pp. 141–42.

13 'never more delighted,' he wrote: CCP, vol. 12, no. 3564, Leach, *Bright Particular Star,* p. 147.

'*success in London*': CC to her mother, 2 March 1845, CCP, vol. 1.

sympathy again!: 'To Miss Cushman. On seeing her play "Bianca" in Milman's tragedy of "Fazio,"' CCP, vol. 10, no. 2972.

14 embossed within the book: 'Cxxxxxxx Cxxxxxx,' CCP, vol. 10, no. 2973. The poem later published in slightly altered stanza form.

15 Burned letters: Cushman's daybook for 1844, Columbia. The dates in July, in the order that I place the entries in my text, are, respectively, Sunday the fourteenth, Saturday the thirteenth, Tuesday the twenty-third, and Wednesday the twenty-fourth.

16 daily visits to their house: Anne Hampton Brewster's journals in the Manuscript Collection at the Library Company of Philadelphia inform this discussion.

'in some respectable graveyard': Stebbins, *Cushman,* p. 50.

'death to end my misery': Rosalie Sully to CC, Saturday, 11 May 1845, CCP, vol. 14.

17 L.O. slept with me: Daybook for 1845, among entries from Saturday, 22 Mar., through Tuesday, 25 Mar.

as any British aristocrat: Charles Augustus Cushman was born in 1818.

'as he will come': CC to her mother, London, 1 Mar. 1845, CCP, vol. 1.

not one to be alone: Letter from Charles Augustus Cushman to Miss Stebbins recalling Charlotte's first years in England, written after Charlotte's death in 1876, CCP, vol. 8.

18 'you will never get over': Brewster, 'Miss Cushman,' p. 16; Leach, *Bright Particular Star,* p. 159.

18 'should be my triumph': Charlotte's words to Anne Brewster, 'Miss Cushman,' pp. 12–13. This determination to reroute defeat was a great constant in Cushman's nature and she often repeated this story.

stared at for profit: *Evening Mirror,* 1 Feb. 1845, JLP.

19 a respectable British debut: CC to George Combe, 21 Nov. 1845, NLS, ms. 7275, no. 28.

man in the moon: Kemble, *Records of Later Life,* vol. 3, p. 118.

complained to a friend: Leach, *Bright Particular Star,* p. 169.

20 'played by Miss Cushman': Ibid., p. 178.

'the tomb': The Sully family was vacationing in Newport, Rhode Island, in the heat of July when Sully's son caught the fever and died. The fact that Rosalie died scant weeks later leads one to believe it was of the same cause, though there is no specific mention of cause that I could find.

'wretchedness of separation!': 2 June 1847.

21 masculine-looking young women: Leach, *Bright Particular Star,* pp. 188–89.

22 'ever walked the earth': Charles Cushman to Emma Stebbins, CCP, vol. 8.

'meant to crush me': CC to Grace Greenwood, 15 June 1854, Columbia.

'so dependent upon her': See preceding note.

23 'progress in art is wonderful': 2 Mar. 1854, Carr, *Hosmer,* p. 69.

24 'fatherly care of me': 2 Mar. 1854, Carr, *Hosmer,* p. 30.

'*his* Mr. Crow': 12 Oct. 1854, Carr, *Hosmer,* pp. 38–39.

28 'no weight to a book': GEJ to publishers Chapman and Hall, 1 July 1844, PM. Geraldine's letters to her publishers concerning *Zoe* are from 9 August 1844, when she writes, 'I shall be very glad to meet with your wishes,' through 26 October 1844, when she returns the proofs.

29 'well as she does': CCP, vol. 11, no. 3449.

'ever told you in words': CCP, vol. 11, no. 3437.

'they cannot be now': Ireland, p. 347.

30 Jane growled: JWC to her cousin 'Babbie' Welsh, 19 Jan. 1846, CL, vol. 20, p. 109.

Adelaide Anne Procter: See Gill Gregory essay on Adelaide Procter in *Victorian Women Poets,* particularly p. 88.

31 Wood's 'harem (scarem)': W. W. Story to James Russell Lowell, 11 Feb. 1853, Hudson, *Browning,* p. 270.

32 sister Mary Garland noted: Garland.

33 Miss Stebbins' '*inner* needs': See preceding note.

under the pines: Leach, *Bright Particular Star,* p. 272.

'on every level': Faderman, *Surpassing the Love of Men,* p. 255.

35 'closed too soon,' Stebbins remembered: Carr, *Cushman,* p. 108.

Lady Love

37 dramatic return to the stage: Leach, *Bright Particular Star,* p. 274.

38 lined with books: Ibid., p. 279.

they were due: Wayman Crow (1808–1884). Clippings of his obituary and the deposition of his will are among the Charlotte Cushman Papers.

'. . . Wayman Crow was born in Hartford, Ky., March 7, 1808, and when he was 6 years old his family moved to Hopkinsville, Christian County, Ky. At the age of 7 he began to attend the district school and there acquired the rudiments of education. In 1819 his father removed to a farm about six miles from Hopkinsville and the boy spent one year there, attending school in the winter and working on the farm in summer. In 1820, when he was 12 years old, he was apprenticed to a country store keeper . . . and there gained his first knowledge of the management of a business, a knowledge which he absorbed thoroughly and which afterwards made him one of the foremost business men of this city. In about one and one half years his master retired from business and young Crow was transferred by agreement to a firm which had previously been engaged in a wholesale business and were necessarily unfamiliar with the ins and outs of the retail trade. Wayman Crow's thorough knowledge of his business stood him in good stead, and he assumed chief control of the firm's business, although he was only 15 years of age. At the expiration of his apprenticeship he was engaged permanently by the firm on a salary, and soon after they established a branch store at Cadiz, Ky., giving him entire control of it with a share of the profits. Their confidence in his integrity and faithfulness was such that, though only twenty miles away, his employers delayed six months before paying him a visit. In 1828 his employers sold out their interest to him on credit, though he was still a minor, and the notes were paid before they reached maturity. In 1835 he sold out his business, finding himself then the possessor of $21,000. . . . He was appointed Postmaster of Cadiz, Ky., when only 19 years old, and held this trust for six years, when he was removed from office in consequence of his support of Henry Clay [a fellow Whig] for the Presidency.'

Of his time in St. Louis: 'In 1840 he was elected President of the St. Louis Chamber of Commerce and held that position for ten years. During that same year he was elected to the State Senate, and again in 1850 on the Whig ticket. It was during this last term that the present railroad policy of the State was inaugurated, and Mr. Crow was prominent as one of the organizers of the Hannibal and St. Joseph and Missouri Pacific Railroads. It was also during this period that he obtained the charters for the St. Louis Asylum for the Blind and for the Mercantile Library. . . . It is principally by his magnificent donations to educational institutions that Mr. Crow was best known, and his donations to the Washington University in particular are an exemplification of his liberality for the cause of education. . . . Altogether his endowments to this one institution amount to more than $200,000. . . . '

39 'my young life': 'Charlotte Cushman: A Memory' by Emma C[row] Cushman, 1918, unpublished typescript, CCP. The following account of Emma's first reactions is taken from this 'Memory.' Almost sixty years had passed, but the emotions appear fresh.

41 a 'new world': Brewster, 'Miss Cushman,' p. 41.

41 overlooking the Mississippi: Leach, *Bright Particular Star,* pp. 279–80.

'But you will come to Rome': New Orleans, 22 Feb. [1858], CCP. The dated letters between Charlotte Cushman and Emma Crow are presented chronologically in the first eight volumes of the Cushman Papers and are noted here by date.

42 country in June: CC to Emma Crow, 3 Feb. 1858, CCP.

from Emma's lips: CC to Emma Crow, Memphis, 21 Mar. 1858, CCP.

pleasure was rare: See preceding note.

'don't like in love!': Nashville, 31 Mar. 1858, CCP.

43 'when I see you': See preceding note.

'you are not ill': Baltimore, 3 May 1858, CCP.

'of my left hand?': Baltimore, 27 Apr. 1858, CCP.

45 'I would have': Sunday, 20 June 1858, CCP.

'hero-worship for her': Charlotte's verbal recollections written down by Miss Stebbins ca. 1875, 16 pp., CCP. This section about Kemble is crossed out.

human, natural voice: Leach, *Bright Particular Star,* p. 11.

'goes to the Theatre!': Charlotte's verbal recollections to Miss Stebbins, CCP.

46 'you please, dear': Leach, *Bright Particular Star,* p. 116.

47 but the mind: Gilbert Abbott à Beckett, quoted by Leach, *Bright Particular Star,* p. 178.

'of yours already': CCP, vol. 9, no. 2806.

48 'obliged to admit': CCP, vol. 9, nos. 2808–9.

'in regard to me': New Orleans, Feb. [1858], CCP.

49 '*regrets* missing you!': New York, 30 June 1858, CCP.

'admire Emma for her taste': HH to Wayman Crow, 17 July 1858, SLRC, quoted by Sherwood, *Hosmer,* p. 167.

'destroy the old one': New York, 20 June 1858, CCP.

50 'cannot be controlled': Rome, 26 Nov. 1858, CCP.

'making you wait!': Great Malvern, 12 Aug. 1858, CCP.

51 'where she is?': Malvern, letter of 18 Sept. 1858, continued on 19 Sept., CCP.

'a private opinion': Rome, 11 Nov. 1858, CCP.

'speak from experience': 2 Dec. 1858, SLRC; Sherwood, *Hosmer,* p. 169.

52 'continue to do so': Rome, [Feb. ?] 1859, CCP.

'Can I say more?': Rome, 11 Nov. 1858, CCP.

'All will be well!': [Autumn 1859], CCP.

'to his staff': This and the following description of their life on Via Gregoriana are from Stebbins, *Cushman,* pp. 117–21.

53 'family or books': Rome, 20 Mar. 1860, CCP.

54 'strange coincidence': Rome, 18 Mar. 1859, CCP.

'force of character to be a life companion': W. Derby, [1858?], CCP.

55 her mother and brother Charlie: Mary Eliza was the widower Elkanah Cushman's second wife. There was an age difference of close to twenty-five years between them and he had an adult son and daughter by a first marriage. Susan stayed in the household of her half siblings, where the father himself seemed to live after he failed in business.

56 'blame attached to any one': Leach, *Bright Particular Star*, p. 66; also see p. 67.

at the Park Theatre: Ibid., p. 91.

57 Rosalie, bless her: Susan's first daughter with Muspratt, Ida, died in her first years. During Charlotte's long American tour beginning in 1849, she had returned to Liverpool when Ida became ill—an illness she survived. It was during that visit that she saw how withdrawn Ned had become. She adopted him in New York a year or so later. It was after she realized he would not live with her and Matilda in England, but wished to go to the newly formed Naval Academy at Annapolis, that she met and took Hattie Hosmer under her wing.

'was laid upon her': To Emma Crow, 12 May 1859, CCP.

58 'very good care of them': 17 Aug. 1859, CCP.

'struggling with circumstances': Rome, [Oct. ?] 1859, CCP.

'Art of Sculpture': Carr, *Hosmer*, pp. 144–45.

'You fiend!': Ibid., p. 152.

59 'friend Miss Cushman': Rome, 8 May 1860, CCP.

'a fireish planet': Friday, 9 Mar. 1860, CCP.

'completely won over': Stebbins, *Cushman*, p. 121.

'all genuine dog-lovers': Ibid., p. 123.

'enervating Italian climate': Ibid., p. 131.

60 'earth to heaven': Ibid., p. 133.

61 'intense deep rest': Anne Brewster's journal, 31 Dec. 1859–New Year's Day, 1860, Brewster.

'marble in its points': Brewster, *Compensation*, p. 86.

'so help me God': Ibid., p. 284.

'mistress-mother': Ibid., p. 294.

'Tante Octavie's daughter': Ibid., p. 284.

62 'but modesty forbade': [Florence, Mar. 1860], Field, *Selected Letters*, p. 18.

'of the girl's nature': Whiting, *Field*, p. 46.

63 'who was not': Kate Field to her mother Eliza Riddle Field, [Florence, Jan. 1860], *Selected Letters*, p. 16.

'for our set': 15 Mar. 1860, CCP, vol. 11, no. 3295.

64 'and truest marriage': *Dearest Isa*, p. xxii.

64 'bust of Miss Cushman': Whiting, *Field,* p. 101; also Field, *Selected Letters,* [Florence, Mar. 1860], where the editor does not put quotes around 'wonderful.'

'her other half': 15 Mar. 1860, CCP. vol. II.

65 'oh my darling': Friday, 9 Mar. 1860, CCP.

'& its expression!': Rome, 5 Apr. 1860, CCP.

'demonstrate too clearly': Rome, 3 May 1860, CCP.

66 'full full of ecstasy': 25 July 1860, CCP.

'engaged to me now?': Rome, 17 Apr. 1860, CCP.

'more money first!': Sunday, 10 June [1860], CCP.

67 'I pray God': Knotting Cross, near Liverpool, 12 June [1860], CCP.

68 'some more money first': Sunday, 10 June [1860], CCP.

69 'but we shall see': Off Queenstown, 24 June [1860], CCP.

A Fashionable Wedding

71 'is made for him': 20 June 1860, CCP.

'hour without you': 27 July 1860, CCP.

'your father's permission': 12 Sept. 1860, CCP.

'can or will': Montreal, 6 Sept. 1860, CCP.

'to repay them?': 30 Aug. 1860, CCP.

72 Sarah, 'Pinny': See Levine, *A Guide to Writers' Homes,* p. 162.

74 'always want company': 20 W. 16 St. [New York], 13 Oct. 1860, CCP.

'been my opinion!': New York, 6 Nov. 1860, CCP, vol. I.

75 'old as she is': New York, 24 Nov. 1860, CCP.

76 'healthy as Missouri': 26 Oct. 1860, CCP, vol. I.

'get a foothold': 6 Nov. 1860, CCP, vol. I.

'it may change': Boston, 20 Dec. 1860, CCP.

'will you not?': New York, 15 Nov. 1860, CCP.

77 'artist and the sitter': See Milroy, 'The Public Career of Emma Stebbins: Works in Marble,' pp. 6–7.

'grow with years': Philadelphia, 16 Jan. 1861, CCP.

'around me last night': 29 Jan. 1861, CCP.

78 'in *white,* eh!': New York, in the letter of 26 Feb. 1861 dated 'Thurs morning Feb. 28,' CCP.

79 'will permanently reside': Clipping enclosed by CC to Mr. Crow, Tremont St., Boston, 8 Apr. 1861, CCP, vol. I.

'else I am well': See letter in preceding note.

79 'delighted with *her*': CC to Mr. Crow, 1 May 1861, CCP, vol. 1.

81 'or perish': See preceding note.

'before it is over': Stebbins, *Cushman,* p. 141.

'tired it very much': [New Bedford, Thursday], May 1861, CCP.

82 'sweet darling? No!': City Hotel, Providence, 4 June 1861, CCP.

'"*in the whole*"': 6 June [1861], CCP.

'all her shortcomings?': 26 June [1861], CCP.

'often been with me': 20 W. 16 St., New York, 27 June 1861, CCP.

83 'way of their knowing': Baltimore, 29 June 1861, CCP.

In Walked Jane Carlyle

85 'very very much': At sea, 26 July [1861], CCP.

86 'contributed to it': Derbyshire, 16 Aug. 1861, CCP.

'curious problems': 7 Sept. 1861, CCP.

'fed on milk': Howe, *Jewsbury,* pp. 69–70.

'three perfect days': Stebbins, *Cushman,* pp. 83–84.

87 on Jane's part: Miss Stebbins in her *Charlotte Cushman,* p. 84, seems to suggest by her placement of CC's letter to an unnamed correspondent—'On Sunday who should come self-invited to meet me but Mrs Carlyle'—that CC and JWC met in London in the late 1840s, and Joseph Leach picked up on this assumption in his biography and carried it along. They did not meet till the summer of 1861. On 30 August 1861, in describing that same Sunday to Emma Crow Cushman, Charlotte wrote: 'I met a person whom I have longed for 12 years to know, Mrs Carlyle.'

88 'and *I* conquered!': Isle of Wight, 30 Aug. 1861, CCP.

89 a stern face: GEJ, 'In Memoriam Jane Welsh Carlyle,' incorporated into the beginning of Carlyle's 'Reminiscence of JWC,' p. 37.

90 'let me be a boy!': See preceding note.

constellations to her: Hanson, *Necessary Evil,* p. 9.

'could and did think': Cushman's verbal recollections transcribed by Miss Stebbins, CCP.

91 'bewailed in an outcry': JWC notebook, Froude, *Carlyle,* vol. 1, p. 98.

92 'instantly put an end to': Carlyle, 'Reminiscence of JWC,' p. 53.

93 'being to the grave': JBW to TC, 21 July [1823], *CL,* vol. 2, pp. 403–4. All references from the Duke/Edinburgh edition of the Carlyles' letters will be referred to by date and volume number.

'it was waeful!': Hanson, *Necessary Evil,* p. 29.

'respect in this manner': 7 May 1862, CCP.

'never leave this place': JBW to Eliza Stodart, [26? Sept. 1819], *CL,* vol. 1, p. 200.

93 comforted her through letters: That Edward Irving offered his comfort is evident. Jane wrote to her grandmother Elizabeth Welsh on 5 October 1819 that she understood the meaning of her father's death: 'The ways of the Almighty are mysterious—but in this instance, *though* He has left thousands in the world whose existence is a burden to themselves & those around them,' God cut short the life of a man 'who was the Glory of his family, & a most useful member of society.' Why?

Jane finds God's intentions 'clear and intelligible': 'Could the annihilation of a Thousand useless and contemptible beings have sent such terror & submission to the hearts of the survivors as the sudden death of one whom their love would if possible have gifted with immortality?'

'Oh no,' she answers, '—Hard it is—but we must acknowledge the wisdom of his sentence even while we are suffering under it—We must kiss the rod even while we are writhing under the tortures which it inflicts—'

Almost fifty years later, reading this letter Jane wrote to her paternal grandmother, Thomas Carlyle, who well knew the unabated pain the death caused her, was quite jolted by the unaccustomed religious language she used in it. Such ponderous religious expressions 'she seldom or never gave utterance to.'

Nowhere in her correspondence, before or after, does Jane ever write in so labored and ponderous a style. Never again does she claim to understand such punishing ways of God to men. The language of the letter is not hers. It was the ministerial language of Edward Irving, the language the twenty-seven-year-old Edward used to comfort her. In the future, as his own children succumbed to TB, it was the language he used to comfort himself. And being *his* words, they did comfort Jane at the time—as did ruins in the moonlight and thoughts of her own death. Thomas Carlyle seems not to have recognized the familiar and long-silenced voice of his best friend.

95 release him from his engagement: Jane sent Edward a lock of her hair, to which Edward replied in a sonnet entitled, quite appropriately, 'To a Lock of My Lady's Hair.' Jane saved the sonnet to his 'Queen of Love,' tearing it from the letter. On the back are broken lines from the letter, two of which read: 'I have resolved neither to see Isabella or her father before I' and 'cannot brook the sight of either until this be explained and until.'

It would be particularly difficult for Edward to ask for his release from his commitment to Isabella Martin in person, for he was a man who loved to make those he was with at the time happy. That was his nature.

read her life: See JBW to Eliza Stodart, [Jan. 1822], *CL*, vol. 2, pp. 16–19.

96 'praise another man': Hanson, *Necessary Evil*, p. 28.

97 'marry without love': JBW to TC, [ca. 17 Jan. 1822], *CL*, vol. 2, p. 20.

98 'be very laughable': JBW to TC, [14 Oct. 1823], *CL*, vol. 2.

99 'seraphic Mrs Montagu'?: TC to JBW, 22 Oct. 1823, *CL*, vol. 2.

'all to him': [12 Nov. 1832], *CL*, vol. 2, p. 470.

100 'thing so insufferable?': [Nov. 1823], *CL*, vol. 2, p. 481.

'a noble woman': [14 Oct. 1823], *CL*, vol. 2, pp. 450–51.

100 'for my industry': 11 Nov. [1822], *CL,* vol. 2, p. 196.

101 'for your head!': 13 Nov. 1823, *CL,* vol. 2, p. 471.

'correspond with you': 18 Sept. 1823, *CL,* vol. 2, pp. 432–33.

102 'bewail his absence': TC to JBW, 20 Dec. 1824, *CL,* vol. 3, pp. 233–34.

'*all* his creatures': 9 Jan. 1825, *CL,* vol. 3, p. 244.

104 'receive a home': 26 Feb. 1826, *CL,* vol. 4, pp. 40–41.

105 'letter to himself': 30 May 1825, NLS, vol. 1776, no. 3. Also see *CL,* vol. 3, p. 335, n. 3.

'all my life': JBW to TC, 12 June 1825, *CL,* vol. 3, p. 335.

'"is not here"': 24 June 1825, *CL,* vol. 3, p. 341.

106 'sooner the better': 3 July 1825, NLS. Also see *CL,* vol. 3, p. 355, n. 4.

107 'passionately loved him': [24 July 1825], *CL,* vol. 3.

'break my heart?': [30 July 1825], *CL,* vol. 3, pp. 360–61.

108 'I destroy you?': 29 July 1825, *CL,* vol. 3.

'you will love': 4 Aug. [1825], *CL,* vol. 3, p. 361.

'deathlike cold eclipse': 10 Aug. 1825, *CL,* vol. 3, p. 367.

109 'humoured man alive': [25 Oct. 1825], *CL,* vol. 3, pp. 393–95.

'should alarm her': 12 Nov. 1825, NLS.

110 'is no equality': 9 Sept. 1826, NLS.

'out of darkness': 3 July 1825, NLS.

'cannot spare them': 26 Feb. 1826, *CL,* vol. 4, p. 43.

'as much before?': JBW to TC, [31 Jan. 1826], *CL,* vol. 4, p. 29.

'Law of Nature': 2 Apr. 1826, *CL,* vol. 4, p. 69.

'I can do': JBW to TC, 10 [Apr. 1826], *CL,* vol. 4, p. 71.

111 'of tremendous interest': JBW to TC, 28 June [1826], *CL,* vol. 4, p. 111.

'of any sort': JBW to TC, [3 Oct. 1826], *CL,* vol. 4, p. 148.

112 'back to my bed': Frank Harris quotes Jane's physician Dr. Richard Quain in *My Life and Loves,* on page 210 of that picaresque novel he made of his life. Given its context, it is no wonder the passage has been consigned to footnotes ever since, that is, when it is not decried altogether—its more usual fate. But ironically, in this instance—when Harris himself is not center stage exaggerating his accomplishments—he seems to be using his unusually retentive memory, his keen intelligence, and his bawdy wit—to tell the truth. Naturally Harris quotes Quain from memory and Quain quotes Jane from memory. No doubt, the *direct* quotes are somewhat altered from the original telling. Still, I find what Harris reports to be essentially verifiable in every primary record I came across—including still unpublished portions of letters that I doubt Harris or Quain could have seen. All the evidence points to the fact that both Quain and Harris were telling the truth—and obviously enjoying it. Recounting to Harris that Jane found Carlyle 'jiggling like' on his wedding night, Dr. Quain posits, 'I guessed

what she meant, the poor devil in a blue funk was frigging himself.' ('Frigging' is one of Harris' favorite words.) Still, Carlyle, for all his physical dysfunction, most likely was attempting to arouse himself on his wedding night in order to fulfill his matrimonial duty. I will again use Harris' reporting of Quain's words in the chapter "The Red Bedroom," during the period when Jane, in mental and physical agony, most probably told Dr. Quain about her wedding night. Certainly, by her own accounts to her confidante Mary Russell, she was morbidly embarrassed afterwards, and for a long time, remembering all she had told him in her diseased state, became quite agitated and refused to see Dr. Quain when he called.

112 'shall see good': TC to Margaret A. Carlyle, 19 Oct. 1826, *CL*, vol. 4.

114 'full of hope': TC and JWC to Margaret A. Carlyle, 16 Nov. 1826, *CL*, vol. 4.

115 'a relative existence': Emerson, *English Traits*, pp. 9–12.

116 'Burn our Ships!': 'Reminiscence of JWC,' p. 67.

'one-oared boats!': 3 July 1825, NLS, Procter, who died of TB before her fortieth birthday, dedicated her last book of poetry, *Legends and Lyrics*, to Matilda M. Hays in 1858 with the following quote from Emerson: 'Our tokens of love are for the most part barbarous. Cold and lifeless, because they do not represent our life. The only gift is a portion of thyself. Therefore let the farmer give his corn; the miner, his gems; the sailor, coral and shells; the painter, his picture; the poet, his poems.'

Swearing Eternal Friendship

117 'not know me': 30 Aug. 1861, CCP.

118 'Sir' to her: Ms., Turnbull Library.

119 quipped William Wordsworth: See Macfarlane, *Reminiscences*, vol. 2.

120 Hero-Worship: Campbell, *Thomas Carlyle*, p. 105.

'Hot cross buns!': Hunt, *Autobiography*, vol. 2, p. 264.

121 'sphere of *possibility*': JWC to TC, [5 Oct. 1845], *CL*, vol. 20, p. 12.

'been more explicit': Leach, *Bright Particular Star*, pp. 190, 191.

'to me alone': TC to GEJ, *CL*, vol. 12, p. 297.

123 'made her idol!': GEJ to JC, 15 Apr. 1841, Ireland.

124 'interminable seams!': [29 Oct. 1841], Ireland.

'little of mine': JWC to Babbie Welsh ("My best Babbie!"). Jane's maternal cousin Jeannie Welsh will always be referred to in the text and notes by her nickname, 'Babbie,' to differentiate her from JWC, who as a maiden was also 'Jeannie Welsh.' JWC's parents, though not related, shared the same last name, 'Welsh,' before marriage as well, which gave JWC Welsh relatives on both sides of her family.

In this dialogue in the text I take the liberty of altering TC's 'You had Jeannie besides you' to 'You had cousin Babbie beside you' for clarity, and JWC's response beginning 'Jeannie! Jeannie' to 'Babbie! Babbie.'

125 '*grande toilette*': JWC to Babbie, [2 Mar. 1843], *CL*, vol. 16, p. 69.

125 insight and élan: Woolf, 'Geraldine and Jane.'

the twentieth century: Ms. letter from T. S. Eliot to Leonard Woolf, 26 Apr. 1932, Berg Collection, New York Public Library.

'about her novels': All quotations from Virginia Woolf are from 'Geraldine and Jane.' The essay can also be found in Virginia Woolf, *The Second Common Reader.*

126 'women *as women*': See JWC to Babbie [18 or 19 Jan. 1843], *CL,* vol. 16.

'do me pleasure': [21 June 1843], *CL,* vol. 16, pp. 211–12.

'their own level': [11 June 1849], Ireland, p. 129.

127 was very disappointed: See JWC to Babbie, [27 May 1843], *CL,* vol. 16, pp. 181–85, marked private, and nn. 13 and 15.

128 'distinguished Authoresses': JWC to Mary Russell, 30 Dec. [1845], *CL,* vol. 20, p. 85.

subsequently told him: JWC to Babbie, [27 May 1843], *CL,* vol. 16, p. 184.

'It's full': See Houghton, 'Harriet, Lady Ashburton,' pp. 225–57, particularly p. 242.

129 '*tragic* about it': [Ca. 12 June 1844], *CL,* vol. 18, pp. 62–65.

he answered: Letters between the Carlyles between 26 and 27 June 1844, *CL,* vol. 18, pp. 85–89.

130 'slumbering till then': [21 June 1844], Ireland, p. 133.

'do so!': See JWC to TC, [12 July 1844], *CL,* vol. 18, p. 131. I turned JWC's reporting of GEJ's words 'If I *wished* to *sacrifice* her' into direct dialogue.

'*going mad*!': See preceding note.

another man!: JWC to TC, [15 July 1844], *CL,* vol. 18, p. 138.

'principal character absent': *CL,* vol. 18, p. 153, n. 2.

131 fast as possible: JWC to Babbie, [9 July 1845], *CL,* vol. 19, p. 92.

great big fire: Geraldine wrote to Charlotte Cushman about the extraordinary atmosphere of Seaforth, CCP, and Jane wrote to Carlyle, [3 Aug. 1845] *CL,* vol. 19, p. 126.

132 '*happy*': [5 Aug. 1845], *CL,* vol. 19, pp. 129–30.

'so trifled with!': [10 Aug. 1845], *CL,* vol. 19, p. 137.

'freedom in that': [13 Aug. 1845], *CL,* vol. 19, p. 142.

'my feet rubbed': JWC to Babbie, [19 Aug. 1845], *CL,* vol. 19, p. 156.

133 world put together: JWC to TC, [20 Aug. 1845], *CL,* vol. 19, p. 58.

'would be welcome': 1 Sept. 1845, *CL,* vol. 19, p. 187.

'at Seaforth House!!': [15 Sept. 1845], *CL,* vol. 19, p. 197.

'ever did before': 13 Sept. 1845, *CL,* vol. 19, p. 191.

loved to parody: JWC to Babbie, [6 Feb. 1845], *CL,* vol. 19, p. 26.

134 '*man* marrying her!': JWC to Babbie, [15 June 1845], *CL,* vol. 19, p. 80.

'*spoke no truth*': Hanson, *Necessary Evil,* p. 374.

134   for Miss Cushman: [19 Jan. 1846], *CL*, vol. 20, p. 109.

135   'breadth of': GEJ to CC, CCP, vol. 11, no. 1435.

     'the magic ring': CCP, vol. 11, ca. no. 1437.

     'minding its clamour': CCP, vol. 11.

     'frightened of it': 4 July 1846, CCP, vol. 11.

136   'explosion of jealousy': [23 Feb. 1846], Ireland, p. 188.

     'of woman-nature!': JWC to Helen Welsh, [24 Apr. 1846], *CL*, vol. 20, p. 180.

     'from a Geraldine': JWC to Babbie, [5 Feb. 1846], *CL*, vol. 20, p. 119.

137   '—literally,—Nothing!': 6 July 1846, *CL*, vol. 20, p. 220.

     'only knows what': CCP, vol. 11.

     'very unwell!': 15 July 1846, *CL*, vol. 20, p. 237.

     'if I cannot': 22 July 1846, *CL*, vol. 20, p. 254.

138   'yet forever no!': 28 July 1846, *CL*, vol. 20, p. 262.

     'make-believe to sleep': JWC to TC, [13 Aug. 1846], *CL*, vol. 21, p. 15.

139   'for some years': CCP, vol. 11, no. 1435.

     'them to touch!': [The year 1846], Ireland, pp. 244–45.

140   'shocked with *me*': [7 Oct. 1844], *CL*, vol. 18, p. 235. I changed 'I have seen him' to direct dialogue: 'I have seen you.'

The Meeting of the Half Sisters

142   'an "emancipated" woman': [26?] Feb. 1848, *CL*, vol. 22, pp. 254–55.

     the respectable housewife: Her name is Alice Bryant in the novel. Her husband Mr. Bryant is at first called 'William' and then 'John,' but basically, like Carlyle, he is referred to by his last name.

143   'strong bass note': Jewsbury, *Half Sisters*, p. 31.

144   'over her crime': Ibid., pp. 283–86.

     'it had turned': Froude, *Carlyle*, p. 23.

     'than I deserve': Jewsbury, *Half Sisters*, p. 291.

145   'you left her': Ibid., p. 294.

     women abandoned in novels: Charlotte Cushman's life offered Geraldine an option for Bianca that went beyond the fate of Corinne in Madame de Staël's *Corinne; or, Italy,* the pivotal novel on which *The Half Sisters* is based. In Jewsbury's novel, the housewife Alice Bryant forgets the time of day while reading *Corinne,* just as Jane Baillie Welsh had done when she was younger. And in *The Half Sisters* the narrator remarks that reading *Corinne* marks an epoch in every woman's life. As well it might. Where else but in this French novel published in 1807 could an intelligent young woman of the time find a heroine who was a *genius,* a woman who led her less cultured British lover to the discovery of the ancient wonders of Italy. Corinne, a thinking, feeling, free-moving human being, was adored and honored by Rome as a great performance artist in de Staël's novel. She moved freely through society without seeming to lose her reputation through her independence. Yet even Madame de Staël could offer the brilliant Corinne no solution but to fade away from life and art after her British lover breaks her heart. However, when the dashing British military man breaks Bianca's heart, instead of giving up and dying, Bianca goes to work. Geraldine presented a woman who survived heartbreak through the sweat of her brow. In this sense Geraldine offered the novel reader a 'new woman' character, one that went further than de Staël's.

Corinne; or, Italy's importance for and influence on nineteenth-century women of genius cannot be overemphasized. See Sara Foose Parrott's discussion in her doctoral dissertation 'Expatriate and Professions: The Careers in Italy of Nineteenth-Century American Women Writers and Artists.'

145 'kept from harm': GEJ to ES, CCP.

146 'light *forces* me!': Manchester, July 1846, CCP.

'come to a woman': Rome, 21 May 1862, CCP.

not beyond them: How good a novelist was Geraldine Jewsbury? She certainly was a prodigious worker, as Mazzini came to realize. Over two thousand of her anonymous reviews appeared in the *Athenaeum;* there were also translations, novels, and children's books. With that much solid work behind her, her enthusiasms, empathetic nature, and adventurous spirit would have made her come down to us as a daring and romantic figure had she been born a man. As a woman, basically seen through Jane Carlyle's shifting point of view, Carlyle's relatives' defense of Carlyle as a husband, and Virginia Woolf's condescending yet good-natured portrait, Jewsbury comes down to us as a rather scattered, silly, unreliable woman, rather than the intellectual she was.

Geraldine's novels were popular in her time. They were novels of ideas. And because Geraldine's genius was speculative more than it was aesthetic (and perhaps because she had bad eyes to proofread with), there is a slight sloppiness in her details. Small points. Alice's husband Mr. Bryant is first called 'William' and then 'John.' And rather humorously, three of her minor characters in *The Half Sisters,* two sister-in-laws and one maid, share the name 'Margaret.' Obviously Geraldine's mind is elsewhere, busy with what these characters represent, what they have to say. They butler forth ideas. They, like the main characters, can be chameleon-like. She bases them at times on real-life prototypes without preparing the reader for their fictive presence. For example, Bianca is extremely poor at the beginning of the book, yet her maid suddenly appears as if she were a fixture in the actor's life. It makes perfect sense if you know Sallie's role in Cushman's life.

The author is definitely interested in fleshing out her main characters. Yet there are inconsistencies in characterization as well. Psychology is tipped when need be to present dominant ideas. And some of Geraldine's ideas appear to be ambivalent. Take Bianca, the pure-hearted actress, who at the same time strikes a "strong bass note," for she has more knowledge of society and life than women usually do. Obviously modeled on Cushman, this 'foreigner' comes to London, where she rises from a circus performer [Geraldine was enthusiastic about the circus in those days] to become a great tragic actress. It is her respect for her art that impels her, yet at the same time, the *reason* this woman becomes an actor is a purely unselfish one. She works to support her mother. Unselfishness in women, Earnestness, Duty—these are primary moral values underlining every variation of Victorian thought, from the most conservative to the most radical. Speaking of a Manchester dinner party she attended, Geraldine wrote to Charlotte of the Englishman sitting next to her:

'He had never seen you, and for many years had given up going to theatres, as he is faithful to the memory of Mrs. Siddons and all that generation, and has even preserved her playbills. But he talked very well and most enthusiastically, and listened to all I said with great faith, and the next time you come here he is fully purposed to go. We were settling *you* the whole dinner-time, and I could not help laughing to see how people instinctively find their point of sympathy. Although he had not been to see you act, he felt a sympathy with you for what you had done for your family; he said he had heard of *that,* and it happens that all his family had been thrown on him, and he behaved in a most worthy way. He was intended for the church, and had a most decided inclination for it; but whilst he was at college his father died . . . and this man was obliged to leave college, and go behind a counter and drudge for years to retrieve his affairs and bring up the rest of his family, hating it all the time. . . . He *knew* what it was you had done, and could appreciate it' (Stebbins, *Cushman,* p. 74).

The point of sympathy the novelist finds in Bianca is the same point of sympathy Charlotte Cushman shrewdly exploited and at the same time wholeheartedly believed: she had gone on the stage not for any kind of self-aggrandizement, but out of earnest unselfishness, to do her duty to her family. This runs through the novel.

Concurrently, the profession of acting for women is seen realistically. The inferior moral surroundings, the tinsel of costuming, the 'business' disgusts Bianca. But this does not excuse polite, albeit philistine, society, which is reprimanded by the narrator for not understanding that a woman actor, just as a woman writer, is pursuing an Ideal of aesthetic perfection, a Platonic Truth that goes beyond the workaday world of specific details.

There is a careless quality to Bianca's quick reversal from professional woman to wife, just as there is a melodramatic quality to Alice's fate. When the relationship between character and destiny conflicted with social norms, Jewsbury tended to become too conscious that it was, after all, just a novel she was writing, and to rely on the *conventions,* not on the integrity, of the form. Perhaps that was what Virginia Woolf meant in 1929 when she wrote that Geraldine would be surprised that anyone had dusted off her books at that late date—though I suspect she did not take Geraldine seriously enough, relying on Jane's words about her friend (when she was upset with her), rather than on the profound nature of Jewsbury's lifelong friendship with *both* the Carlyles and the respect she garnered from such as Mazzini and her close friend and admirer, Carlyle's biographer J. A. Froude.

147 'with an amiability!!': JWC to Babbie, [27 Feb. 1849], *CL,* vol. 23, pp. 243–44.

148 claimed Rousseau again: Jane's letter to Babbie (see preceding note) pictures Carlyle happy with 'four riding horses which he might by turns gallop to death—and I had a

pony which took me as fast as Anthony could *walk* at his head, over the beautiful hills in the neighbourhood—and we sat and smoked in *the carpenters shop* Capt S has fitted up for himself—and I learned to *turn* and shoot with a bow—and shot—*myself* in the cheek!—as a green mark can testify to this hour: and indeed indeed—I felt like little Macready [her goddaughter, Lydia Jane] on its late three day visit to myself—with no end of wishes and whim and a childish surprise and felicity to find them all immediately gratified.'

149 'about the writer': GEJ to JWC, 20 Mar. 1845, Ireland, p. 159.

150 'upon *my* honour': Journal entitled 'Much Ado About Nothing,' *LM*, vol. 2, p. 75.

152 'most fragrant flowers': JWC journal, 26 Mar. 1856, *LM*, vol. 2, p. 270.

   very little cas: See preceding note, 5 Nov. 1855, p. 261.

153 'were better not!': JWC journal, 15 May 1856, NLS, The rest of the text in *New LM*, p. 15, May 1856. Alexander Carlyle published the entire journal in order, he claimed, to prove that Froude's view of the Carlyles' difficult marriage was unfounded.

   'has accepted me': Surtees, *Ludovisi Goddess*, p. 56.

155 'your dearest life': Ibid., p. 35.

   '. . . have you?': Ibid., p. 54.

   'for his aunt': Ibid., p. 58.

   'in my heart': Ibid., p. 70.

   unhappy *at first:* Ibid., p. 71.

156 in exclamation points: Ibid., p. 78.

   'in Babyless Places!': Hanson, *Necessary Evil*, pp. 487–88.

157 'of the day': Stebbins, *Cushman*, p. 84.

159 'upon *my* honour!': JWC to CC, 5 Cheyne Row, Chelsea, Friday, [Sept. 1861], CCP.

   'makes one start': Robert Browning to HH, Carr, *Hosmer*, p. 60.

161 'old Rosa Bonheur': Klumpke, *Bonheur*, p. 71.

   'of wild things': CC to JWC, Rome, 16 Nov. 1861, NLS, ms. 1774.

162 'unto her highness!': See preceding note.

163 '"*think shame*"!': JWC to CC, 31 Jan. [1862], CCP.

   'on Monday afternoon': CC to JWC, Saturday morning, 12 July 1862, NLS.

164 'would write me!': 19 Feb. 1863, CCP.

165 'a little alarming': Oliphant, *Autobiography*, p. 74.

   'made in vain': Ibid., 11–12.

166 'can tell you': TC note, *LM*, vol. 3, p. 177.

   'talent to be': Froude, *Life in London*, pp. 230–31.

   'luxury in comparison!': *LM*, vol. 3, p. 179.

   'you were mad!!!': *New LM*, vol. 2, p. 282.

167 'Never': Carlyle, 'Reminiscence of JWC,' p. 145.

168 'did you expect?': Harris, *My Life,* pp. 209–10. See also my endnote for 'back to my bed' on page 300.

'worse than pain': GEJ to Walter Mantell, Turnbull Library.

169 'am suffering torments': 25 Apr. 1864, NLS.

170 'for the child!': JWC to Mary Russell, 12 Nov. 1864, NLS.

'is too disgusting': See preceding note; and partially published in *LM,* vol. 3.

'you cannot!': 16 Nov. 1861, NLS, no. 1774.

The Roman Mosaic

172 'winter after winter': 24 Apr. 1862, CCP.

'in the summer': 24 Apr. 1862, CCP.

173 'we *will* do': 18 Apr. 1862, 'Good Friday!,' CCP.

'death, called *Woffles*': Cobbe, *Life,* vol. 2, p. 358.

174 'universally cheerful': 7 May 1862, CCP.

175 been 'stupid' enough: CC to ECC, 15 Jan. 1862, CCP.

'I say less?': 16 Aug. 1861, CCP.

'believe this—': 23 Jan. 1862, CCP.

176 'best for us': CC to ECC, 13 Mar. 1862, CCP.

'as one can': CC to ECC, 30 Apr. 1862, CCP.

'of my friends': CC to ECC, 30 Jan. [1862], CCP. Part of this letter dated 'Friday morning, Jany 31.'

'could speak then': 30 Jan. 1862, CCP.

'"Ladie Mamma"': 20 Mar. 1862, CCP.

177 'little Carlotta somewhere': 13 Mar. 1862, CCP.

'to his caressing': CC to ECC, 20 May 1862, CCP.

'hope, my help': 21 May 1862, CCP.

178 '*will come again!*': 12 Dec. 1862, CCP.

'*ruler* you know': 22 Jan. 1863, CCP.

in the world: 7 Nov. 1862, CCP.

'for a man!!': 21 Nov. 1862, CCP.

179 'of punishing her!': 31 Jan. 1863, CCP.

'Mrs Carlyle says': 3 Apr. 1863, CCP.

'man about her': 27 Mar. 1863, CCP.

'behind in England': 7 Feb. 1863, CCP.

180 'than Miss Blagden': 3 Apr. 1863, CCP.

180 'in his face': ECC, 'Charlotte Cushman: A Memory,' typescript, pp. 11–12, CCP.

181 '"not to tell"': See preceding note, p. 13.

'shall Sallie do?': See preceding note. The telegram also can be found at CCP.

'then suddenly extinguished': See preceding note, p. 14.

'than her husband': Howe, *Memories,* pp. 219–20.

184 'he might be': ECC, 'Charlotte Cushman: A Memory,' p. 5, CCP.

'at the theatre': See preceding note, p. 6.

185 'is a sensualist': CC to ECC, 26 Dec. 1863, CCP.

186 'can bear this!': 5 Dec. 1862, CCP.

187 'see were delusions': 'Melancholy Death of a Gentleman at Leamington,' clipping, CCP.

'darling this summer': 13 Nov. 1863, CCP.

'her physical requirements': Paris, 16 Dec. 1863, CCP.

188 'not fail me': 9 Jan. 1864, CCP.

'sorry for her': Rome, 30 Jan. 1863 [*sic:* should be 1864], CCP.

189 'an inferior caliber': 22 Jan. 1864, CCP.

'with full power!': 30 Jan. 1863 [*sic:* should be 1864], CCP.

190 'she is plunged': See preceding note.

'a woman worker': 9 Mar. 1864, CCP.

191 'to do it': 4 Feb. 1864, CCP.

'ideas for himself': Leach, *Bright Particular Star,* pp. 327–28.

incompetence to Seward: Ibid., pp. 318–19.

193 'upon my soul': 20 May 1864, CCP.

'under my roof': 22 June 1864, CCP.

196 '*your father's daughter*': 3 Mar. 1865, CCP.

'mind the cost': 22 June 1864, CCP.

pearls, 'Big ones': See preceding note.

'does it?': Brixton, 9 June 1864, CCP.

197 '*to be together*': See preceding note.

'across the room': Sherwood, *Hosmer,* p. 235.

'to have babies': Ibid.

198 a little Charlotte?: Ibid., p. 226.

'really wanted rest': 2 Dec. 1864, CCP.

'the *best* society': 23 Dec. 1864, CCP.

'dependent on it': CC to ECC, 3 Jan. 1865, CCP.

199 'health by exercise': CC to ECC, 26 Jan. 1865, CCP.

199 'claims upon you': 4 Feb. 1865, CCP.

200 '*enough* for *him*': CC to ECC, 9 Feb. 1865, CCP.

201 'Anglo Saxon virtue': 4 Feb. 1865, CCP; 'Pluck,' rather than 'pluck,' as CC uses it twice in this letter, making a point of it.

    'lovers this winter': 30 Mar. 1865, CCP.

    'Seward is better!': 28 Apr. 1865, CCP.

203 'grateful to her': 11 May 1865, CCP.

    'dear Mrs Carlyle': 18 Aug. 1865, CCP.

    'Mrs Carlyle's present': 'Monday P.M., 1865 Aug.' CCP, no. 817.

204 'in my happiness': N. Wales, 29 Sept. 1865, CCP.

    'convulsion of suffering': 17 Sept. 1865, CCP.

    her from drowning: 4 Oct. 1865, CCP.

The Red Bedroom

205 'to send you': Sarah Dilberoglue to CC and ES, 22 Apr. 1866, CCP.

206 ' "shadow of Marriage" ': Hanson, *Necessary Evil*, p. 405.

208 '*detestable*—upon *my* honour!': 2 Aug. [1849], *CL*, vol. 24, pp. 159–71.

209 'burst into tears!': Hanson, *Necessary Evil*, p. 431.

    'never to be measured': Oliphant, *Autobiography*, p. 75.

211 'know it fine': 3 Mar. 1863, *NL*, vol. 2, p. 285.

    'shot away': TC, note, *LM*, vol. 3, p. 201.

    'as by enchantment': JWC to TC, [15 July 1864], *LM*, vol. 3, pp. 202–3.

212 'lonely and miserable': The Gill, [21 July 1864], NLS.

    'charge of me': See preceding note.

    ' "the world began"!!!': Holm Hill, 23 July 1864, NLS.

213 'no such nursing': JWC to TC, Holm Hill, 25 July 1864, NLS.

    'nothing had happened!': 24 Aug. 1864, NLS.

214 'but still I slept': JWC to TC, Holm Hill, 25 July 1864, NLS.

    'at my heart': Holm Hill, Thursday, 28 July 1864, NLS.

    'not right itself': 2 Aug. [1864], *LM*, vol. 3, pp. 205–6.

    'and God's mercy': JWC to TC, [29 July 1864], NLS.

    'alter their figure': JWC to TC, Holm Hill, 16 Aug. 1864, NLS.

215 'I am seeing': JWC to TC, 11 Aug. [1864], NLS.

    'expected me *home*': JWC to TC, Holm Hill, 12 Aug. 1864, NLS.

    'in my dreams': 19 Aug. 1864, NLS.

    'of primeval innocence!': JWC to TC, 20 Sept. [1864], NLS.

215 'and the Dr!': JWC to MR, Oct. [18]64, NLS.

217 'rubbing in': JWC to TC, 28 Apr. 1864, NLS.

'a grim hold': JWC to TC, 8 Sept. 1864, NLS.

'reflections like *that*!': JWC to TC, 9 Sept. [1864], NLS.

'red-hot torture': 16 Sept. [1864], *LM*, vol. 3, p. 210.

'That sofa!': 22 Sept. [1864], NLS.

218 'their habit is': 5 Sept. 1864, *NLM*, vol. 2, p. 299.

'sort of suicide': JWC to TC, *LM*, vol. 3, p. 212.

'returning no more': JWC to Mrs. Austin, Sunday, 9 Oct. [1864], NLS.

'for the better': Monday, 3 Oct. 1864, *NLM*, vol. 2, pp. 216–17.

'of *Consideration*': 30 Nov. 1864, (p.m. 1 Dec. 1864), NLS.

220 'a fee from me!': JWC to Mary Russell, 28 Feb. 1865, NLS.

'to know that!': 3 June 1865, NLS.

'her and me': Written by Carlyle on 12 Aug. 1869, *LM*, vol. 3, p. 215.

221 'Oh mercy!': JWC to TC, 2 Apr. 1866, *LM*, vol. 3, p. 316.

222 'with great glee': JWC to TC, 3 Apr. 1866, *LM*, vol. 3, p. 318.

224 fit the line: Letters of the Carlyles to John Forster, Miscellaneous Letters, no. 11, at the Victoria and Albert Museum. Coincidentally, on the same page to which this letter is attached, there is also the letter to Forster from B. W. Procter, 'Barry Cornwall,' telling of the death of his daughter Adelaide Anne Procter. She died in 1864, not yet forty, of the consumption her grandmother Mrs. Montagu early feared. Her father's distress is visible in his handwriting, which exhibits a painful lack of control and contrasts with the meticulous hand of TC, who was deeply distressed and stunned as well.

225 'gone from him': 22 Apr. 1866, CCP.

Changing Times

227 'my wretched heart': CC to Fanny Seward, Liverpool, 11 May 1866, CCP.

229 '& my own': CC to ECC, 25 Oct. 1866, CCP.

'about my neck!': See preceding note.

'to be refused': 21 Sept. 1866, CCP.

230 'daughter is coming': Brighton, 25 Sept. [1865], CCP.

'feel for me': CC to ECC, Paris, 6 Nov. 1866, CCP.

'movements—perhaps': 18 Sept. 1866, CCP.

'is now away': Rome, 1 May 1867, CCP.

231 'want him dismissed': Leach, *Bright Particular Star*, p. 337.

'it for me': 21 Oct. 1867, CCP.

232 bouts of depression: Leach, *Bright Particular Star*, p. 338.

232 ' "we will talk" ': Philadelphia, 30 Dec. 1867, Cushman Club.

'of my childhood': CC to ECC, 4 July [1868], CCP.

233 'a true man': CC to ECC, 13 July 1868, CCP.

'worth struggling for': CC to ECC, Newport, Saturday, 4 Feb. [186?], CCP.

'Washington for Ned': 218 E. 17th St., New York, 21 July 1868, CCP.

'*fast* people either': CC to ECC, 13 July 1868, CCP.

234 'may lose herself': CCP, no. 987.

235 'can harm you': Hyde Park, 27[?] July 1868, CCP.

236 'careful of yourself': 31 Aug. 1868, CCP.

'until that time': CC to ECC, 6 Sept. 1868, CCP.

237 'the whole world': Boston, 28 Sept. 1868, CCP.

'care of myself': CC to ECC, at 'Sister's—Cambridge,' CCP, vol. 3.

'with you here': St. Louis, 9 Oct. 1868, CCP.

238 'my head open': St. Louis, 15 Oct. 1868, CCP.

'nicer ever since!': Hyde Park, 31 Oct. 1868, CCP.

'cook & waiter': CC to ECC, New York, 25 Oct. 1868, CCP.

'well with *me*!': CC to ECC, Hyde Park, 31 Oct. 1868, CCP.

'things went ill': Philadelphia, 8 Nov. 1868, CCP.

239 'it's a girl': Washington, D.C., 17 Nov. 1868, CCP.

'& this season': Malvern, 23 June 1868, CCP.

'your father's regard': See preceding note.

9 May 1869: Leach, *Bright Particular Star,* p. 341.

240 'dread and fear': Ibid., p. 342.

'out for them': Malvern, 27 June 1869, CCP.

241 'this mortification would': Great Malvern, 28 June 1869, CCP.

242 her during childbirth: Leach, *Bright Particular Star,* p. 343; also see CC to Mr. Crow, 11 Aug. [1869], CCP.

243 'own loving Auntie': Edinburgh, 19 Aug. [1869], CCP.

'from the College!': Edinburgh, 20 Aug. 1869, CCP.

'on heavy paper': Edinburgh, 23 Aug. 1869, CCP.

'*to be, entirely*': CC to ECC, Edinburgh, 24 Aug. [1869], CCP.

'Your loving Auntie': [Aug. 1869], CCP, no. 1179.

244 'will see tomorrow': CC to ECC, [Oct. 1869], CCP.

'sooner the better': Great Malvern, 1 Nov. 1869, CCP.

'strangers and knaves': Hempstead, 22 Nov. 1869, CCP.

245 'ways I could': CC to ECC, [8 Oct. 1870], CCP.

245 '& united sway': Harrogate, 9 Oct. 1870, CCP.

246 'keen, dark eyes': Carr, *Hosmer,* p. 355.

'so beautifully housed': HH to Lady Loo, Northampton, 28 Dec. 1867 (Carr, *Hosmer,* p. 267, dates the letter 23 Dec.). All the following quotations from HH's letters to Lady Loo are from the same source. Very few are dated.

250 'with the Tiarra!!!': Carr, *Hosmer,* p. 283.

'to be remembered': Ibid., pp. 296–97 and 272.

251 as of nature: Ibid., p. 309.

'perhaps not': Ibid., p. 190.

253 'Your very lovingest, H.G.H.': Ibid., pp. 275–78.

'Laocoön once more': This letter states 'Lady Loo' has 'booked for 27th May.' This *might* be a letter of 1870 as CC left Rome on Sunday, 22 May 1870.

254 'on my side': CC to ECC, 10 July 1870, CCP.

'half an hour': CC to ECC, 28 July 1870, CCP; and see Monday, 1 Aug. 1870.

255 'to little purpose': Malvern, Saturday, 27 Aug. 1870, CCP.

The Door of Exit

256 'up these crumbs': Newport, 2 Feb. 1871, CCP.

257 '*me* any more': Newport, 22 Jan. 1871, CCP.

'my feet again': CC to ECC, New York, 7 Mar. 1871, CCP.

'in my life': Stamford, Connecticut, 24 Mar. 1871, CCP.

258 'an unutterable state': CC to ECC, Sunday, 26 Mar. 1871, CCP.

'violence to myself': 29 Mar. 1871, CCP.

'not overdo myself': Leach, *Bright Particular Star,* p. 349.

'cancer this morning?': News clipping, CCP.

'as a *finality*': Leach, *Bright Particular Star,* p. 350.

259 'were $4,935!': CC to ECC, New York, 5 Nov. 1871, CCP.

'$50,000 this season': CC to ECC, New York, 28 Oct. 1871, CCP.

'satisfies me better': CC to ECC, 14 Nov. 1871, CCP.

'it is over': CC to ECC, 3 Dec. 1871, CCP.

'choice of seats!!': CC to ECC, 22 Dec. 1871, CCP.

260 'if I could': 13 Mar. [1872], CCP.

'*printed* of me': Stebbins, *Cushman,* p. 238.

'but almost imperious': Howe, *Memories,* pp. 224–25.

261 'else need be!': Cincinnati, 2 Nov. 1872, CCP.

'test of feeling': CC to ECC, 20 Apr. 1872, CCP.

261 'studio in Rome': News clipping, CCP.

264 'a happy life': Copy of letter dated 21 July 1874, Newport, JLP.

'Fame's good queen!': From one of two sonnets Sidney Lanier wrote about Charlotte Cushman, Stebbins, *Cushman*, pp. 268–69.

265 'achieved without it!': Ibid., p. 263. I use the dash and exclamation point in '—you will . . . myself!' from the news clipping, JLP, rather than Stebbins' punctuation, as it better reflects CC's style.

266 'until 2 o'clock': CC to ECC, Philadelphia, 9 Nov. 1874, CCP.

267 'not my forte': CC to ECC, Philadelphia, 15 Nov. 1874, CCP.

'has frightened me': CC to ECC, Cincinnati, 24 Nov. 1874, CCP.

'the reading-desk': Stebbins, *Cushman*, p. 264.

268 'through the play': CC to Charles Cushman, Chicago, 10 Feb. 1875, CCP.

'little bushes budding': CC to Charles Cushman, Pittsburgh, 2 Apr. 1875, CCP.

'each other first': 6 Apr. 1875, CCP.

'in New York': Stebbins, *Cushman*, p. 274.

'baleful to her': Ibid., p. 276.

269 'inclination & *pleasure*': CC to ECC, CCP; see 'Lenox, Fri, 24 Sep 1875,' and 'Lenox Sat 25 Sep 1875.'

'apparently unnecessarily': CC to ECC, Boston, 15 Oct. [1875], CCP.

'We shall see': CC to Ned and ECC, Boston, 12 Oct. [1875], CCP.

270 'am not so': CC to ECC, 16 Oct. [1875], CCP.

'sorts of fun': 27 Oct. 1875, CCP.

271 'his fights alone': See penciled letters of 22 Dec. and 23 Dec. [1875].

all mankind: 24 Dec. [1875], CCP.

'left it alone': 30 Dec. 1875, CCP.

272 'looks like progress': CC to ECC, 27 Jan. 1876, CCP.

'bright glancing eyes': Stebbins, *Cushman*, pp. 282–83.

'I get thinner?': 9 Feb. 1876, CCP.

274 'Punch with care': Leach, *Bright Particular Star*, p. 295.

Life and Letters

275 'of either sex': Memorial card, CCP.

'"the dramatic stage"': Leach, *Bright Particular Star*, p. 398.

'make an attempt': Ibid., p. 391.

276 'whatever I was': ES to Sidney Lanier, 1 Mar. [1876]. All the letters from Emma Stebbins to Sidney Lanier are at Johns Hopkins University and are quoted from Jennie Lorenz's transcripts of the same at JLP.

278 'I dropped asleep': Selections from CC's daybook while at sea, Columbia.

each of her belongings: Brother Charlie was to receive $1,500 yearly during his lifetime, Miss Stebbins the same. Sallie was to have $500 a year—interest on $50,000—plus free rent of a house in Philadelphia. Charlotte's nieces Rosalie and Mabel Muspratt were also to receive $500 a year; married, $750. Her half nephew Alexander was to have $333 yearly, and there were smaller bequests.

279 'of whatever nature': 2 July 1876, JLP. I spell out 'E[mma] C[row] Cushman.'

'prove a failure': 8 July [18]76, JLP.

'weakly or capriciously': 14 July [1876], JLP.

'of all kinds': Lenox, 6 July 1876, JLP.

'have not got': Lenox, 27 July 1876, JLP.

'medicine or doctors': New York, 18 Feb. 1877, JLP.

280 hurry the book: Villa Cushman, Newport, 29 Nov. 1877, JLP.

'"written a book"'!': Villa Cushman, Newport, 10 Apr. 1878, JLP.

Afterword

281 'very striking portrait': *The Theatre: A Monthly Review and Magazine,* vol. 1, new ser. (Aug. 1878–Jan. 1879), JLP.

282 'of singular beauty': 'The Poetry of Mrs. Cushman' by Lilian Whiting, Boston, review of *Shadows in the Glass* after the author's death, news clipping, JLP.

283 'impersonal ghost hero': Froude, *Thomas Carlyle: A History of the First Forty Years of His Life,* vol. 1, p. xi.

287 'the consolidating knot': Carr, *Hosmer,* p. 35. 'The latter' in original has been changed to 'a good artist' for clarity.

Bibliography

Manuscripts and Unpublished Letters Consulted

Brewster
: The Anne Hampton Brewster Manuscript Collection owned by the Library Company of Philadelphia and housed in the manuscript department of the Historical Society of Pennsylvania. The extensive collection includes correspondence, journals, diaries, commonplace books, copybooks, miscellaneous article drafts, and newspaper clippings.

CCP
: The Papers of Charlotte Saunders Cushman (1816–1876), Manuscript Division, Library of Congress.

Letters of Charlotte Cushman to Emma Crow Cushman, arranged chronologically, vols. 1–8.

Letters *to* Charlotte Cushman, listed alphabetically by last name of correspondent, vols. 9–14.

Newspaper clippings, vols. 19–20.

Columbia
: Cushman daybook for 1844–45 and letters to Grace Greenwood, Brander Matthews Dramatic Museum Collection, Rare Book and Manuscript Library, Columbia University.

Cushman Club
: Letters of Charlotte Cushman to Nannie Lemmon.

Garland
: 'Notes on the Art and Life of Emma Stebbins' by Mary Garland, 8 mspp. dated 10 April 1888. Miscellaneous Papers—Stebbins, Emma. Manuscripts and Archives Division, The New York Public Library, Astor, Lenox and Tilden Foundations.

JLP
: Jennie Lorenz Papers, Manuscript Division, Library of Congress. An accumulation of research on the life of the actress by JL from ca. 1830 to 1960.

NLS The George Combe Papers, National Library of Scotland.

Northampton Letters of Harriet Hosmer to Louisa Lady Ashburton.

PM Geraldine Jewsbury's letters to her publishers Chapman and Hall, The Pierpont Morgan Library, New York.

SLRC Harriet Hosmer Papers, Schlesinger Library, Radcliffe College.

Turnbull Library Letters of Geraldine Jewsbury to Walter Mantell and correspondence with Thomas and Jane Carlyle, Alexander Turnbull Library, National Library of New Zealand.

Published Letters

CL *The Collected Letters of Thomas and Jane Carlyle.* Duke/ Edinburgh ed. Edited by Kenneth J. Fielding et al. Vols. 1–26 (up to 1851).

Ireland *Selections from the Letters of Geraldine Jewsbury to Jane Welsh Carlyle.* Edited by Mrs. Alexander Ireland. London and New York: Longmans, Green, 1892.

LM *Letters and Memorials of Jane Welsh Carlyle.* Edited by James Anthony Froude. 3 vols. London: Longmans, Green, 1883.

New LM *New Letters and Memorials of Jane Welsh Carlyle.* Annotated by Thomas Carlyle and edited by Alexander Carlyle. 2 vols. London: John Lane, 1903.

Selected Books and Articles

Brewster, Anne H. *Compensation; or, Always a Future: A Novel.* Philadelphia: J. B. Lippincott, 1860.

———. 'Miss Cushman.' *Blackwood's Magazine,* August 1878. Typescript, CCP.

Campbell, Ian. *Thomas Carlyle.* Edinburgh: Saltire Society, 1993.

Carlyle, Thomas. 'Reminiscence of Jane Welsh Carlyle.' In *Reminiscences,* edited by C. E. Norton with an introduction by Ian Campbell. London: J. M. Dent & Sons, 1972.

Carr, Cornelia, ed. *Harriet Hosmer: Letters and Memories.* New York: Moffat, Yard, 1912.

Cobbe, Frances Power. *Life of Frances Power Cobbe, by Herself.* Vol. 2. Boston: Houghton Mifflin, 1894.

Eliza Cook's Journal. Edited and written by Eliza Cook. May 1849–May 1854. (Entire file at New York Public Library.)

Cushman, Emma Crow. *Insight: A Record of Psychic Experiences.* Boston: Christopher Publishing House, 1917.

————. *Shadows in the Glass.* Boston: Christopher Publishing House, [1920].

Dearest Isa: Robert Browning's Letters to Isabella Blagden. Edited by Edward C. McAleer. Austin: University of Texas Press, 1951.

Emerson, Ralph Waldo. *English Traits.* London: Harrap Library, n.d.

Faderman, Lillian. *Surpassing the Love of Men.* New York: William Morrow, Quill, 1981.

Field, Kate. *Selected Letters.* Edited with an introduction by Carolyn J. Moss. Champaign: University of Illinois Press, 1996.

Froude, James Anthony. *My Relations with Carlyle.* Reprint. New York: Books for Libraries Press, 1971.

————. *Thomas Carlyle: A History of His Life in London, 1834–1881.* 2 vols. in one. New York: Charles Scribner's Sons, 1884.

————. *Thomas Carlyle: A History of the First Forty Years of His Life, 1795–1835.* 2 vols. New York: Charles Scribner's Sons, 1906.

Gardner, Albert Ten Eyck. *Yankee Stonecutters: The First American School of Sculpture, 1800–1850.* Reprint. New York: Books for Libraries Press, 1968.

Gregory, Gill. 'Adelaide Procter's "A Legend of Provence": The Struggle for a Place.' In *Victorian Women Poets: A Critical Reader,* edited by A. Leighton. Oxford: Blackwell Publishers, 1996.

Hanson, Laurence and Elizabeth. *Necessary Evil: The Life of Jane Welsh Carlyle.* London: Constable, 1952.

Harris, Frank. *My Life and Loves.* Edited by John F. Gallagher. New York: Grove Press, 1963.

Houghton, Lord. 'Harriet, Lady Ashburton.' In *Monographs,* 2d ed. London: John Murray, 1873.

Howe, M. A. De Wolfe, ed. *Memories of a Hostess* [Mrs. Anne Fields]. Boston: Atlantic Monthly Press, 1922.

Howe, Susanne. *Geraldine Jewsbury: Her Life and Errors.* London: George Allen & Unwin, [1935].

Hudson, Gertrude Reese, ed. *Browning to His American Friends.* London: Bowes & Bowes, 1965.

Hunt, Leigh. *The Autobiography.* Vol. 2. New York: Harper and Bros., 1850.

James, Henry. *William Wetmore Story and His Friends.* 2 vols. Boston: Houghton Mifflin, 1903.

Jewsbury, Geraldine. *The Half Sisters*. Edited with an introduction by Joanne Wilkes. Oxford: Oxford University Press, 1994.

———. *Zoe: The History of Two Lives*. London: Virago Press, 1989.

Kaplan, Fred. *Thomas Carlyle: A Biography*. Ithaca, N.Y.: Cornell University Press, 1983.

Kemble, Frances Anne. *Records of Later Life*. Vol. 3. 2d ed. London: Richard Bentley and Son, 1882.

Klumpke, Anna. *Rosa Bonheur*. Translated by Gretchen von Slyke. Ann Arbor: University of Michigan Press, 1997.

Larrabee, Denise M. *Anne Hampton Brewster, 19th-Century Author and 'Social Outlaw.'* Exhibition, 16 March–31 August 1992. Philadelphia: Library Company of Philadelphia, 1992.

Leach, Joseph. *Bright Particular Star: The Life and Times of Charlotte Cushman*. New Haven, Conn.: Yale University Press, 1970.

Levine, Miriam. *A Guide to Writers' Homes in New England*. Cambridge, Mass.: Apple-wood Books, 1984.

Markus, Julia. *Dared and Done: The Marriage of Elizabeth Barrett and Robert Browning*. New York: Alfred A. Knopf, 1995.

Milroy, Elizabeth. 'The Public Career of Emma Stebbins: Works in Bronze.' *Archives of American Art Journal*, vol. 34, no. 11 (1994): pp. 2–13.

———. 'The Public Career of Emma Stebbins: Works in Marble.' *Archives of American Art Journal*, vol. 33, no. 3 (1993): pp. 2–12.

Oliphant, Mrs. [Margaret]. *The Autobiography and Letters of Mrs. M. O. W. Oliphant*. Edited by Mrs. Harry Coghill. 3d rev. ed. Edinburgh: William Blackwood and Sons, 1899.

———. *The Life of Edward Irving*. London: Hurst and Blackett, n.d.

Parrott, Sara Foose. 'Expatriates and Professionals: The Careers in Italy of Nineteenth-Century American Women Writers and Artists.' Ph.D. diss., George Washington University, 1988.

Richardson, Robert D., Jr. *Emerson: The Mind on Fire*. Berkeley: University of California Press, 1995.

Rubinstein, Charlotte Streifer. *American Women Sculptors*. Boston: G. K. Hall, 1990.

Sherwood, Dolly. *Harriet Hosmer: American Sculptor 1830–1908*. Columbia: University of Missouri Press, 1991.

Stebbins, Emma. *Charlotte Cushman: Her Letters and Memories of Her Life*. Edited by her Friend, Emma Stebbins. Reprint. New York: Benjamin Blom, 1972.

[Sterling, Anthony C.] *Metrical Miscellanies* by A. C. S. Printed for private circulation, 1854.

Stillman, William James. *The Autobiography of a Journalist*. 2 vols. Boston: Houghton Mifflin, Riverside Press, 1901.

Surtees, Virginia. *The Ludovisi Goddess: The Life of Louisa Lady Ashburton*. London: Michael Russell Publishing, 1984.

Whiting, Lilian. *Kate Field: A Record*. Boston: Little, Brown, 1899.

Woolf, Virginia. 'Geraldine and Jane.' *Times Literary Supplement*, 28 Feb. 1929. In *The Second Common Reader*. San Diego: Harcourt Brace Jovanovich, 1960.

Index

Note: Page numbers in *italics* refer to illustrations.

Illustration Credits

Illustrations in this work are used by permission and courtesy of the following:

Charlotte Cushman Theatre Club, Library Committee: page 62

Columbia University Rare Book and Manuscript Library: pages 151, 158, 210, 221, 225, 251

The Folger Shakespeare Library: pages 182, 262 (top)

Fraser's Magazine: pages 102, 113 (right), 122 (bottom left)

The Harvard Theatre Collection, Houghton Library: page 10

The Library Company of Philadelphia: page 15

Library of Congress, Manuscript Division, Charlotte Cushman Papers: pages 19 (both), 21, 263, 266 (both), 277 (left)

Library of Congress, Prints and Photographs Division, Charlotte Cushman Photo Album: pages 11, 25 (top), 44, 64, 72 (right), 75, 78, 174, 183, 200, 234, 242

Collection of Elizabeth Millroy: page 34

National Portrait Gallery, London: pages 122 (top left), 148, 284

Schlesinger Library, Radcliffe Institute, Harvard University: pages 23, 194, 195, 247, 248 (all)

Smithsonian Institution, Archives of American Art, Emma Stebbins Scrap Album: pages 55, 192 (both), 203, 273, 285

Smithsonian Institution, Archives of American Art, John Neal Tillton Scrap Book: page 8

Washington University Archives: page 72 (left)

Washington University Gallery of Art: pages 25 (both), 185

Watertown Library: page 27

Author's collection: pages 207, 216 (top)

Private collections: pages 40, 48, 94, 113 (left), 115, 122 (top right and bottom right), 127, 154, 160, 162, 216 (bottom), 219 (both), 262 (bottom)

A NOTE ON THE TYPE

THIS BOOK was set in Adobe Garamond. Designed for the Adobe Corporation by Robert Slimbach, the fonts are based on types first cut by Claude Garamond (c. 1480–1561). Garamond was a pupil of Geoffroy Tory and is believed to have followed the Venetian models, although he introduced a number of important differences, and it is to him that we owe the letter we now know as "old style." He gave to his letters a certain elegance and feeling of movement that won their creator an immediate reputation and the patronage of Francis I of France.

Composed by North Market Street Graphics,
Lancaster, Pennsylvania
Printed and bound by Quebecor Printing,
Fairfield, Pennsylvania
Designed by Virginia Tan